The American Kitchen
1700 *to the* Present

❦

FROM HEARTH TO HIGHRISE

The American Kitchen 1700 to the Present

FROM HEARTH TO HIGHRISE

ELLEN M. PLANTE

Facts On File®

AN INFOBASE HOLDINGS COMPANY

The American Kitchen 1700 to the Present: From Hearth to Highrise

Copyright © 1995 by Ellen M. Plante

Facts On File, Inc.
460 Park Avenue South
New York, NY 10016

Library of Congress Cataloging-in-Publication Data

Plante, Ellen M.
    The American kitchen 1700 to the present / Ellen M. Plante.
        p.   cm.
    Includes bibliographical references and index.
    ISBN 0-8160-3038-3
    1. Kitchens—United States—History.   2. Cookery—United States—
History.   3. United States—Social life and customs.   I. Title.
TX653.P56   1995
643′.3′0973—dc20   94-33235

Text and jacket design by Catherine Rincon Hyman
Printed in the United States of America

MP FOF 10 9 8 7 6 5 4 3 2 1

This book is printed on acid-free paper.

In memory of my grandmothers who labored in their kitchens—and for my mother, whose career as a nurse manager and accomplishments as a watercolor artist taught me there is indeed much, much more to life than the kitchen.

ACKNOWLEDGMENTS

Without the help of others this work would have been impossible to complete. A special thank you to my editor, Caroline Sutton, for the opportunity to write this book and guidance along the way. Thank you to the numerous museums, living-history museums and historic house museums across the country that responded to my requests for information and photographs, especially Mimi Sherman, Curator of Old Merchant's House in New York City; Herbert S. Gary of President Warren G. Harding's Home in Marion, Ohio; Jacki Sullivan at Storrowton Village Museum in West Springfield, Massachusetts; Phyllis P. Shaw, Superintendent, John Muir National Historic Site in Martinez, California; Eric Freeman, Public Relations Manager for Conner Prairie in Noblesville, Indiana; Robert L. Barrett, Curator, Museum Village in Orange County, Monroe, New York; Jan Joseph Losi, Curator, Banning Residence Museum in Wilmington, California; and Elizabeth D. Kennedy, Associate Director of Old Cowtown Museum, Wichita, Kansas. I'd also like to thank Franklin Friday of Friday Historical Business Archives in Louisville, Kentucky for his kind interest in this project and help in obtaining photos of early twentieth-century GE appliances and kitchen displays and to Carina C. Thate of Gabrielle Bamberger Public Relations who was instrumental in securing vintage Maytag photographs for my use. Finally, a special thank you to my family—my husband, parents and children—for moral support and help along the way.

CONTENTS

INTRODUCTION

The history and evolution of the American kitchen indicate that the concept of this area as a family-oriented space has come full circle. Like the early eighteenth-century "hall" with massive cooking hearth, today's kitchen is often planned as the core of the home. Houses are designed with large, functional and comfortable kitchens that combine open food preparation centers with eating areas that extend into family rooms or other areas of family activity.

In the almost three hundred years of development explored in this book, the kitchen passed from the Colonial hall or keeping room to expanded, factory-like work centers located in basements or separate buildings during the early Victorian period. After the advent of gas lines and indoor plumbing in the early 1870s, kitchens were routinely placed on the first floor, at the rear of the home, where disagreeable odors and daily activities would not intrude upon the rest of the household.

The nineteenth-century industrial revolution ushered in cookstoves, mass-produced gadgets and utensils, and eventually iceboxes that brought marked change and improvement to the domestic sphere. Before the end of the nineteenth century, domestic science experts and architects were exploring "planned" space in the kitchen. Historians have noted that the study of sanitation during the 1890s took the kitchen from a factory-like series of workrooms to a laboratory-like, sterile center of culinary and cleaning operations, and introduced the concept of a "scientific" approach to household routines. This same period saw increased production of canned and packaged foods, which ultimately led to a shift in the housewife's role from producer to consumer.

The dawn of the twentieth century found the emphasis on technology pervading the home and the eventual introduction of electric appliances altering the physical aspects of the kitchen as well as the manner in which "housewifery" was performed. Freestanding cupboards gave way to built-in cabinets with a continuous counter area and gas or electric stoves replaced their coal and/or woodburning counterparts. By the

1920s serious thought was being given to decorating the kitchen and color began to invade flooring, appliances, furniture and kitchen tools.

The modernistic kitchen of the 1940s and 1950s benefited from continual advancements and improvements in appliances and this second half of the century has brought us microwave ovens, energy-efficient appliances and state-of-the-art kitchenware.

The history of the American kitchen is entrenched in the sociological, cultural and economic factors that dictated or determined American everyday life. For the purposes of this book, the middle-class and their homes are examined and explored as they've long been the target of those who would dispense domestic advice and create advertising for new or improved products and services.

While the Colonial kitchen and early American cookery have been the subject of numerous reference books written since the late 1800s, the kitchen of the Victorian period has remained obscure. Hidden away in sub-basements and the subject of few photographs, the nineteenth-century kitchen has held little of the romance associated with the glowing embers of the Colonial hearth. This is not at all surprising since the Victorian kitchen was viewed as the domain of "domestics" while family life centered around the parlor and the dining room. Therefore, in researching the nineteenth-century kitchen, numerous domestic manuals and cookbooks have been examined for recommendations regarding the physical appearance of the room, necessary kitchen equipment, cookery, the manner in which household chores were conducted and by whom.

The continued publication of domestic guides and home manuals, textbooks for home economics courses, as well as the proliferation of women's magazines during the early twentieth century provided volumes of notes on the kitchen of the early 1900s. Advertisements, magazines and the history of related industries aided greatly in exploring the kitchen from the 1930s through modern day.

The manner in which domesticity has been perceived since the late 1700s has also had a direct impact on the development of the American kitchen. While the post-Revolution Colonial kitchen was subject to subtle change in American cookery thanks to a new emphasis on patriotism, the early 1800s saw cooking methods improved with the introduction of the range and cookstove. This was the most significant development during the early Victorian period, as little thought was given to the drudgery of kitchen work performed, for the most part, by domestic servants. Change, however, was marked, once the middle-class mistress returned to her kitchen as a shortage of "domestics" plagued the urban areas during the late 1800s. As a result, those chapters devoted to nineteenth- and early twentieth-century kitchens are the longest.

The housewife's increasing status as a consumer during the early 1900s spurred additional advances in appliances and packaged goods. Early on, change in the kitchen was sporadic, but came in great waves as a "scientific" approach to cooking and housework was called for. The "modern" kitchen of the 1930s and 1940s was the forerunner of today's kitchen.

In short, we shall examine the evolution of the kitchen as a "room," the women and servants who labored there, cooking and other household tasks as well as the cultural and industrial changes that affected the kitchen's growth and development.

1

The Colonial Kitchen 1700–1839

". . . WOMAN'S WORK IS NEVER DONE"

The McClure (a fictitious family) log cabin hall is typical of the 1836 Northwest Territory. As the center of home life this large room includes a brick cooking hearth, wall cupboard for earthenware and staples and table for family meals.

Walls are whitewashed and flooring is wide wooden planks. Atop the mantel a mortar and pestle, sadiron, storage containers and teapot are kept handy.

Courtesy of McGuire Photography, Conner Prairie, Noblesville, Indiana.

The world corrupts; home should refine . . .

Domestic Duties Or Instructions To Young Married Ladies
—Frances Parkes, 1829

*W*hile the first homes the colonists hastily constructed during the Early American period of the seventeenth century provided temporary shelter in the form of crude log cabins or sod huts, housing in the colonies during the 1700s took on the characteristics of permanent dwellings. Farmhouses in the North, plantation homes in the South and Georgian and Federal-style buildings in growing urban centers all had a common center of activity—the massive cooking hearth.

During the first years of the eighteenth century, purely functional housing throughout vast rural areas consisted of a family home with one large room or "hall" on the ground floor and a sleeping loft above. Some homes also included a small bedroom off the hall for the adults in the family. The hall served as the center of family activity; meals were cooked at the fireplace and then eaten at a table close by, spinning and sewing were done near the light of the fire and the family came together for prayer, home instruction and conversation near the warmth of the hearth.

The Colonial home was indeed the focus of the family, serving their material needs as well as their social needs. There were few if any outside activities to draw them away from home, with the exception of weekly religious services. Social clubs, community groups and formal entertainment did not exist.[1]

Since the hall was literally the center of the home, everyday items such as tools for indoor and outdoor use were hung from pegs or hooks about the room and meat and vegetables were often hung from poles strung up near the ceiling. A spinning wheel, flax wheel and/or loom were placed in the corner. Furnishings were simple and utilitarian. A trestle table with benches and perhaps a few stools provided seating as well as a worktable and place for meals, a chest stored family belongings and a corner cupboard served to house the wooden and pewter tablewares. Occasionally a separate worktable stood against a wall for meal preparation and washing dishes in a wooden bucket. Floors were crafted from wide wooden planks and kept sparkling clean with a daily sprinkling of sand, which acted as a scouring compound and prevented the wood from absorbing cooking odors.

As families prospered houses became larger. While no specific division of rooms was recognized during the early 1700s, by the 1720s modest Colonial houses were being constructed with two separate rooms on the ground floor. Regarding the saltbox style so popular in the Northeast, author and historian Mary C. Crawford wrote that "between 1675 and 1775 . . . from the end of King Philip's War until the outbreak of the Revolution, such houses were frequently amplified so as to include a second ground floor room, which was used as a parlor."[2] The all-purpose hall then ceased to exist and cooking was conducted in what came to be called the "keeping room." The hall, or parlor, functioned as an area for family gatherings and entertaining guests.

On plantations and in smaller homes throughout the southern colonies the kitchen was often located in a separate building or cookhouse attached to the rear of the main building through a breezeway.

After the Revolution homes grew even larger, incorporating four rooms in organized ground floor plans. There were rooms for the specific activities of cooking, dining, socializing and a large chamber for sleeping.[3] In growing towns and cities American domestic architecture closely resembled that of upper-class English homes and the resulting townhouses built during the late eighteenth century for both the wealthy and middle class had kitchens located in the basement (which was partially above ground with windows and a door). Not only was the basement relatively cool, a definite advantage during the warm summer months when the cooking hearth was still in constant use, but it also served to protect the rest of the household from unpleasant cooking odors.

The pantry was incorporated into the kitchen during the late 1700s for storage, and to guard against the theft of costly staples and spices it was often outfitted with a lock.

This "keeping room" in the 1776 Potter Mansion at Storrowton Village Museum features a large cooking hearth with a brick bake oven. An iron swinging crane holds a kettle over the fire and a "roasting kitchen" sits in front of the hearth. Wooden storage cupboards run across the top of the chimney and a large crane, which can be seen at the top of the photo, is designed to swing out into the room and, with a blanket thrown over it, creates a warm spot in front of the fire.

Courtesy of Storrowton Village Museum, located on the grounds of the Eastern States Exposition, West Springfield, Massachusetts.

The kitchen in the reconstructed 1794 Gilbert Farmstead at Storrowton Village includes a brick cooking hearth and bake oven with an iron door. A pine scrubtop table holds earthenware, dried herbs and a wooden bowl full of eggs. A step-back cupboard stores kitchen necessities and homemade brooms are stacked in a corner. A built-in corner cabinet located in the dining room can be seen through the doorway.

Courtesy of Storrowton Village Museum, located on the grounds of the Eastern States Exposition, West Springfield, Massachusetts.

In both rural and urban areas, existing homes were being extended with a kitchen wing or enclosed lean-to kitchen/storage area in order to convert the keeping room into a dining room or additional parlor.

Regarding the all-important cooking hearth, Early American homes had clay-lined wooden chimneys with a green-wood lug pole placed across the hearth's wide expanse to hold hooks that supported kettles and other cookware. Vast improvements were achieved during the eighteenth century when stone or locally handcrafted (or imported) bricks were used in chimney construction and the hand-forged iron lug pole replaced wooden saplings.

While it may appear that during this pre-industrial period there were few significant changes in the cooking hearth, this is far from true. Necessity truly being the mother of invention, colonists were continually attempting to improve fireplace cooking by experimenting with chimney designs, size of the fireplace and the introduction of more modern and convenient tools. For example, the forged-iron lug pole was improved upon with the introduction of the swinging iron crane, which proved far safer and advantageous in placing heavy pots to cook over the fire.

The early hearth was quite large, usually 8 to 10 feet wide and 5 to 6 feet tall. Brick bake ovens were often built into the fireplace either at the side or rear, with an ash pit and separate flue channeled into the chimney. Next to the hearth might be a "chimney cupboard" in which cooking utensils could be stored or benches to provide seating near the warmth of the fire.

Prior to 1700, fireplace walls were whitewashed just as the other plastered walls in the hall or keeping room were but by the early eighteenth century it became fashionable to panel and paint them—dark blue, olive green or a brown-red color. By the 1750s lighter colors for the interior of the home were in vogue. Fireplace walls were then painted a subtle shade of gray, blue, mustard, salmon or buff and regular cleaning kept them free of soot and dirt. At the same time improvements in chimney design led to smaller hearths with a bake oven (often in the shape of a beehive) now located at the front of the fireplace and accessorized with a small iron door.

Wooden flooring in the keeping room or kitchen wing continued to be popular in the north while southern regions often used brick in the cookhouse or summer kitchen.

In the pre-industrial eighteenth and early nineteenth century, the majority of the population was engaged in farming. Home-based agricultural businesses had to provide for their own needs and the kitchen

A close-up view of a Colonial log cabin cooking hearth made of stone with hand-forged hooks for hanging kettles, pots and so forth over the fire. Footed skillets can be seen on the floor next to *the hearth and iron tongs hang from the wooden beam. A primitive early mantel holds candle molds and early candlesticks.*

Courtesy of Museum Village in Orange County, Monroe, New York.

garden, poultry yard, smokehouse, root cellar and dairy room provided the staples so vital to everyday existence.

While it is difficult to imagine today, the Colonial-era family had no such luxury as ready-made goods to fall back on in case of emergency. Their existence was dependent upon raising and curing their own meat, growing fruits and vegetables to be stored or made into preserves and tending the wheat and corn fields so the family would have flour for the all-important breads the housekeeper made.[4]

The kitchen garden was located just outside the kitchen or keeping room and fruits and vegetables were grown for family meals while herbs were cultivated for medicinal purposes and food flavoring.

A small poultry yard was maintained for raising chickens and securing the eggs so important to a variety of recipes.

Large farms or plantations had a separate building to serve as a smokehouse for curing hams and other meats. Smaller homes and those located in growing towns and cities utilized attic space next to the chimney as a mini-smokehouse. Since smoking and curing were the most reliable means of preserving meats, the smokehouse was a vitally important part of every home.

Early root cellars or larders were constructed underground, next to the house or in a hillside nearby rather than beneath the house. These storage areas with dirt or stone walls often had protruding stone shelves on which to place storage containers and the below-ground setting kept perishables cool and helped preserve fruits and root vegetables. As homes grew during the 1700s, small cellars were incorporated underneath the kitchen with access through an outside door.

Northern colonies created icehouses built into the earth where slabs of ice chipped from a lake or pond could be buried in layers of straw or sawdust to preserve meats and other perishables. In his book *A Field Guide to America's History*, Douglass L. Brownstone tells us that "farmers frequently put the cooling microclimate of the icehouse to a variety of uses. On a farm, where everything was patched and repatched, used and reused . . . it was inconceivable that an icehouse would serve merely as a repository for ice. A cool chamber was usually built, or excavated, below the icehouse's main floor for the storage of such perishables as fruit and dairy products. On some farms the icehouse's cool chamber eliminated the need for a springhouse in which to chill milk."[5]

In the South the stone springhouse with cool spring waters channeled through it was the primary means of preservation since ice was unobtainable.

The dairy room or buttery was a small room located off the kitchen or keeping room where butter was churned and cheeses made.

Wells and cisterns provided water for cooking, washing and bathing and large wooden buckets were used to transport the water into the kitchen.

With the dawn of the nineteenth century cooking continued to be done at the cooking hearth but the kitchen was enhanced with a dresser or large step-back cupboard for additional storage, as well as a primitive pie safe with wood-slat doors to provide circulation for the baked goods placed within. A worktable continued to function as the center of meal preparations but meals were now served at a gateleg table (a table with drop leaves supported by extra legs that swung out gate-style) situated close to the warmth of the fire. In large homes, the family came together in the dining room. Wooden buckets and benches for washing dishware were replaced by crude sinks carved from stone and hand-sewn curtains and rugs dressed small windows and wood floors.

The Colonial Cooking Hearth and Kitchen Equipment

Clarissa, said my judicious mother, by not knowing how to make puddings and pies, you may be occasionally mortified, but if you are ignorant of roasting and boiling, you may be annoyed every day.

Recollections of a Housekeeper
—Clarissa Packard, 1834

The fire at the Colonial cooking hearth was kept burning day and night. Not only was it in constant use for cooking, baking, making soap, candles and so on, but it was relied upon for warmth and light within the home. Perhaps more importantly, the fire was closely guarded to prevent the embers from dying out because it was a difficult, time-consuming process to light a new fire. In the age before matches, the family tinderbox of twigs and rags stood ready along with flint and steel should the need arise to start a fire, but more often than not, hot coals were retrieved from a neighbor and quickly transported home instead.

At the hearth stood and hung the family's valuable array of iron pots, kettles, frypans, trivets and utensils. Much of the forged iron cookware was passed on from one generation to the next, and for many of the middle- and upper-class households, copper and brass vessels were

This Colonial cooking hearth is on exhibit in the Visitor's Center at Museum Village in Orange County. The brick hearth includes a large brick bake oven and within the hearth can be seen the iron crane used to hang pots of stew and the andirons used to support the logs for the fire. A large "roasting kitchen" (a tin vessel placed in front of the fire to roast meat) and various cooking utensils are on display. A two-drawer worktable can be seen and the mantel holds assorted pottery, pewter and woodenware items.

Courtesy of Museum Village in Orange County, Monroe, New York.

utilized as well. The items found at the hearth were not excessive, each piece having a specific function. Within the hearth stood a pair of andirons or firedogs that not only served to hold logs for the fire, but could also support a spit or various utensils. Utilitarian wrought iron firedogs were typically found at the cooking hearth but the fireplace in the parlor was often outfitted with more decorative brass examples.

From first the lug pole, and then later the swinging crane within the hearth, could be hung the mammoth pots and kettles used to prepare the one-pot meals so typical during the early 1700s. Footed pots and cauldrons of various sizes were a necessity, not just for cooking, but for making soap and candles. Large examples often weighed as much as 30 or 40 pounds when empty and it was a back-breaking job to lift them up to the lug pole or iron crane.

Round or triangular footed trivets in assorted sizes and heights stood next to the hearth for use with iron skillets or kettles that cooked food or heated water directly over the burning embers.

In those homes where the cooking hearth did not contain a built-in bake oven, a "Dutch oven" was put to use. These large, footed vessels were made of sturdy iron and had tight-fitting concave lids. They were commonly used for baking breads and cakes and were placed among the ashes of the fire with hot coals spooned atop the concave lid.

Footed gridirons for cooking meats could be placed over the hot coals as could long-handled iron toasting forks and waffle irons.

By the eighteenth century roasting meat had progressed from the more primitive methods of using strong string to suspend the meat over the fire (which needed constant attention) to revolving spits or the use of a "roasting kitchen." The tin roasting kitchen was a footed, box-like container with a rounded back, open on one side to receive the heat of the flames when set in front of the fire. A spit inside held the meat in place and a small door in the back allowed the cook to check her meat and baste as needed. Roasting kitchens were made by tinsmiths in various sizes to meet the needs of each household.

Iron utensils such as long-handled forks, skewers, skimmers and ladles were usually hung next to or above the hearth.

In general, meats were roasted, broiled or fried at the fire or cooked in stews. Vegetables were boiled in the large iron pot suspended over hot coals. Some andirons were equipped with small pull-out drawers in front where potatoes could be placed for baking.

Preparing breads and cakes in the brick fireplace oven demanded a skill acquired over time. A small fire of twigs and hot coals was built in the oven and allowed to burn for a specified period so the bricks would absorb the heat. The fire, ashes and all, was then removed so the bread, cake or pie could be inserted and baked. The experienced housekeeper had several ways of testing the heat within the oven to make sure it was hot enough for baking. One popular method was to sprinkle some flour on the oven floor, close the door and then check the flour a moment later. If brown, the oven was suitable, but if the flour burned, the oven was too hot and had to be allowed to cool.[6]

The iron cookware and utensils used at the hearth were indeed the most important kitchenware items during the Colonial period but other necessities were called for as well. Lidded pantry boxes, either round or oval in shape, were used to store spices, herbs, flour, cheese and butter. They were crafted from strips of wood in graduating sizes so they could be stored in "nests" to save space.

The stone, wood or iron mortar and pestle was used to mash and grind herbs for cooking and home remedies and a wooden salt box hung close to the hearth for flavoring meats, stews, hash and broth.

Assorted wooden bowls and spoons were used for mixing, and in the Northeast, Virginia and Ohio, redware pottery, the first earthenware made in America (from red clay), was readily available in the form of large bowls, molds, pie plates, platters, pitchers, jars and bean pots. Redware, however, was not a sturdy pottery and by the early 1800s stoneware made of gray clay proved to be a more practical alternative. The majority of stoneware pieces, crocks and jars, were used to store foodstuffs but hard-working vessels such as butter churns, molds, pots and pitchers were turned out by potters as well.

Hand-crafted wooden sieves, rolling pins, apple parers, food choppers and "beetles" or mashers were all used in preparing meals and preserves.

Tinware was not widely used until the early 1800s but once introduced, its light weight was appealing to Colonial women accustomed to heavy iron pots. Tin measuring cups, candlesticks, graters, pie plates, candle molds, coffee bean roasters and roasting kitchens were common items in the early nineteenth-century kitchen and in rural areas they were often obtained by bartering with the traveling tinsmith or peddler.

When the family sat down to dinner during the early 1700s, the long trestle table was covered with a homespun tablecloth, and napkins were in place for each family member. The salt cellar stood at the center of the table and large wooden trenchers held the stew, hash or other dish that had cooked all afternoon at the hearth. Wooden bowls or plates were used for individual servings and drinking cups held cider or ale. At the same time, pewter dishware was used in the homes of the wealthy, but it was the mid-eighteenth century before it was commonly found in

The kitchen in the 1823 William Conner brick home at Conner Prairie features a massive brick cooking hearth with a bake oven. An iron swinging crane supports a kettle and pots over the fire. Iron forks and ladles hang from the mantel and additional cookware sits by the hearth. To the right of the mantel is a small built-in storage cupboard and the mantel holds a copper tea kettle, pewter platter, mortar and pestle and a large mechanical device with a chain and turn-wheel that is used to rotate a spit at the hearth. A table in front of the window holds a sugar "firkin" or bucket and wooden chopping bowl.

Courtesy of McGuire Photography, Conner Prairie, Noblesville, Indiana.

middle-class homes. Between 1750 and 1800 pewter was widely available and several pieces were often given as a wedding gift. At the fully dressed dinner table could be found pewter plates, bowls, mugs, spoons, porringers, shakers and a teapot, sugar, creamer and pitcher.

In her book *Home Life in Colonial Days,* Alice Morse Earle tells us, "It was not until Revolutionary times that china was a common table furnishing; then it began to crowd out pewter. The sudden and enormous growth of East India commerce, and the vast cargoes of Chinese pottery and porcelain wares brought to American ports soon gave ample china to every housewife. In the southern colonies beautiful isolated pieces of porcelain, such as vast punch bowls, often were found in the homes of opulent planters; but there, as in the north, the first china for general table use was the handleless tea-cups, usually of some Canton ware, which crept with the fragrant herb into every woman's heart—both welcome Oriental waifs."[7]

Whether the middle-class dining table was set with pewter handed down by family or a popular china, by the 1830s dinner had become an increasingly formal, elaborate affair in urban areas, especially in those middle-class and upper-class homes where "domestics" were employed. A large assortment of foods and sweets was presented as cooking became more of an art form.

Women's Role in the Colonial Kitchen

St. Paul knew what was best for women when he advised them to be domestic. There is something sedative in the duties which home involves. It affords security not only from the world, but from delusions and errors of every kind.

Godey's Lady's Book, II
—"Woman" by Mrs. Sandford, August 1831

During the early 1700s when the family home and farm or business was being established, husband, wife and children labored for the common good of their home-based industry. Women in rural areas took part in planting and harvesting as needed; they prepared meals, tended the garden, poultry yard and dairy; made clothing, linens and bedcovers; prepared medicinal remedies and tended the sick; did the laundry; made the household supplies of soap and candles; put up preserves; and instructed children in deportment, religion and occasionally the basics of reading and arithmetic. With the exception of laboring over the crops, life in the growing urban areas was not so very different for the housewife.

In *Woman's Life in Colonial Days,* Carl Holliday points out that in the twentieth century it is difficult for us to understand the harsh reality of the physical labor and constant drudgery the Colonial woman was subject to. In addition to her long hours of work, she constantly had to deal with pregnancy and infant mortality, as well as natural disasters, illness and disease and the adjustments to be made by leaving family and friends behind to venture off to a new country.[8] That it was indeed a hard life for the early Colonial housekeeper would seem an understatement.

In order to accomplish the endless tasks that very often determined the family's survival and well-being, by the eighteenth century many women were subscribing to a weekly housekeeping ritual. For the majority of families, Sunday was a day of worship with lengthy religious services to attend. The rest of the week found the Colonial housewife doing the wash on Monday, ironing on Tuesday, baking on Wednesday, preparing brews on Thursday, churning butter and making cheese on Friday and devoting Saturday to sewing and mending that required regular attention. As the eighteenth century progressed, growing villages, towns and cities attracted merchants who made available everything from cloth to produce, meats, dairy products, cider and so forth. Families had the option of purchasing various necessities rather than turning them out at home. As a result, the housekeeping ritual was altered somewhat during the late 1700s and early 1800s to meet individual family's needs.

Monday, or wash day as it was commonly called, was devoted to the most tedious of tasks. Rainwater was collected for the wash or obtained from a nearby stream and, weather permitting, the laundry was done outdoors. A small fire was prepared to heat the heavy iron wash pot and slivers of lye soap were added to the boiling water. Additional buckets or kettles containing rinse water and starch were prepared and the clothing and linens sorted. Laundry was boiled, vigorously rubbed against the wooden scrubboard, rinsed, starched and either hung on a line or spread out on the grass to dry.

Just making the lye soap in order to do the wash was a major undertaking. The housekeeper would carefully save cooking grease and ashes from the hearth until she'd accumulated enough to make a batch of soap. Lye was created from water poured over the ashes and allowed to drain into a container underneath. The lye was then added to boiling water and several pounds of grease and the entire concoction cooked and stirred for the better part of a day. Once the lye and grease were well

Costumed interpreters at Conner Prairie's 1836 village prepare ginger-bread and spice cake for a celebration. Dough is rolled at the worktable, a dry sink sits in front of the window and a step-back cupboard holds staples, dishware and spoons. A small wooden pantry box and sugar "firkin" or bucket can be seen on the worktable.

Courtesy McGuire Photography, Conner Prairie, Noblesville, Indiana.

At Conner Prairie's Living History Musuem, costumed interpreters help visitors in hands-on activities such as churning butter. Pictured here, an earthenware butter churn with wooden plunger.

Courtesy of McGuire Photography, Conner Prairie, Noblesville, Indiana.

mixed, salt was added to the pot in order to make the "soap" rise to the top. The soap was then removed to a primitive mold where it was allowed to cool. To make soap for bathing, bayberry was often added to a small portion that was allowed to cook a little longer in an effort to break down the harshness of the lye.

When the ironing was done on Tuesday, starch made at home from wheat flour was used until the early 1800s when store-bought starch made from corn became available. Hollow box irons heated by inserting hot coals from the hearth were commonplace until hand-forged irons complete with an iron slug were introduced. The slug could be heated in hot embers and inserted into the iron in place of hot coals. These box irons were eventually replaced by solid irons (often called sadirons), which were heated directly in front of the fire.

The tabletop or an old board suspended between two stools served as an ironing board and the housekeeper, a daughter or perhaps a young girl hired as "help" would labor all day ironing linens, shirts, dress clothing and so on.

When baking was done on Wednesday (this would eventually be changed to Saturday), dough was prepared for several loaves of bread and these were baked in the "Dutch oven" or the hearth's bake oven. If time allowed, the housekeeper might also prepare a cake or pie, but her objective was to turn out the bread for the coming week.

The early colonists devoted Thursday to brewing common drinks such as beer, ginger beer and cider. Making apple cider was the most time-consuming, often involving the entire family. After apples were gathered from the trees, a circular trough and large pressing stone were used to mash the apples into pulp. This in turn was pressed into cakes with layers of straw placed between them so pressure could be applied to draw out the apple juice. The juice was then strained through a primitive sieve and placed in casks for fermentation.

As the eighteenth century progressed, the middle-class farmer could take his apples to a mill located in town to have his cider made. As store-bought goods and staples flooded the shelves of the general store and small, specialized shops, Thursday became a popular day for going to the market.

Although Friday was set aside for making cheese and churning butter, these processes could actually take several days of preparation. In turning out butter, the housekeeper had first to allow milk to sour in the butter churn. Within a few days this could be "worked" in the tall wooden vessel with the plunger. Children were often responsible for the "churning," which often had to be done for hours at a time in order for the butter to rise to the top. This was then removed to a wooden bowl where the housekeeper would work the excess milk out of the butter with the aid of small wooden paddles. The butter was then placed in hand-crafted wooden butter molds. To preserve butter for the winter months, it was packed in lidded crocks with layers of salt or a brine made of water, salt and saltpeter.

Making cheese was as time-consuming as turning out butter but the majority of women prided themselves on their ability to produce good dairy products. A gentle touch was needed to separate the curds of the warmed milk so the whey could break free. The curds were then gathered together in a cheesecloth and placed in a special cheese basket that sat atop a small tub. The cheese was then pressed into a wooden tool made specifically for that purpose and allowed to sit for a few days. Once removed from the press, cheese was aged for six months or so in a cool, dark spot. Sage juice created from sage leaves was often added during the cheese-making process to create a flavorful sage cheese and cottage cheese was made by adding cream and salt to curds of milk.

In the early eighteenth century when Saturday was devoted to mending, it was time well spent since spinning and weaving to produce clothing materials were hard work and cloth was at a premium. No scrap of material was wasted and along with the family's clothing, which was constantly patched and repaired, the Colonial wife also made curtains, napkins, bedding, tablecloths and small rugs. In their book *Artists in Aprons*, authors C. Kurt Dewhurst, Betty MacDowell and Marsha Mac-Dowell explain that "In attaining economic self-sufficiency, it was crucial for the production of textiles to be conducted in the home . . . Here, a mother could tend to her homemaking chores and still supervise the carding, spinning and weaving processes. Much of the work in domestic wool spinning and weaving was done by young girls, thereby providing their economic contribution to the family unit and freeing up the already over-burdened work load of the mother."[9]

Although flax was easy to grow in the colonies, it was a several-step process to bring it to the point where it could be spun and turned into thread. The thread was then dyed with natural ingredients such as berries or tree bark before it was used in making linens and clothing. Young women often found employment as "spinners" and would travel from house to house spinning the thread the housekeeper would later use at her loom.

Preparing wool was somewhat less tedious than the steps involved in processing flax, and once the sheep had been sheared the wife could begin sorting the fine wool from that of a lesser quality. The wool was dyed and then "carded" into rolls for spinning. Cards were hand-held wooden paddles with wire teeth used to comb the wool and this job was often delegated to the children in the family. During the evening hours wool was spun into yarn, the loom was used to fashion woolens or the housewife might spend time on a quilt made from scraps of fabric and material.

Along with the designated weekly chores and the grueling hours spent at the cooking hearth on a daily basis, the Colonial housekeeper also had to find time to make a large quantity of candles. It was especially important to have an abundant supply on hand for the winter months when darkness came early. Tallow from animal fat was kept warm in an iron pot over the fire while the holes in the arms of a wooden candle dipper/dryer were threaded with wicks. These in turn were dipped into the tallow and placed on a stand to dry. The procedure was repeated a number of times until the candles were of the proper size.

In the Northeast where bayberry bushes were plentiful, a cup or two of bayberry was added to the tallow in an attempt to mask its unpleasant odor.

With the advent of tin candle molds during the eighteenth century, the art of candle making became more efficient. Tallow could be poured directly into molds of a required size and allowed to dry.

Many middle-class Colonial homes in the North had hired help to assist the wife with seasonal chores. In other homes either a young girl or an indentured servant lived with the family to provide daily assistance. Nonetheless, the housekeeper's life revolved around the completion of tasks and never-ending manual labor. The housekeeper in the South, while perhaps relieved somewhat regarding hands-on labor, had to acquire strong managerial skills in order to keep a plantation with numerous slaves running smoothly. She had the additional responsibility of seeing to the slaves' welfare—food, clothing and shelter—along with that of her immediate family.[10] But because the role of domestic manager on the plantation was less physically demanding on the mistress than on the workers themselves, she didn't suffer the same physical hardships as women in the northern colonies.[11]

By the early 1800s the population of towns along the eastern seaboard and urban centers such as New York, Philadelphia and Baltimore was increasing at a steady rate. The middle- and upper-class families of these areas had access to a growing number of markets offering meats, fruits and vegetables, household goods etc., and "going to the market" became commonplace. Many of the auxiliary functions of the cooking hearth in middle-class homes became passé as mass-produced goods steadily increased.

In the North, indentured servitude was on the decline but young farm girls moving to the cities in search of employment found work as "hired help" in individual households. During the 1820s and 1830s the increasing number of immigrants arriving in America provided a readily available source of "domestics," and this, combined with growing movement towards an industrialized society, altered the course of domesticity.

Development of American Cookery

The American Citron—Take the rind of a large watermelon not too ripe, cut it into small pieces, take two pound of loaf sugar, one pint of water, put it all into a kettle, let it boil gently for four hours, then put it into pots for use.

American Cookery
—Amelia Simmons, 1776

Prior to the 1742 American publication of an English cookbook entitled *The Complete Housewife,* by Eliza Smith, Colonial women relied on their own handwritten recipes, memory and their best judgment when preparing family meals.

While many middle- and upper-class homes subscribed to the English cookery methods they'd long been familiar with, the majority of households found it necessary to make adjustments in meal planning due to the unavailability of certain items and the abundance of others. Colonial cooks substituted native American fruits and vegetables where they could and became inventive when they had to.

Early colonists grew the herbs and vegetables they'd known in England but in addition, they adapted recipes to include corn, pumpkins, beans, sweet potatoes, cranberries, blueberries and elderberries. By the mid-eighteenth century, families living in urban centers dined on the fish that were so plentiful along coastal regions, as well as poultry and beef.

In rural areas, where the majority of the population was still engaged in farming, large quantities of pork were served as well as the "one-pot" meals that were so popular. In addition, baked beans, corn bread, puddings and chowder became staples of the Colonial diet.

It is not at all surprising that when Eliza Smith's book was published in America it became a moderate success. Even though her recipes were for strictly English fare, her book no doubt proved very helpful to many a Colonial housewife who'd had no previous experience with a printed guide. Given the popularity of *The Complete Housewife,* it wasn't long before other English cookbooks became available in the colonies. For example, *The Frugal Housewife* by Susannah Carter was at hand by 1772 and *The New Art of Cookery* by Richard Briggs was in use by 1792. Finally, in 1796, *American Cookery, or the Art of Dressing Viands, Fish, Poultry, and Vegetables, and the Best Modes of Making Pastes, Puffs, Pies, Tarts, Puddings, Custards and Preserves, and All Kinds of Cakes from the Imperial Plumb to Plain Cake. Adapted to this Country, and All Grades of Life* by Amelia Simmons was published.

Recognized by historians as the first truly American cookbook, Simmons' work was a 48-page text that combined noted English dishes with recipes calling for native American ingredients such as cornmeal.[12] The author was so convinced that a need existed for a book of American cookery that she invested her own money in seeing the work brought to print by Hudson & Goodwin of Hartford, Connecticut. She was indeed correct for the initial publication was followed by several editions up until the 1830s.

In an essay written by Mary Tolford Wilson, which appears as an introduction to the 1958 reprint of *American Cookery* by Oxford University Press, she explains that "the originality of Amelia Simmons' work lies in its recognition that an American could not find in a British

A costumed interpreter displays the foods for a celebratory feast in the 1830s living-history village at Conner Prairie. With baking done at the hearth or in the bake oven, it took several days to prepare a large selection of *foods for a social gathering. Wooden bowls, pewter cups and china dishware are used at the table in front of the hearth.*

Courtesy McGuire Photography, Conner Prairie, Noblesville, Indiana.

cookbook recipes for making dishes that she as an American had known and eaten all her life. The deficiencies of British works stemmed largely from one source: Americans used ingredients that Europeans did not ordinarily employ. Amelia Simmons was the first writer of cookery books to set to work with that fact in mind."[13] For example, *American Cookery* included recipes for Indian pudding, Indian slapjacks and "Johny Cake," all of which called for the use of cornmeal.

A NICE INDIAN PUDDING

3 pints scalded milk, 7 spoons fine Indian meal, stir well together while hot, let stand till cooled; add 7 eggs, half pound of raisins, 4 ounces butter, spice and sugar, bake one and a half hour.

From *American Cookery*

Simmons' work also offered recipes for dishes using native squash, pumpkin and berries. Noteworthy, too, is that four of her recipes call for the use of pearl ash, a chemical leaven made of refined wood ash, to produce a lightness in baked goods. Pearl ash was first used in America in the 1790s and was soon being exported to England and European countries.

MOLASSES GINGERBREAD

One table spoon of cinnamon, some coriander or allspice, put to four teaspoons pearl ash, dissolved in half pint water, four pound flour, one quart molasses, four ounces butter . . . knead well till stiff, the more the better, the lighter and whiter it will be, bake brisk fifteen minutes; don't scorch; before it is put in, wash it with whites and sugar beat together.

From *American Cookery*

By the year 1800 a second, revised edition of Simmons' book had been published and the new spirit of republicanism that echoed throughout the country could be glimpsed in her recipes for "Independence Cake" and "Election Cake."

Wilson's 1958 introductory essay mentioned above summarized that *American Cookery* established a model others soon followed. She notes that "in time, the awareness of indigenous cookery extended even to geographical differences and regional works began to appear. But Amelia Simmons still holds her place as the mother of American cookery books."[14]

It is interesting to note that *American Cookery* as well as other recipe books attempted early on were primarily composed of ingredients with

This costumed interpreter presents the sweets prepared for an 1836 Christmas Eve celebration at Conner Prairie. Shown on the worktable next to the cooking hearth is treasured fine china *that will be used for the special cakes that have been baked.*

Courtesy McGuire Photography, Conner Prairie, Noblesville, Indiana.

little or virtually nothing in the way of actual instructions. Cookery methods were handed down from mother to daughter until domestic servants took over in the kitchen during the 1830s and 1840s and prior to this it was assumed women knew how to cook but needed a helping hand with what to cook.

Regarding regional cooking, the slaves on plantations developed a style of southern cooking that included the use of rice, black-eyed peas, corn, wild greens and pork to make such dishes as hush puppies (deep-fried corn bread batter) and hopping John (a mixture of rice and black-eyed peas).

The Pennsylvania Dutch made use of cabbage, sausage and apples in many of their dishes and became noted for their sauerkraut, waffles, scrapple (fried cornmeal and pork), apple butter and shoofly pie (made with brown sugar and molasses).

The early colonists who settled in the North developed recipes for Boston baked beans, brown bread and seafood chowder that became associated with the New England region.

In 1824 *The Virginia Housewife, Or Methodical Book of 1824* by Mary Randolph was published and according to Barbara L. Feret, author of *Gastronomical and Culinary Literature*, Randolph's book may be considered the first southern cookbook. Feret writes that "whereas Amelia Simmons mentions specialties of New England, Mary Randolph put in print for the first time dishes typical of the south—catfish soup, turnip tops, beaten biscuits, field peas and ochra soup . . . polenta, curry and Indian meal pudding."[15]

With increasing wealth among the middle-class and the tendency of the new "genteel" Americans to host elaborate dinner parties with a variety of sweets offered for dessert, the 1828 publication of *Seventy-Five Receipts for Pastry, Cakes, and Sweetmeats* by Eliza Leslie was well received. Her second book, *Domestic French Cookery,* released in 1832 was especially popular in the South where an elevated interest in French cooking was noted.

By the late 1830s many cookbooks included lengthy essays on cultural trends. For example, in both the 1837 publication of *The Housekeeper's Book* by Frances McDougall and *The American Frugal Housewife* by Lydia Child, which was published the following year, the authors expressed deep concern over the excessive extravagance that was replacing the more humble Colonial cooking of the eighteenth century. These same views would persist and were evident in the works published by Catharine Beecher during the 1840s as well as several lesser known cookbooks that targeted the temperance movement.

Today, Colonial cooking is viewed by many food historians as a form of folk art as in the 1989 book by William Ways Weaver, *America Eats: Forms of Edible Folk Art.*

Notable Changes: The New Concept of "Home" and the Transition from "Hired Help" to "Domestic Servants"

Young ladies should be taught that usefulness is happiness, and that all other things are but incidental.

The American Frugal Housewife
—Lydia Marie Child, 1832

The pre-industrial Colonial era from 1700 until the dawn of the Victorian period in the late 1830s was a time of marked change in domesticity and the broader concept of "home." While the cooking hearth continued to be the center of domestic activities and the techniques employed in performing household chores altered very little during this time span, economic prosperity and notable "political" efforts made by women brought "home" to the forefront of American culture. This move in turn transformed the middle-class woman's way of life.

The wearisome tasks of the Colonial housewife were performed to assure her family's survival. Mary Beth Norton tells us in *Liberty's Daughters: The Revolutionary Experience of American Women, 1750–1800* that each task "was conceived to be an end in itself, rather than as a means to a greater or more meaningful goal."[16] As such, cooking, sewing, making candles, tending the garden and even producing large numbers of children were utilitarian functions directly linked to the welfare of the home, having little to do with the community at large. Nor did the housewife view any portion of her work to be a "craft" or personal expression of a special ability or talent.

As a home-based industry, a married couple worked together for the family and its prosperity, albeit in very different roles. Woman's work was for the most part confined indoors, and once the kitchen was removed to the keeping room or a wing, she was increasingly isolated from the rest of the family. Daughters worked alongside their mother to become skilled in domestic undertakings and boys worked outdoors with their father to tend the livestock, care for crops etc. That is not to say the Colonial family, or more specifically, the Colonial housewife did not have contact with the outside world. Several household tasks eventually provided the impetus for social gatherings that Colonial women no doubt looked forward to for both companionship and a break from the daily routine. For example, in Holliday's *Woman's Life in Colonial Days,* he explains that certain work often required a spirit of cooperation between neighbors and as women gathered together to spin or sew, a social climate developed. The end result was the group quilting bee or spinning bee that women undoubtedly began to look forward to for friendship outside the home. The "bee" had the added attraction of lessening the sense of "work" associated with it since the women could visit, exchange news and share their concerns while they were sewing, quilting and so on.[17]

In growing urban areas, middle-class merchants and tradesmen's wives would often gather together for a social hour at which tea was the favored drink. Available and in use in many Colonial households of the early eighteenth century, tea had become especially popular among women by the 1750s and 1760s and it was common practice among them to carry a small teacup, saucer and spoon when going visiting, as such items were then scarce and each household might have just one or two.[18]

It was by these two avenues—the increased production of homespun cloth in response to high duties being levied on imports, and the widespread boycott of tea—that politics first entered the home. (These actions on the part of women would ultimately influence their homes as well as their role.) For example, Holliday notes " . . . the well-to-do Americans of the eighteenth century at length adopted the custom of importing the finer cloth, silk, satin and brocade; but after the middle of the century the anti-British sentiment impelled even the wealthiest either to make or buy the coarser American cloth. Indeed, it became a matter of genuine pride to many a patriotic dame that she could thus use the spinning wheel in behalf of her country. Daughters of Liberty, having agreed to drink no tea and to wear no garments of foreign make, had spinning circles . . . and it was no uncommon sight between 1770 and 1785 to see groups of women, carrying spinning wheels through the streets, going to such assemblies."[19]

Regarding the boycott of tea, an agreement published in the February 12, 1770 edition of the *Boston Evening Post* perhaps says it best. Over 300 women penned their names to the following, which was dated January 31, 1770:

> At a time when our invaluable Rights and Privileges are attacked
> in an unconstitutional and most alarming Manner, and as we find
> we are reproached for not being so ready as could be desired, to

lend our Assistance, we think it our Duty perfectly to concur with the true Friends of Liberty in all measures they have taken to save this abused Country from Ruin and Slavery. And particularly, we join with the very Respectable Body of Merchants and other inhabitants of this Town, who met in Faneuil Hall the 23rd of this Instant, in their Resolutions, totally to abstain from the Use of Tea; And as the greatest part of the Revenue arising by Virtue of the late Acts, is produced from the Duty paid upon Tea, which Revenue is wholly expended to support the American Board of Commissioners; WE, the Subscribers, do strictly engage, that we will totally abstain from the Use of that Article (sickness excepted) not only in our Respective Families, but that we will absolutely refuse it, if it should be offered to us upon any Occasion whatsoever. This agreement we cheerfully come into, As we believe the very distressed Situation of our Country Requires it and we do hereby oblige ourselves religiously to observe it till the late Revenue Acts are repealed.[20]

Notable too is that many women worked the family farm or ran the family business while husbands and sons fought the Revolutionary War. For the good of the country, for the sake of their family, they suffered the hardships of additional labor and a shortage of necessities for the cause at hand.

So it was, in the late 1700s, that hearth and home combined with politics—first in protest and then pursuit of freedom. As a result, women saw themselves in a new light and their domestic role expanded to include sending good citizens out into the world. In addition, religious overtones fostered "Christian" homes where morality and politics were closely intertwined. For example, consider these early nineteenth-century words of noted cookbook author Mary Randolph. On the subject of domesticity she wrote, "the prosperity and happiness of a family depend greatly on the order and regularity established in it. The husband . . . will feel pride and exultation in the possession of a companion, who gives to his home charms that gratify every wish of his soul, and render the haunts of dissipation hateful to him. Sons bred in such a family will be moral men, of steady habits; and daughters will each be a treasure to her husband; and being formed on the model of an exemplary mother, will use the same means for securing the happiness of her own family which she has seen successfully practiced under the paternal roof."[21]

The new spirit of patriotism encouraged an increasing awareness of native foods and as we've already seen, Amelia Simmons' second edition of *American Cookery* included recipes for cakes named in honor of the new republic. Also noteworthy is that in the preface of Simmons' first edition, published in 1776, she refers to the female character as "virtuous," a descriptive term commonly applied to the housewife through the mid-nineteenth century.

Coinciding with this new wave of republicanism was an economic prosperity that fostered genteel femininity. As the authors tell us in *Artists in Aprons,* "As mills and factories were established that offered greater rewards for the laborer and cheaper goods for the consumer, it no longer was necessary to produce some items at home. As the new incentives for income and spending progressed, woman and her hearth began to be regarded as the ideal vehicles for the display of wealth . . . Both house and woman were adorned with the accouterments of position and prosperity attained by socially rising merchants, farmers and craftsmen. The American dream of affluence for all . . . was on its way to becoming a reality."[22]

While the eighteenth century was witness to the northern housewife working side by side with the "help," and indeed a young farm girl or indentured servant was often considered a part of the family, this scheme changed dramatically during the early 1800s. As the housewife made the subtle shift from laborer to manager, the "help" became the "domestic servant." This transition was noted in Faye Dudden's 1983 publication, *Serving Women: Household Service in Nineteenth Century America.* Dudden writes that, "beginning in the 1820s and more noticeably in the 1830s, Americans began to hire more servants to work in an explicitly domestic sphere. Abandoning the language of help, they began to call them 'domestic servants' . . . In hiring domestics middle-class women found the means to make domesticity more flexible, accommodating roles of authority and activity, rather than passivity and isolation."[23]

During the early 1800s the majority of "domestics" were young women moving from rural America to towns and cities in search of employment. By the 1840s the immigrant population began to fill these roles as native-born daughters turned to other avenues for work.

Even with "domestics" the housewife usually continued to do her own baking but she often turned the everyday cooking and mundane tasks of laundry, cleaning and so on over to servants. With the increased awareness of cookery via the cookbook and more time to devote to the brick bake oven, many a mistress took pride in her ability to turn out fine cakes and bread or serve an elaborate dinner she'd supervised.

Houses began to increase in size as the middle and upper class became more affluent. Women in turn devoted time to decorating their homes and entertaining. Populations in urban areas continued to grow and "ceremony" became an increasingly significant portion of a home life that was viewed as a safe haven from the encroaching industrial revolution.

Virtuous women were guided in their new roles by a large number of etiquette manuals, magazine articles and novels that became common-place by the 1830s. One such publication, *Godey's Lady's Book*, was destined to be a strong voice for American women for decades to come. Editor Sarah Josepha Hale supported the political connection between good citizenry and domesticity and the magazine advised women through editorials and information on decorating, needlework, fashions etc. There was, however, cause for concern regarding the middle-class woman's new life-style and noted authors of early nineteenth-century domestic manuals voiced their opinion in the pages of their text. They worried that the concept of genteel feminism and extravagance were detrimental to women's health and that young daughters would not be properly trained in household skills.

With these thoughts in mind, it's interesting to note that Catharine Beecher took a romanticized view of early Colonial women in her 1869 *American Woman's Home*. Beecher wrote, "In those former days most women were in good health, debility and disease being the exception. Then, too, was seen the economy of daylight and its pleasures. They were used to early rising, and would not lie in bed, if they could. Long years of practice made them familiar with the shortest, neatest, most expeditious method of doing every household office, so that really for the greater part of the time in the house there seemed, to a looker-on, to be nothing to do. They rose in the morning and dispatched husband, father, and brothers to the farm or woodlot; went sociably about, chatting with each other, skimmed the milk, made butter, and turned the cheeses. The forenoon was long . . . they had leisure for an hour's sewing or reading before it was time to start the dinner preparations."

Beecher went on to express her concern over deteriorating female health by writing "The race of strong, hardy, cheerful girls, that used to grow in country places, and made the bright, neat, New-England kitchens of old times—the girls that could wash, iron, brew, bake, harness a horse and drive him, no less than braid straw, embroider, draw, paint, and read innumerable books—this race of women, pride of olden time, is daily lessening; and in their stead come the fragile, easily-fatigued, languid girls of a modern age, drilled in book-learning, ignorant of common things."

Catharine Beecher proposed the mid-nineteenth-century woman should be as skilled as her Colonial ancestors. She advised that "cultivated, intelligent women, who are brought up to do the work of their own families, are labor-saving institutions. They make the head save the wear of the muscles. By forethought, contrivance, system, and arrangement they lessen the amount to be done, and do it with less expense of time and strength than others." Regarding excess and extravagance, Beecher proposed "a moderate style of housekeeping, small, compact, and simple domestic establishments, must necessarily be the general order of life in America."[24]

Letters to Young Ladies by Mrs. L. H. Sigourney (sixteenth edition, published in 1854) offered a more practical and realistic view of the Colonial household as the author discussed "industry." Sigourney wrote:

> . . . I have seen no class of people, among whom a more efficient system of industry and economy of time was established, than the agricultural population of New England. Their possessions are not sufficiently large to allow waste of any description. Hence, every article seems to be carefully estimated, and applied to its best use . . . The farmer, rising with the dawn, attends to those employments which are necessary for the comfort of the family, and proceeds early with his sons or assistants, to their department of daily labour . . . Fitting tasks are proportioned to the youngest ones, that no hand may be idle. In the interior of the house, an equal diligence prevails. The elder daughters take willing part with the mother, in every domestick toil . . . The sound of the wheel and the vigorous strokes of the loom, are heard . . . In the simple and abundant supply of a table, from their own resources . . . all are interested . . . The active matron strives to lessen the expenses of her husband, and to increase his gains. She sends to market, the wealth of her dairy, and the surplus produce of her loom. She instructs her daughter by their diligence to have a purse of their own, from which to furnish the more delicate parts of their wardrobe . . . In the long evenings of winter, she plies the needle, or knits stockings with them, or maintains the quiet musick of the flax-wheel, from whence linen is prepared for the family. She incites them never to eat the bread of idleness, and as they have been trained, so they will train others again; for the seeds of industry are perennial.[25]

While Beecher expressed concern over the new breed of young women with fragile health and expanding interests that hampered training within the domestic sphere, Mrs. Sigourney was more direct in pointing out it was women's patriotic duty to tend the domestic altar. She noted that "as surely as the safety and prosperity of a nation depend on the virtue of its people, they, who reign in the retreats where man turns for his comfort, who have power over the machinery which stamps on the infant mind its character of good or evil, are responsible, to a fearful extent, for that safety and prosperity."[26]

As the Victorian period approached, the invention and widespread use of the cookstove and mass-produced kitchen gadgets and utensils would alter the kitchen and woman's work considerably.

Colonial Household Hints and Recipes

❦HOUSEHOLD HINTS❦

OBSERVATION

All meat pies require a hotter and brisker oven than fruit pies, in good cookeries, all raisins should be stoned [crushed to remove seeds] . . .

American Cookery
—Amelia Simmons, 1776

HERBS, USEFUL IN COOKERY

Thyme, is good in soups and stuffings. Sweet Marjoram, is used in Turkeys. Summer Savory, ditto, and in sausages and salted beef, and legs of pork. Sage, is useful in cheese and pork, but not generally approved [thought to be too strong or overpowering]. Parsley, good in soups, and to garnish roast beef, excellent with bread and butter in the spring . . . Sweet Thyme, is most useful and best approved in cookery.

American Cookery
—Amelia Simmons, 1776

Tight, waxy, yellow butter is better than white or crumbly, which soon becomes rancid and snowy. Go into the center of balls or rolls to prove and judge it; if in firkin [a lidded, wooden container], the middle is to be preferred, as the sides are frequently distasted by the wood of the firkin—altho' oak and used for years. New pine tubs are ruinous to the butter. To have sweet butter in dog days and thro' the vegetable seasons, send stone pots to honest, neat, and trusty dairy people, and procure it pack'd down in May, and let them be brought in the night, or cool rainy morning, covered with a clean cloth wet in cold water, and partake of no heat from the house, and set the pots in the coldest part of your cellar, or in the ice house. Some say that May butter thus preserved, will go into the winter use, better than fall made butter.

American Cookery
—Amelia Simmons, 1776

The grand arcanum of management can be stated in three simple rules: let every thing be done at a proper time, keep every thing in its proper place, and put every thing to its proper use.

The Virginia Housewife
—Mary Randolph, 1824

If you would avoid waste in your family, attend to the following rules, and do not despise them because they appear so unimportant . . . Buy your woolen yarns in quantities from someone in the country, whom you can trust. The thread stores make profits upon it, of course. After old coats, pantaloons etc. have been cut up for boys, and are no longer capable of being connected into garments, cut them into strips, and employ the leisure moments of children, or domestics, in sewing and braiding them for door mats.

The American Frugal Housewife
—Lydia Marie Child, 1832

That part of mutton called the rack . . . is cheap food. It is not more than four or five cents a pound; and four pounds will make a dinner for six people . . .

The American Frugal Housewife
—Lydia Marie Child, 1836

Keep yeast in wood or earthen. Keep preserves and jellies in glass, or china or stoneware. Keep salt in a dry place. Keep meal in a cool dry place. Keep ice in the cellar, wrapped in flannel. Keep vinegar in wood or glass.

The Good Housekeeper
—Sarah J. Hale, 1839

❧ RECIPES ❧

TO ROAST A LARGE FISH

Take a large fish (pike), gut it and clean it, and lard it with eel and bacon, as you lard a fowl; then take thyme and savory, salt, mace, and nutmeg, and some crumbs of bread, beef-suet and parsley; shred all very fine, and mix it up with raw eggs; make it a long pudding, and put it in the belly of your pike, skewer up the belly, and dissolve anchovies in butter, and baste it with it; put two splints on each side of the pike, and tie it to the spit; melt butter thick for the sauce, or, if you please, oyster sauce, and bruise the pudding in it. Garnish with lemon.

The Complete Housewife
—Eliza Smith, 1742

TO ROAST BEEF

The general rules are, to have a brisk hot fire, to hang down rather than to spit, to baste with salt and water, and one quarter of an hour to every pound of beef, tho' tender beef will require less, while old tough beef will require more roasting; pricking with a fork will determine you whether done or not; rare done is the healthiest . . .

American Cookery
—Amelia Simmons, 1776

BREWING SPRUCE BEER

Take four ounces of hops, let them boil half an hour in one gallon of water, strain the hop water then add sixteen gallons of warm water, two gallons of molasses, eight ounces of essence of spruce [concentrated flavoring from sap], dissolved in one quart of water, put in a clean cask, then shake it well together, add half a pint of emptins [a semi-liquid yeast], then let it stand and work one week, if very warm weather less time will do, when it is drawn off to bottle, add one spoonful of molasses to every bottle.

American Cookery
—Amelia Simmons, 1776

A STEW PIE

Boil a shoulder of Veal, and cut it up, salt, pepper and butter half a pound, and slices of raw salt pork, make a layer of meat, and a layer of biscuit, or biscuit dough into a pot, cover close and stew half an hour in three quarts of water only.

American Cookery
—Amelia Simmons, 1776

A CROOKNECK, OR WINTER SQUASH PUDDING

Core, boil and skin a good squash, and bruise it well; take 6 large apples, pared, cored, and stewed tender, mix together; add 6 or 7 spoonsful of dry bread or biscuit, rendered fine as meal, half pint milk or cream, 2 spoons of rose-water, 2 do. [ditto] wine, 5 or 6 eggs beated and strained, nutmeg, salt and sugar to your taste, one spoon flour, beat all smartly together, bake. The above is a good receipt for Pompkins, Potatoes or Yams, adding more moistening or milk and rose water, and to the two latter a few black or Lisbon currants, or dry whortleberries scattered in, will make it better.

American Cookery
—Amelia Simmons, 1776

CHERRY BOUNCE

Take a peck of morella cherries, and a peck of black hearts. Stone the morellas and crack the stones. Put all the cherries and the cracked stones into a demi-john, with three pounds of loaf-sugar slightly pounded or beaten. Pour in two gallons of double-rectified whiskey. Cork the demi-john, and in six months the cherry bounce will be fit to pour off and bottle for use; but the older it is, the better.

Seventy-Five Receipts for Pastry, Cakes, and Sweetmeats . . .
—Eliza Leslie, 1833

NEW YEAR'S CAKE

Seven pounds of flour, sifted. Half pound of butter. Half a pound of lard. Two pounds and a half of White Havanna Sugar. Having sifted the flour, spread the sugar on the paste-board, a little at a time, and crush it to powder by rolling it with the rolling pin. Then mix it with the flour. Cut up in the flour the butter and lard, and mix it well by rubbing it in with your hands. Add by degrees enough cold water to make a stiff dough, then knead the dough very hard, till it no longer sticks to your hands. Cover it, set it away for an hour or two, and then knead it again in the same manner. You may repeat the kneading several times. Then cut it into pieces, roll out each piece into a sheet half an inch thick. Cut it into large flat cakes with a tin cutter. You may stamp each cake with a wooden print, by way of ornamenting the surface. Sprinkle with flour some large flat tin or iron pans, lay the cakes in them, and bake them a pale brown, in an oven of equal heat throughout. These cakes require more and harder kneading than any others, therefore it is best to have them kneaded by a man, or a very strong woman . . .

Seventy-Five Receipts for Pastry, Cakes, and Sweetmeats . . .
—Eliza Leslie, 1833

2

The Early Victorian Kitchen 1840–1869

"A PLACE FOR EVERYTHING AND EVERYTHING IN ITS PLACE"

This circa 1832 kitchen is an excellent interpretation of an early kitchen with cooking hearth that was updated during the Victorian period. The fireplace, 65 inches wide by 46 inches high by 24 inches deep, now houses an Abendroth York cast-iron stove. The kitchen also includes a reconstructed sink with a hand pump and over the sink are bells, once part of the call system for the upstairs rooms. Worktables, a small rocker and assorted cookware can be seen in this photo, as well as the small cupboard in the brick wall behind the bake oven, which most likely was used to store and dry wood.

Courtesy Old Merchant's House Museum, New York City.

What has made this nation great? Not its heroes but its households.

Godey's Lady's Book
—Editorial by Sarah J. Hale, July 1869

*T*he mid-nineteenth century was a transitional period for the Victorian kitchen. Those with older homes where the kitchen had progressed from the hall to the keeping room continued to build additions to the back of the house or a "wing" for the kitchen and its utility rooms. In the warmer climates of the southern states a separate kitchen or cookhouse building remained popular to avoid the threat of fire to the main building and to contain heat in the hot summer months. In the ever-expanding urban centers where building was taking place at a fast and furious pace, kitchens were built at the rear of the house or in the basements of city townhouses and brownstones.

Basement kitchens were either dark, cavernous series of adjoining utility rooms, or, if constructed in the English style, actually a half-basement with windows above or at ground level and a door leading outside at the rear of the building.

Very distinct differences marked the rural or country kitchen, which was still an important setting for family meals and activities, and the urban, middle-class kitchen, which was given over to domestic servants as the parlor and dining room became the focus of family interaction.

Although the iron cookstove and range were available, many households were hesitant to forsake reliable cookery methods and continued to rely on the cooking hearth. This attitude, however, changed during the late 1840s as the merits of the new cookstove were quickly recognized, and by the late 1850s a range or stove could be found in homes everywhere.

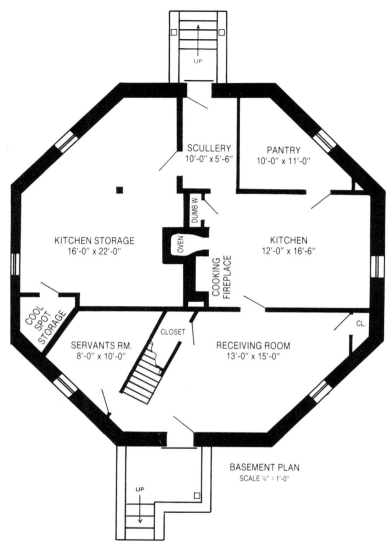

UP

SCULLERY
10'-0" x 5'-6"

PANTRY
10'-0" x 11'-0"

DUMB W

KITCHEN STORAGE
16'-0" x 22'-0"

OVEN

KITCHEN
12'-0" x 16'-6"

COOKING FIREPLACE

COOL SPOT STORAGE

CLOSET

CL.

SERVANTS RM.
8'-0" x 10'-0"

RECEIVING ROOM
13'-0" x 15'-0"

BASEMENT PLAN
SCALE ¼" = 1'-0"

UP

This basement plan for the Rich-Twinn Octagon House located in Akron, New York is commonly referred to as an "English-style" basement because it is half above ground level and has several windows. The kitchen includes a cooking hearth with bake oven, a dumbwaiter to transport meals upstairs to the formal dining room, a pantry, scullery, large storage area with a "cool spot" for fruits and vegetables, servant's chamber and a receiving room, which served as an informal family dining/sitting area.

Courtesy of James Stapleton, Restoration Director, Newstead Historical Society.

With over half the population still engaged in farming during the mid-1800s, the 1852 publication of *Rural Architecture* by Lewis F. Allen offered designs for homes to meet the needs of the middle-class farming family. Of his Design II the author wrote,

> It [the house] has a subdued, quiet, unpretending look; yet will accommodate a family of a dozen workmen, besides the females engaged in the household work, with perfect convenience; or if occupied by a farmer with but his own family around him, ample room is afforded them for a most comfortable mode of life, and sufficent for the requirements of a farm of two, to three or four hundred acres. This house is, in the main body, 36x22 feet, one and a half stories high, with a projection on the rear 36x16 feet, for the kitchen and its offices; and a still further addition to that, of 26x18 feet, for wash-room . . . the style of this establishment is of plain Italian, or bracketed [a Victorian architectural style popular from 1850–1880 and characterized by a square, box-like design embellished with decorative brackets], and may be equally applied to stone, brick, or wood.[1]

In writing about the kitchen, Allen expressed the view that in rural areas the kitchen was indeed the heart of the home. He described it as

> the grand room of this house. It is 24x16 feet in area, having an ample fireplace, with its hooks and trammels, and a spacious oven by its side. It is lighted by a double window at one end, and a single window near the fireplace. At one end of this kitchen is a most comfortable and commodious family bedroom, 13x10 feet, with a large closet in one corner, and lighted by a window in the side . . . A passage leads by the side of the oven to a sink-room, or recess, behind the chimney, with shelves to dry dishes on, and lighted by the half of a double window, which accommodates with its other half the dairy, or closet adjoining. A door also opens from this recess into the closet and dairy, furnished with broad shelves, that part of which, next to the kitchen, is used for dishes, cold meat and bread cupboards; while the part of it adjoining the window beyond, is used for milk . . . a door opens, also, from the kitchen into a passage four feet wide and twelve feet long leading to the wash-room, 18x16 feet, and by an outside door, through this passage to the porch . . . in the wash-room are two windows. A chimney at the far end accommodates a boiler or two, and a fireplace, if required. A sink stands adjoining the chimney . . . in this wash-room may be located the cooking stove in warm weather, leaving the main kitchen for a family and eating room.[2]

Whether a kitchen was located in the growing town or city, or in the country, these factory-like centers of operation shared some common features during the period 1840–1869. In general, the kitchen proper had an adjoining pantry or store-closet and oftentimes a washroom (commonly called "scullery," an old British term) for laundry and/or preparation of fruits and vegetables for cooking. The Colonial kitchen root cellar became simply the "cellar" and most kitchens took advantage of this underground space for storage and preservation of certain foodstuffs.

Catharine E. Beecher advised housekeepers on the subject of the pantry in *Miss Beecher's Domestic Receipt Book*. She told her readers, "It is best to have a store-closet [pantry] open from a kitchen, because the kitchen fire keeps the atmosphere dry, and this prevents the articles stored from moulding, and other injury from dampness. Yet it must not be kept warm, as there are many articles which are injured by warmth. A cool and dry place is indispensable for a store-room, and a small window over the door, and another opening out-doors is a great advantage, by securing coolness, and a circulation of fresh air."[3]

The store-closet or pantry was used to keep staples such as flour, cornmeal, rye, oatmeal, salt, macaroni, rice and sugar in barrels or covered crocks or jugs. Herbs and spices were stored in the pantry in wooden or tin containers or in small glass jars with cork stoppers. Preserves, jelly, cakes and bread were also kept in the pantry.

The cellar, usually dark and cool, was the ideal spot for storing vinegar, oil, molasses, smoked meats and root vegetables.

Laundry work was done in the washroom if one was available, or in the kitchen.

As in Colonial days, the kitchen garden remained an important part of domestic undertakings throughout the mid-century. Mass-production of packaged goods was not yet a reality and the kitchen garden provided the household with the various berries and vegetables used in everyday cooking. This was especially so in rural areas but by the 1860s the city dweller could visit the farmer's market to purchase fresh produce.

A well-tended garden reflected upon the household and this thought was conveyed by Joseph and Laura Lyman in their 1869 publication, *The Philosophy of Housekeeping*. The Lymans proposed that "Good housekeeping does not begin or end with the front and back doorsteps of one's home. The same spirit of system, the same thoughtfulness and care, the economy and forethought that reign within, infusing a tone and, so to speak, a soul through the well-kept house . . . will expand into the dooryard and bloom in the garden . . . all a lady has to do . . . is carry her system and the maxims of thrift, and order, and thoroughness out among her currant-bushes, her cherry-trees, her vines, and her beds."[4]

The kitchen itself was of a large size with walls painted in light to moderate tones of beige, tan or cream and woodwork painted in slightly darker shades. Kitchen flooring was either brick or wood, and wooden floors were often painted either gray, mustard, green or a dark shade of red and then covered with an oilcloth or scattered rag rugs. Oilcloth proved to be popular in the kitchen and was recommended by Catharine Beecher when she wrote, "The kitchen floor should be covered with an oil cloth. Carpets, or bits of carpet, are not so good, because of the grease and filth that must accumulate in them, and the labor of sweeping, shaking, and cleansing them . . . if the cook is troubled with cold feet in winter, small bits of carpeting can be laid where she sits and stands the most. Otherwise they had better be kept out of the kitchen."[5]

The cooking hearth remained the center of activity until the cookstove or range became commonplace and at that point many fireplaces were either bricked up or served to house the larger range. The cast-iron cookstoves manufactured during this time period burned wood or coal (coal was abundant and readily available by the mid-nineteenth century) and while most urban dwellings took advantage of the new fuel, rural kitchens often continued to cook with wood.

The range and the cookstove were two very different appliances, although both included an oven and burners. "Range" referred to large, brick-set, iron structures where flues and draughts were located in the brickwork. The range was most often placed within an existing hearth. Early "stoves" were totally constructed of iron, having flues within and smaller in size than the range. Housekeeping experts of the mid-Victorian period differed in their opinion of which was preferable, but many believed the range inferior to the stove because the mortar and brickwork absorbed heat that should be directed at cooking, thus making the range less economical than a stove. In addition, popular household manuals noted an increased risk of clothing catching fire when standing before the range, the inability of the range to keep a fire burning all night long, and, although a range could keep the kitchen warm in the winter, it made it unbearably hot during the summer.

In the 1869 publication of *The American Woman's Home* by Catharine E. Beecher and Harriet Beecher Stowe, Catharine's strong opinion that every housekeeper should be adept at operating her stove in the most economical manner possible was clearly conveyed in Chapter V, THE CONSTRUCTION AND CARE OF STOVES, FURNACES, AND CHIMNEYS. She informed her readers that after having investigated and operated various

cookstoves, she'd discovered one "constructed on true scientific principles, which unites convenience, comfort, and economy in a remarkable
manner." The stove illustrated here (as it appears in Beecher and Stowe's
work), was reported to be made of "fine castings and nice-fitting
workmanship, all the parts liable to burn out are so protected by linings,

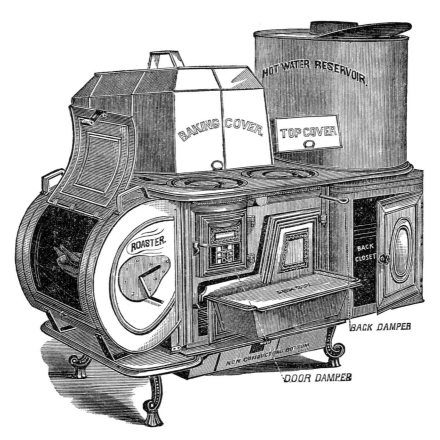

*This ideal cooking stove was illustrated
in both the* American Woman's Home
*by Catharine E. Beecher and Harriet
Beecher Stowe and the 1873*
Housekeeper's Manual *by Catharine
Beecher. This durable, well-constructed
model would allow the housekeeper to
perform several functions at once, such
as bake bread in the oven, roast meat in*
*the tin roaster, make tea on a top
burner, warm sadirons underneath the
back cover, keep water hot in the reservoir, and burn for twenty-four hours on
one coal hod. According to Beecher, this
illustration "exhibits the stove completed, with all its appendages, as they
might be employed in cooking for a
large number."*

and other contrivances easily renewed, that the stove itself may pass from one generation to another . . ."

Realistic in her understanding that not all housekeepers would carefully study the methods of operating this stove (or teach their cooks), Miss Beecher also recommended it because "it also can be used satisfactorily even when the mistress and maid are equally careless, and ignorant of its distinctive merits." Outfitted with every possible attachment, this stove would, with proper management of dampers, perform multiple functions at the same time, such as burn for 24 hours on one coal hod, keep 17 gallons of water hot in the reservoir, bake pies in the warming closet, warm sadirons underneath the back cover, bake bread in the oven, roast meat in the tin roaster and make tea on a top burner or under the baking cover.[6]

Hundreds of founderies were turning out ranges and cookstoves by the 1850s and it is therefore not suprising that numerous models existed and improvements were being made at such a rapid pace that a stove could become outdated in a year or two and quickly traded for a modern version.

Kitchen furnishings throughout the period 1840–1869 included a large worktable for preparing meals and baked goods, a pie-safe (also called a tin-safe) which was a freestanding cupboard, 5 to 6 feet tall, with shelves and two cupboard doors made of pierced tin. This pie-safe, used to store fresh baked goods, would allow air to circulate throughout the cupboard while at the same time protecting the contents from flies and mice.

If it was necessary for domestics to sleep in the kitchen to tend the fire or due to lack of space, a bunk-settee might also be found near the warmth of the hearth, stove or range.

One item that remained in constant use throughout the nineteenth century was the kitchen clock, which was relied upon when cooking and for the preparation of timely meals.

A step-back cupboard (or china closet) was used in the majority of kitchens to store dishware, everyday tableware, cutlery and table and kitchen linens.

A sink made of iron, soapstone or granite was encased in a wooden "dry sink," which was a low cupboard housing the sink, with additional space located to the side of the sink and down below. Early in the nineteenth century water was carried into the kitchen from the well and later a pipe ran from the well to a pump at the kitchen sink. During the 1850s windmill power pumped water to receptacles on the roof top and indoor piping and kitchen faucets brought water to the sink.

In many kitchens pegs were hung near the stove to dry kitchen towels and limited shelving was used to store necessities while utensils were hung on the wall near the hearth and then the cookstove. The kitchens in larger homes also included a linen press for storing napkins, table-cloths and linens.

The early Victorian kitchen was lacking in planned organization and space but toward this end, the 1860 third edition of *Beecher's Domestic Receipt-Book* (first published in 1849), offered suggestions for work areas and storage centers. The author's instructions for building a kitchen worktable with built-in shelves and drawers above would provide "an invaluable aid to system, and it would save many steps, and much inconvenience." The table was to be 6 feet in length and 30 inches tall, made with three pull-out drawers in front for kitchen tools such as the rolling pin, coffee stick, mush stick, gridiron scraper and mashers. A second drawer would hold cutlery and the third was proposed for dish cloths and towels.

Above the table Miss Beecher recommended shelves nailed or screwed to the wall with doors or a sliding curtain to protect the contents from dust. These shelves could keep a ready supply of sugar, spices, coffee, tea and so on at the cook's fingertips and enough room would remain for a receipt book and household account book.[7]

This same publication included practical instructions and advice on building a kitchen closet which would be a "great aid to system and order." Miss Beecher suggested this large, square and open area have pegs to hang brooms and mops and the area given over to shelving could neatly store cleaning, laundry and ironing supplies such as the skirt board, bosom board (for ironing blouses), carpet stretcher, scrubbing brushes etc. Of her recommendations Catharine Beecher wrote that "by thus arranging articles together in one place, and with so complete an assortment, much time and many steps are saved, while they are preserved in good order.

"A housekeeper who chooses to do without some of these conveniences, and spend the money saved in parlor adornments, has a right to do so, and others have a right to think she in this shows herself deficient in good sense."[8]

Although the ice chest was introduced during the 1860s, thus making it possible to keep perishables fresh for longer periods of time, they were found in few homes until later in the century.

During the 1840s–1860s change was virtually nonexistent in the kitchen as a room. Before the Civil War (1861–1865), there was a surplus of "domestics" to carry out the tedious, mundane and endless variety of household chores. Whether those domestics were slaves on southern plantations or immigrants flooding America in search of a new

The kitchen plan as illustrated in the 1869 publication American Woman's Home *by Catharine E. Beecher and Harriet Beecher Stowe. The kitchen proper includes an innovative, built-in "cooking form" with sink, storage areas for flour, rye and cornmeal and a work area to prepare meats, vegetables and so on (designated by "cook" in the illustration). Open shelves were recommended for easy access to kitchenware items and a stove room, separated from the kitchen by sliding doors, would contain heat and odors. Dishes could be washed in the stove room and it provided additional storage space and access to the cellar.*

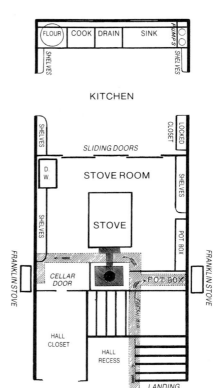

life, household help was not difficult to find. While some mistresses may have made an attempt to provide small comforts in their kitchen, such as a rocker for the weary cook or a colorful gingham curtain dressing a small window, they did not campaign for improvements regarding day-to-day operations. Ever so slowly, and at a time coinciding with the end of the Civil War, did change begin to take place. Slavery was abolished. The industrial revolution was in full swing and increasing numbers of domestics and newly arriving immigrants were opting for employment in factories and mills springing up all across the country.

In their 1869 publication *The American Woman's Home*, noted domestic science authority Catharine E. Beecher and her sister, Harriet Beecher Stowe, described in detail the layout of a "Christian house, that is a house contrived for the express purpose of enabling every member of a family to labor with the hands for the common good, and by modes at once healthful, economical, and tasteful."[9] The sisters proposed some very modern changes regarding the kitchen. For example, they recommended the kitchen should be located on the first floor and include a kitchen area with a separate stove room. They advised readers, "between the two rooms glazed sliding-doors [to allow for light] . . . serve to shut out heat and smells from the kitchen. The sides of the stove-room must

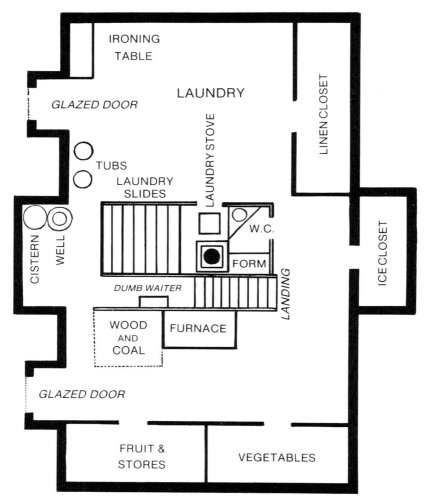

The Beecher sisters included this basement plan in their 1869 publication American Woman's Home. The basement included a laundry area with a stove for heating water and irons, laundry tubs and an ironing table. An ice closet, cistern and well were to be located in the basement of the ideal home, as well as storage areas for fruits, vegetables and staples.

be lined with shelves . . . boxes with lids, to receive stove utensils, must be placed near the stove. On these shelves, and in the closet and boxes can be placed every material used for cooking, all the table and cooking utensils, and all the articles used in house work, and yet much spare room will be left. The cook's galley in a steamship has every article and utensil used in cooking for two hundred persons, in a space not larger than this stove-room, and so arranged that with one or two steps the cook can reach all he uses." The authors were of the opinion that this well-planned and organized space in the stove-room would eliminate the hundreds of extra steps a cook took during the course of a day simply to fetch and put away kitchen items.

The kitchen room (9x9 feet) included a locked closet, shelving, a sink and adjacent "cooking-form." This "cooking-form," an extreme departure from kitchen furnishings and utensils in use up until that time, offered the most modern kitchen plan possible. It was a built-in, counter-like outfit of storage areas for flour, rye and cornmeal with small drawers for towels and scouring equipment, and open shelving below to accommodate sugar containers and assorted buckets and tins. On top of the cooking-form was a "moulding and meat board" to prepare meats, vegetables and bread. Next to the sink was a dish-drainer with grooves that would hold tableware and allow water to run back into the sink.[10]

In the house design the sisters proposed with compact kitchen and stove-room, the laundry room, storage closet and icebox were to be located in the basement and included a separate stove for heating water and irons. They told readers, "If parents wish their daughters to grow up with good domestic habits, they should have, as one means of securing the result, a neat and cheerful kitchen. A kitchen should always, if possible, be entirely above-ground, and well lighted . . . If flowers and shrubs be cultivated around the doors and windows, and the yard near them be kept well turfed, it will add very much to their agreeable appearance."[11]

Others were also beginning to promote the benefits of a well thought-out kitchen. In *The Philosophy of Housekeeping* by Joseph B. and Laura E. Lyman, their 1869 home manual offered several different kitchen plans designed to save steps and energy in cooking and conducting household chores. Directed at those who subscribed to small town living or farming for their livelihood, the authors wrote:

> It may be said, in general, that, in grouping the different rooms of a house plan, the person mainly interested in the result should proceed from within outwardly, rather than the reverse, which is

the natural method of the carpenter. For instance, the house-keeper who is so fortunate as to have it in her power to prescribe the internal arrangement of a house, should begin with her sitting-room and kitchen, as these are practically the nucleus of a dwelling. Let her determine in her own mind of what size she would like to have her kitchen; where she would have her windows; where the fireplace or flue for stove-pipe; where the pump (if this is practicable) and sink; on which side she would like her pantry and closet. Around this let her arrange those rooms which she would have opening to it, as bedroom, sitting-room, wood-house, and the doors leading to the chambers and cellar . . . The first thing to be considered in a plan for the kitchen is saving steps . . . her kitchen is her workshop. Water, fuel, the stove, the dishes, the raw materials of food, are the tools and the stock with which it is her business to concoct the family sustenance. The absolute amount of movement unavoidable in the domestic routine is about the same in families of the average size; but the rapidity and ease with which this is performed in different households vary enormously . . . the time thus rescued from the demands of the kitchen may be so much more pleasantly and profitably employed in little arts of household adornments, in personal accomplishments, or in agreeable conversation . . . to effect a difference so great, is it not worth the while for every housekeeper to plan her work as well as the facilities by which it is done, in the best possible manner? For instance, to have her stove, fuel, and water in the closest juxtaposition that circumstances will allow; to set her table so that dishes can be placed upon it from the closet and the stove, removed to the sink, the cleaning accomplished, and they returned to the closet, with the fewest movements and in the shortest time.[12]

The Philosophy of Housekeeping offered plans for an L-shaped kitchen addition to an older home as well as building plans for an "elegant residence in one of our cities . . . an excellent arrangement for a family that has two or more servants, and entertains a good deal."[13]

The first plan for an L-shaped kitchen addition would provide maximum convenience in the farmhouse. The plan called for a kitchen proper, a pantry, bedroom off the kitchen and wood-house. The plan illustrated here, as it appeared in the 1869 edition of the authors' book, outlines the following:

A   indicates a door to the yard on the north side of house
B   is a door leading into the original structure
C   leads into a small bedroom with window facing south

D opens to the pantry

d a desk where the farmer can keep his papers

DT placement of the dining table

E signifies a window in the pantry

F is a pass-through to the wood-house

S signifies placement of the cookstove

s indicates the sink with pump and waste pipe

w opening behind the stove with access to wood-box

WT is a worktable placed between two windows.

Advantages of this plan include a relatively even temperature during the winter, warmth from the kitchen would pass into the bedroom, during the summer the fresh-air-flow from windows would "keep the

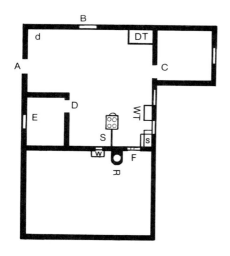

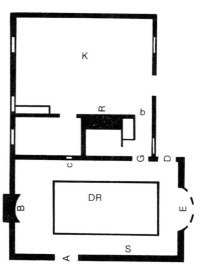

In their 1869 book The Philosophy of Housekeeping, *authors Joseph B. and Laura E. Lyman included this plan for an L-shaped kitchen addition to an existing home. The plan includes a kitchen proper, pantry, bedroom located off the kitchen and a wood-house. The authors suggested this was a most convenient plan for a farmhouse or rural dwelling where the wife did most of her own work.*

In contrast to the illustration for a rural dwelling where the housekeeper did most of the kitchen work, this plan, included in the 1869 Philosophy of Housekeeping *by Joseph B. and Laura E. Lyman, was suggested for an urban kitchen where servants were on hand. The dining room, which features a large bay window, could be entered via the center hall, and the kitchen arrangement includes the kitchen proper, a pantry and a convenient butler's pantry.*

ventilation perfect." The stove, fuel, water, pantry and worktable are all located at the same end of the kitchen, thus providing convenience. For the above kitchen plan, the authors offered the following scenario:

> suppose it is baking day. In winter, by opening the door, it will be warm enough to enable the house-keeper to mould her bread and make her pies and cakes in the pantry. This has a broad shelf running the entire length of the room, under the window "E," which serves at once for shelf and table . . . the shelf is broad enough to hold her moulding-board, and everything she needs can be reached by taking one or two steps to the right or left. If she has a place for everything, and everything in its place, as every good house-keeper should, she will be able to put her hands at once upon the baking-pans, the rolling-pin, the nutmeg-grater, the soda-box, without the loss of a moment in unnecessary and vexatious search. As soon as her pans are ready for the stove, the interval she has to pass in reaching the oven door is very short; and thus saving steps and time and annoyance, at every stage of the work, she may do a large baking in two hours, which under circumstances less favorable, would consume half a day.

The Lymans went on to explain that in doing laundry the kitchen worktable could easily be moved on wash day and the laundry tubs set in place by the sink, close to the stove where water could be heated. The authors recommended that the portion of the kitchen with pantry, stove and sink have an oilcloth floor covering but suggested the space occupied by the table could be carpeted, "without danger from soiling by the usual work of a kitchen."[14]

A second plan typifies the kitchen in a city home where domestic servants are on hand. As illustrated on the previous page, the following represent:

A   is a decorative half-glass door leading from the hall into "DR," the dining room

B   signifies the grate

b   a sliding panel between the kitchen and sink room through which orders may be given to the cook without subjecting guests to kitchen noise etc.

c   is a small opening in the pantry through which dishes can be passed to the dining room

D   a half-glass door leading into the yard

E   is a large bay window

G a door leading through a small sink room into "K," the kitchen. The sink room (later called a butler's pantry) includes a sink and small storage closet

R signifies placement of the range

S is a sideboard.

The authors noted that "In such an arrangement as the above, the cook and dining-room servant cannot possibly interfere with each other. In setting and clearing away the table, the dining-room servant need not enter the kitchen at all. The dishes containing food may be passed to and from the table through the opening 'c,' so that the cook need never enter the dining room. In this way the china, glasses, and silver, which belong in the china-closet and in the pie-safe, never go to the kitchen, but remain entirely in the charge of the trusty dining room servant."[15]

Clearly, from the advice offered by both the Beecher sisters and the Lymans, a first floor kitchen was preferable to one located in the basement. The cellar or basement was, however, a practical location for doing laundry and storing foodstuffs. In addition, the popularity of these household guides indicates a growing interest in making better use of kitchen space to promote economy and system.

Regarding the appearance of the kitchen, painted walls and floors continued to be recommended throughout the 1860s. *The Philosophy of Housekeeping* advised that white was most unsuitable in the kitchen as it grew dull and had to be repainted frequently. The authors advised readers a buff color was preferred, especially if grained in imitation of oak, as this color would hold up well and resist soiling.[16]

Depending upon the size of the household, kitchens and adjoining utility rooms were equipped with an assortment of necessities that are often unfamiliar to us today. The average Victorian kitchen had on hand wooden beetles (mashers), an apple corer, cherry stoner, meat mallet, skewers, a saw knife, butter spade (a hand-held wooden utensil used in making butter), tin jelly (pudding mold), pudding cloths, slaw cutter, balance (scale), lemon squeezer and so on. More common tools such as rolling pins, sifters and the mortar and pestle were also required.

Cookware during the period 1840–1869 was either heavy forged iron (and later cast iron), tin or copper. A long, oval fish kettle was important in any household as was a preserve kettle and at least four saucepans of different sizes. Skillets were on hand for frying and a waffle iron, bread pans, toasting iron and tea kettle were equally important. While cast-iron and tin cookware were found in the majority of kitchens, copper pots and pans were costly and therefore used by the well-to-do.

Small tin items found in most kitchens included cake pans, pie dishes, an oil can, candle box, funnel, egg boiler, scoops, dippers, a colander and large tin boxes to store bread and cakes.

Earthenware jars with lids were commonly used to keep butter, salt and pickles, and woodenware items such as a breadboard, spice boxes and a salt box could be found in the pantry and by the stove.

Baskets of all shapes and sizes were used to store or collect fruit, vegetables and eggs, and the largest were reserved for laundry work.

By the 1850s and 1860s growing industries were mass-producing cast-iron gadgets and utensils that quickly replaced hand-crafted or wooden examples. (See "Notable Changes.")

Catharine E. Beecher— Modern-day Authority

There is nothing which has a more abiding influence on the happiness of the family than the preservation of equable and cheerful temper and tones in the housekeeper.

American Woman's Home
—Catharine Beecher and Harriet Beecher Stowe, 1869

No examination of the history of the American kitchen would be complete without recognizing the significant contributions made by Catharine E. Beecher in the area of domestic science. Catharine's campaign to educate girls and women in all aspects of household management resulted in the early introduction of "domestic science" classes at selected schools across the country. In addition, the 1869 publication of *American Woman's Home,* which Catharine wrote with her famous sister, Harriet Beecher Stowe, proved to be the most complete household manual written during the mid-nineteenth century.

Catharine Beecher (1800–1878), daughter of noted minister, Lyman Beecher, grew up in a spiritually and intellectually stimulating atmosphere. Her early education at Miss Pierce's School for young women included more than just the needlework, language and arts courses deemed appropriate for her sex during the early 1800s. She was also schooled in science and math and here was laid the foundation for her later efforts to improve the moral and practical education of women.

At the age of 22 Catharine experienced the heartbreak of her fiancé's death. Knowing she had to go on without him (and that career choices for single women were few), she turned her attention to the respectable work of opening a school for young women in Hartford, Connecticut where her efforts focused on teaching the importance of the home in fostering morality.

While her sister Harriet managed the school in Hartford, Catharine went on to open schools in Cincinnati, Ohio; Quincy, Illinois; Milwaukee, Wisconsin; and Burlington, Iowa. She often staffed her schools with instructors from back east and endeavored to include household management as an important subject. Toward this end Catharine wrote *A Treatise on Domestic Economy for the Use of Young Ladies at Home and at School,* which was first published in 1841 and went through several editions. The preface of the third edition (published in 1860) reads:

Catharine E. Beecher, noted pioneer of the study of domestic science in America. Her books told women the kitchen should be the most important room in the house and housekeeping was a noble and important position.

Courtesy of the Schlesinger Library, Radcliffe College.

The author of this work was led to attempt it, by discovering, in her extensive travels, the deplorable sufferings of multitudes of young wives and mothers, from the combined influence of poor health, poor domestics, and a defective domestic education ... The writer became early convinced that this evil results mainly from the fact, that young girls, especially in the more wealthy classes, are not trained for their profession ... the measure which, more than any other, would tend to remedy this evil, would be to place domestic economy on an equality with other sciences in female schools. This should be done because it can be properly and systematically taught (not practically, but as a science), as much so as political economy or moral science, or any other branch of study; because it embraces knowledge, which will be needed by young women at all times and in all places ... women will be trained to secure, as of first importance, a strong and healthy constitution, and all those rules of thrift and economy that will make domestic duty easy and pleasant. To promote this object, the writer prepared this volume as a text-book for female schools. It has been examined by the Massachusetts Board of Education, and been deemed worthy by them to be admitted as a part of the Massachusetts School Library. It has also been adopted as a text-book in some of our largest and most popular female schools . . . East and West.[17]

The very ambitious contents of this work included chapters devoted to the responsibilities of American women, difficulties peculiar to American women and remedies for such difficulties, as well as the study of domestic economy, the care of health, foods and drinks, clothing, cleanliness, the practice of early rising, domestic exercise, manners, the preservation of good temper in a housekeeper, habits of system and order in the household, charity work, economy of time and expenses, good mental health, care of domestics, care of children and infants, care of the sick, treatment for accidents and injuries, social duties, home construction, fires and lighting, laundry, ironing, care of all the rooms within the home, sewing, yards and gardens, miscellaneous directions for care of domestic animals, writing party invitations, arranging flower baskets etc.

As a supplement to the above, Catharine then wrote *Miss Beecher's Domestic Receipt-Book,* which was published in 1846. Her goal in writing this follow-up was to provide housekeepers with a variety of recipes written in simple, straightforward fashion to satisfy family needs and offer selections for dinner parties and evening receptions. Her recipes called for the use of native fruits and vegetables rather than offering yet another publication full of British fare.

Miss Beecher took advantage of her published works as a forum for expressing her strong opinions and moral standing. For example, on the subject of temperance, her *Domestic Receipt-Book* advised readers "wine is often useful as a medicine, under the direction of a physician, but its stimulating, alcoholic principle, makes it an improper agent to be drank in health. The same is true of cider or strong beer . . . the general rule is established by an incredible amount of experience and testimony, that alcoholic drinks, in no cases, are needed by those in health, and that the indulgence in drinking them awakens a gnawing thirst and longing for them, that leads the vast majority of those who use them, to disease, debility, poverty, folly, crime, and death."[18]

Moral righteousness and the welfare of the family were to be every woman's prime concern and the author recommended in this same publication, "do not begin housekeeping in the style in which you should end it, but begin on a plain and small scale . . . be determined to live within your income, and in such a style that you can secure time to improve your own mind, and impart some of your own advantages to others. Try to secure symmetry in your dress, furniture, style of living, and charities . . . cultivate a taste for intellectual pleasures, home pleasures, and the pleasures of benevolence. Have some regular plan for the employment of your time . . . have chief reference to making home pleasant to your husband and children. It will save them from a thousand snares, and you from many sorrows."[19]

While Catharine was establishing her schools for young women, writing her books on domestic economy and lecturing across the country, her sister Harriet Beecher Stowe was achieving her own success as a noted author. In 1865 her book *House and Home Papers* was published, offering advice on home decoration and horticulture, but she is of course best known for her 1851 novel, *Uncle Tom's Cabin.*

Catharine and Harriet joined efforts to co-author *The American Woman's Home or, Principles of Domestic Science,* which was released in 1869. Having had several children, Harriet contributed valuable information on child rearing along with ideas on home decoration. Catharine expanded upon her earlier works to create a complete home manual that could be easily understood by those seeking guidance, and once again, her work often echoed her moral philosophy. *American Woman's Home* endeavored to elevate housekeeping to a well-respected profession and advised that every family member, including young children, must be schooled in household activities. For example, in Chapter 1, entitled "The Christian Family," the authors wrote " . . . the higher civilization has advanced, the more have children been trained to feel that to labor . . . is disgraceful, and to be made the portion of a degraded class. Children of the rich grow up with the feeling that servants are to work for them, and they themselves are not to work. To the minds of most children and servants, 'to be a lady,' is almost synonymous with 'to be waited on, and do no work.' It is the earnest desire of the authors of this volume to make plain the falsity of this growing popular feeling, and to show how much happier and more efficient family life will become when it is strengthened, sustained, and adorned by family work."[20]

In regard to the kitchen, we've already seen that *American Woman's Home* was revolutionary with its instructions for a separate stove-room and kitchen with a built-in "cook-form" for storage and meal preparation. This same work was also an encyclopedia of useful and practical recommendations for heating and ventilating the home, personal health care and exercise, healthful foods and drinks, etiquette, care of children,

The Harriet Beecher Stowe House kitchen incorporates many of the recommendations proposed in the American Woman's Home by Catharine Beecher and Harriet Beecher Stowe. Note the open shelving for easy access to kitchenware items, the iron range and wooden flooring. The encased sink includes a drainboard and the whole room conveys convenience and neatness. With a comfortable rocker and bright tablecloth it's also a cheerful room— something the Beecher sisters thought extremely important.

Courtesy the Stowe-Day Foundation, 77 Forest Street, Hartford, Connecticut.

servants, the sick, house cleaning, charitable works and so forth. Catharine Beecher closed this book with a section entitled "Appeal to American Women," in which she reiterated the importance of including the study of domestic science in all schools for girls so they would be capable of managing their own homes. She firmly believed the aristocratic life-style many women chose to lead was responsible for the general decay of female health. Only by way of proper training in the household arts and then practical application could a woman run a successful home and maintain good health. Idleness was considered both physically and mentally debilitating. For example, Miss Beecher wrote,

> let us now look at the dangers which are impending. And first, in regard to the welfare of the family state, the decay of the female constitution and health has involved such terrific sufferings . . . add to these, other influences that are robbing home of its safe and peaceful enjoyments. Of such, the condition of domestic service is not the least. We abound in domestic helpers from foreign shores, but they are to a large extent thriftless, ignorant, and unscrupulous, while as thriftless and inexperienced housekeepers, from boarding-school life, have no ability to train or control. Hence come antagonism and ceaseless "worries" in the parlor, nursery, and kitchen, while the husband is wearied with endless complaints of breakage, waste of fuel and food, neglect, dishonesty, and deception, and home is anything but a harbor of comfort and peace. Thus come clubs to draw men from comfortless homes, and next, clubs for the deserted women. Meantime, domestic service—disgraced, on one side, by the stigma of our late slavery, and, on the other, by the influx into our kitchens of the uncleanly and ignorant—is shunned by the self-respecting and well educated, many of whom prefer either a miserable pittance or the career of vice to this fancied degradation. Thus comes the overcrowding in all avenues for woman's work, and the consequent lowering of wages to starvation prices for long protected toils . . . factory girls must stand ten hours or more, and consequently, in a few years debility and disease ensue, so that they never can rear healthy children, while the foreigners who supplant them in kitchen labor are almost the only strong and healthy women to rear large families.[21]

Clearly the author was concerned not only about unskilled mistresses being unable to train inexperienced immigrant servants, but she also indicates that the shift from "helping" to "serving" drove native-born daughters away from household work and to the factories with their long hours and low pay.

Catharine Beecher's work continued and in 1873, at the age of 73 (five years before her death), her books, *Miss Beecher's Housekeeper and Healthkeeper* and *The New Housekeeper's Manual* were both published. Her pioneering efforts to formally educate young women in domestic science had far-reaching effects that inspired others to take up her cause. Her many books brought valuable advice into the nineteenth-century homes of young housekeepers and helped institute guidelines for "system" in household management. For many, her works no doubt brought encouragement, comfort and applause as they strove to make a comfortable home and nurture a happy family. In addition, her efforts inspired others to focus attention on domestic science. As newer kitchens, household products and appliances became available, additional home manuals and cookbooks were published, cooking schools were established, healthful cooking became increasingly important and extensive studies in domestic science at colleges and universities during the late 1800s continued the work she began.

The Role of Domestic Servants

. . . the whole process of home-making, house-keeping and cooking, which ever has been woman's special province, should be looked on as an art and as a profession . . .

Godey's Lady's Book
—Editorial by Sarah J. Hale, circa 1857

The changes in domesticity that brought about genteel feminism and the widespread use of domestics during the late Colonial period continued on into the Victorian era. Women were encouraged at every turn that their role in the domestic realm was vital not only to their family's well-being but to that of the nation at large. For example, in the 1848 book, *The Young Lady's Guide to Knowledge and Virtue* by Anna Fergurson, home was described as

that place which has the strongest ties upon the feeling, so it is the place in which woman has the power of exerting her influence in the greatest degree. This is her true and proper station; the duties of home are peculiarly hers; and let it not be thought that, in assigning home as the appropriate sphere for her action, we are assigning her a mean and ignoble part. It is, in truth, far otherwise. The sphere of her operation may be a limited one; but as many rivers make up the ocean's waters, so the conjunction of many homes makes up the world; and, therefore, in performing her duties at home, she is performing her part in the world at large; and, as a man carries with him, through the world, those same habits and feelings he has gathered in his home—and as these habits and feelings are principally derived from the influence of woman—woman, in performing her home duties, takes a vast share in the concerns of the community.[22]

During the mid-Victorian period the growing middle-class households had clearly defined roles for family members and servants although daily rituals varied depending upon their location (rural vs. urban), the family's status and the business the husband was engaged in. Especially in the larger towns and cities, the role of the housekeeper was a managerial one: she was overseer of the domestic servants and their daily chores, she was responsible for raising her children and instructing them in acceptable "home culture," she cared for sick family members, was devoted to her husband's well-being, maintained a rigorous or relaxed social calendar (depending upon her locale and the season of the year) while at the same time being careful to follow the strict formality governing a variety of events and occasions, and she was expected to devote considerable time to worthy charitable causes.

Whereas the majority of Colonial women performed their own work with the aid of children, family members and perhaps a hired girl or indentured servant (with the exception of plantations where slaves did the bulk of the work), the Victorian mistress instructed her domestics in cooking and household chores and managed the factory-like operations of her kitchen and laundry area, along with upkeep of the house as a whole. Toward this end she was encouraged to treat her domestics kindly, govern her household with a firm conviction as to how things should be done and, above all, maintain continual patience. This was no small task, especially for an inexperienced housekeeper whose frustrations could often lead to a show of temper or whose fear of losing a skilled and trusted domestic caused her to relinquish authority to a servant or cook. In an attempt to avoid such situations, domestics were often hired on a trial basis so the mistress could have time to determine if they were capable of doing work as instructed.

With the exception of remote rural areas, domestic help was not difficult to find before the Civil War broke out. The wave of immigrants making their way to America made up the majority of domestic workers by the 1840s. Many of the young women lacked skills required for other areas or work of their limited or nonexistent knowledge of the English language left them little choice but to seek employment as domestics. Initially these positions were a stepping stone to other areas of work, or more importantly, they sufficed until the young women married and established middle-class homes of their own. That, however, began to change by the 1850s and as Glenna Matthews points out in her work, a social history of women entitled *Just a Housewife*, "Those housewives who escaped overwork all too often did so at the expense of other women, that is, by the exploitation of servants. As the century wore on and there were increasing class differences between mistress and maid— and eventually ethnic and racial differences as well—women who worked as domestics were increasingly likely to be excluded from the benefits of domesticity they provided for others."[23]

Training new household help was often a time-consuming and frustrating task for the housekeeper with numerous other obligations to fulfill. In the third edition of *Miss Beecher's Domestic Receipt-Book*, published in 1860 and designed as a supplement to her earlier work, *Treatise on Domestic Economy*, Catharine Beecher suggested that to ease the burden of such training, detailed instructions should be written on large cards and carefully reviewed by both the mistress and the servant. These cards could then be hung in the kitchen for the domestics to refer to as needed.[24]

Regarding the above, the author wrote:

nothing secures ease and success in housekeeping so efficiently as *system* in arranging work. In order to aid those who are novices in these matters, the following outlines are furnished by an accomplished housekeeper. They are the details of family work, in a family of ten persons, where a cook, chambermaid, and boy, are all the domestics employed, and where the style of living is plain, by every way comfortable . . . Directions for the Cook—On Sunday, rise as early as other days. No work is to be done that can properly be avoided. Monday—rise early in hot weather, to have the cool of the day for work. Try to have everything done in the best manner. See that the clothes line is brought in at night, and the clothes pins counted and put in the bag. Put the tubs, barrel, and pails used, on the cellar bottom. Inquire every night, before going to bed, respecting breakfast, so as to make preparation beforehand. Tuesday— clean the kitchen and sink-room. Bake and fold the clothes to iron the next day. Wednesday—rise early in warm weather, so as to iron in the cool of the day. Thursday—fold off the clothes. No other special work. Friday—clean all the closets, the kitchen windows, the cellar stairs, and the privies. Try up all the grease, and put it away for use. Saturday—bake, and prepare a dinner for Sunday. Every day but Monday, wipe the shelves in the pantry and kitchen closet. Be careful to have clean dish towels, and never use them for other purposes. Keep a good supply of holders, both for cooking and ironing, and keep them hung up when not in use. Keep your boiler for dish water covered. Sweep and dust the kitchen every day. Never throw dirt, bones, or paper around the doors or yard. Never give or lend what belongs to the family without leave. Try to keep everything neat, clean, and in order. Have a time for everything, a place for everything, and everything in its place. The hour for going to bed is ten o'clock. Those who work hard should go to bed early, or else health and eyesight will fail.[25]

This listing gives little indication of the amount of time the cook devoted to preparing meals, baking, making preserves and so on. A skilled cook was an important asset to the family's well-being and greatly determined the mood of the household. A growing awareness of foods and their effect on the body's health gave rise during the 1840s and 1850s to the importance of variety in meal planning but knowing how to bake good bread was of prime importance. Yeast bread was served daily and thought to be a great source of nutrition. If the cook was unable to produce a satisfactory bread, the housekeeper* would perform this task herself or supervise every step of the process to assure good results. As Catherine Beecher pointed out,

> Perhaps it may be thought that all this is great drudgery, but it is worse drudgery to have sickly children, and a peevish husband, made so by having all the nerves of their stomachs rasped with sour, or heavy bread. A woman should be ashamed to have poor bread, far more so, than to speak bad grammar, or to have a dress out of the fashion. It is true, that by accident, the best of housekeepers will now and then have poor bread, but then it is an accident, and one that rarely happens. When it is very frequently the case that a housekeeper has poor bread, she may set herself down as a slack baker and negligent housekeeper.[26]

The cook's duties, combined with her laundry work and other responsibilities no doubt left her laboring from morning until night. If she was very skilled and organized she might have time in the evenings to devote to a bit of needlework, reading or a family or social life.

---

* Housekeeper is used to refer to the mistress of the house.

The duties of the chambermaid were as time-consuming and tedious as the cook's. She was responsible for general and seasonal cleaning throughout the house as well as daily chamber work, which included emptying and scalding the chamber pots, airing the beds and bedrooms (chambers), washing dishes after meals and collecting lamps each morning to clean them, trim the wicks and refill them with fuel. Depending upon the day of the week the chambermaid also did the sweeping, washed walls, windows and porches, kept the china-closet neat and orderly, put clean laundry away after all was ironed and folded, dusted and polished the furniture.

In order for the domestics to carry out their work in a systematic manner, it was important for the housekeeper to supply them with adequate kitchen tools, cookware and cleaning supplies, and make sure her pantry and storage areas were always well stocked. Household manuals recommended that at least once a month the mistress inspect her home top to bottom to determine any extra work that needed to be done, such as repairs or mending. She was also to take inventory in her pantry and cellar to make a list of items needed for the coming month. A monthly "bill of fare" was then planned so the cook would be preparing a variety of meals the family would enjoy.

The social agenda of the urban, middle-class family was every bit as time-consuming for the help as it was for the mistress. To successfully conduct dinner parties or afternoon teas at home, domestics were trained, supervised and occasionally assisted by the housekeeper in setting the table and making preparations for a several-course meal. After the mistress completed her menu she would check the pantry and cellar to determine what items were needed to prepare a dinner for most often a party of twelve. In addition, the silverware, glassware and dishes were inspected to make sure all was in order.

The typical menu for a dinner party of twelve would include a soup, a selection of four or five meats and/or fish, four or five vegetable dishes and a variety of cakes, pastries and fruit for dessert. The cook would begin preparing these foods the day before the party was to take place, boiling the soup, dressing and cooking meats and baking cakes. The actual day of the event the maid or waiter, under the close eye of the mistress, would gather the tableware together and set the table and sideboard. Since the dinner was as much a reflection and display of one's station in life as it was a social event, an endless variety of vessels, dishes, tableware and so on were called for. Catherine Beecher offered timely advice on setting the table and preparing the dining room for such occasions in *Miss Beecher's Domestic Receipt-Book*. She wrote that the table should be set early in the forenoon . . . the table rug must first be laid exactly square with the room, and the tables also set exactly parallel with the sides of the room. If the tables are handsome ones, put on two white tablecloths, one above the other. If the tables are not handsome, cover them with a colored table-cloth, and put two white ones over. Then set the castors [vessels for condiments] in the exact centre of the table . . . place the plates and knives, with a napkin and tumbler at the right of each plate . . . if it is cold weather, set the plates to warm, and leave them till wanted. Set the salt stands at the four corners, with two large spoons crossed by each . . . place table-mats in the places where the dishes are to be set. The host is to be seated at one end, and the hostess at the other, and at their plates put two knives and two forks. Put a carving knife and fork, and carver stand, at each place where a dish is to be carved. Put the jelly and pickles at diagonal corners . . . if wine is to be used, put two wine glasses by each tumbler. Just before dinner is to be served, a bit of bread, cut thick, is to be laid with a fork on each napkin. Then prepare the side-table thus: As the party, including host and hostess, will be twelve, there must be one dozen soup plates, and one dozen silver spoons. Then there must be two dozen large knives, and three dozen large plates, besides those on the table. This is to allow one plate for fish, and two for two changes of meat for each guest . . . Then, there must be three dozen dessert plates, and two dozen dessert knives and forks. One dozen saucers, and one dozen dessert spoons. One or two extra of each kind, and three or four extra napkins, should be added for emergencies . . . on the side-table, also, is to be placed all articles to be used in helping the dessert; and unless there is a convenient closet for the purpose, the dessert itself must be set there and covered with napkins. All the dishes and plates to be used, except those for desserts and soups, must, in cold weather, be set to warm by the waiter. If coffee is to be served at the dinner-table, the furniture for this must be put on the side-table, or in an adjacent room or closet.[27]

Although meal preparations were under way and the dining table (or tables) set, the domestic's work was far from finished. At the appointed dinner hour the cook would deliver the soup to the dining room prior to the guests taking their seats. If the kitchen was located in the basement she made several trips up and down the stairs during the course of the evening unless a dumbwaiter was available to transport dishes back and forth. After the soup had been served the cook would then deliver the meats, fish and vegetables, with each plate covered to keep it hot until served. The waiter or maid was on hand in the dining room once all guests were seated and would proceed to place dishes before them, place food on the table and remove place settings as each course was completed. Prior to serving dessert, the servant would remove everything from the table, including the top tablecloth, and then place the dessert dishes and silverware around. The guests, with the aid of the host and hostess, could help themselves to pastry, cakes and so on. Finally, after dessert, the servant would again remove everything from the table, including the second tablecloth, and fruit and coffee would be served.

At the end of the evening the domestics faced the task of washing all the dishes and restoring everything to its proper order.

Entertaining in the form of an evening party was also quite popular and proved to be a bit less demanding on the servants. The cook prepared a selection of sandwiches, cakes, pastries etc. but these were laid out buffet style on a long table and guests could help themselves or were assisted by the waiter or maid.

Obtaining and keeping good domestic help was the subject of much discussion and concern throughout most of the nineteenth century. In training her hired help, the mistress was advised to consider it a blessing and social obligation to train a young girl in the art of housekeeping or cooking. In return, domestics were encouraged to view their situation and their employer with patience, avoid gossiping about the family, treat the children in the household kindly, use provisions wisely, keep their chamber neat and tidy and look kindly on the opportunity to learn from the mistress as preparation for the day they might have a home of their own. As mentioned earlier, this advice was well-received by both parties until around the 1850s. After that point in time, mistresses were growing weary of the revolving-door stream of domestics that would come and go in their households, and frustrations over continually having to instruct "Bridget" or "green Erin" (as immigrant girls were collectively referred to) fostered resentment.

Household servants were quick to discover they could increase their earnings by specializing rather than simply being a "maid-of-all-work," or by finding their way up the ladder from perhaps "scullery maid" to chambermaid. As a result, they frequently left one employer in favor of another for economic gain. That in turn prompted many a mistress to complain her "girl" had been stolen away from her just as she'd finished training her to the ways of the household.[28]

Also noteworthy, class distinctions between mistress and maid became more marked, and at a time when domestics were further segregated from the family by the back stairway, their growing discontent with servitude began leading them to other avenues of employment.

An 1854 oil on canvas painting by Lilly Martin Spencer entitled Shake Hands? This housekeeper maintains a sense of humor while preparing the family meal from the assortment of fresh foods in front of her and a pot bubbles away on cast-iron stove behind her.

Courtesy Prints and Photographs Division, Library of Congress.

As the Civil War came to an end and the Thirteenth Amendment freed the slaves, forever altering the way of life on southern plantations, the industrial revolution was swiftly moving ahead and economic uncertainties required many households to simplify their life-style. The Lymans pointed this out in *The Philosophy of Housekeeping* when they wrote, "One of the effects of the war which has just closed has been to bring our American society into much closer resemblance to the European civilization. It has exaggerated the differences between the upper and lower classes, making the rich richer, the poor poorer. By this means, the large middle class . . . has been greatly diminished. A fraction of it has been raised above the modest independence, which they formerly enjoyed, to the possession of wealth and the indulgence in luxury; while by far the larger portion, with incomes but little increased, and prices often more than doubled, have a far harder struggle to make ends meet than they had ten years ago."[29]

As the 1870s approached, domestic help was increasingly difficult to obtain. Those urban housekeepers who grew tired of the search, or had little choice but to manage with limited or virtually no help, began to assume responsibility for a greater number of tasks within their own homes.

Notable Changes: Widespread Use of the Cookstove and Mass-production of Gadgets and Utensils

Another mode of systematizing relates to providing proper supplies of conveniences, and proper places in which to keep them.

American Woman's Home
—Catharine Beecher and Harriet Beecher Stowe, 1869

Between 1840 and the outbreak of the Civil War in 1861, Americans enjoyed a period of relative prosperity. Although the majority of the nation's population was still engaged in farming, urban areas expanded as industries flourished. While economic instability followed the war, it did little to slow the industrial revolution.

The railroad played an important role in expansion and distribution of goods and by 1869 trains were carrying factory-made wares across the country. As foundries, mills and factories sprang up in the shadows of this network system, the number of inventions increased and patents were granted for countless items. Between 1836 (when the patent system was initiated in the United States) and 1869, a total of 98,459 patents were granted, many of which would alter housekeeping and cooking methods by saving time and/or increasing productivity.[30] The most notable of these were cookstoves and cast-iron kitchen tools.

During the early 1700s, Pennsylvania German settlers were using a box-like iron stove for heat and Benjamin Franklin had introduced his heating stove, the "New Pennsylvania Fireplace" by 1742. It was, however, several decades before a cookstove was in use.

Advertisements for cookstoves began to appear in the early 1800s and one such ad, circa 1823, by stove-maker Philip Willcox of Springfield, Massachusetts told readers:

> Philip Willcox Respectfully informs his friends and the public that he has just received from New York an assortment of E. Hoyt's highly approved patent COOKING STOVES. The above mentioned stoves are so constructed as to convey the steam arising from the boilers (which is admitted to be almost the only objection to cooking stoves) directly into the pipe without the least inconvenience to the cooking; also the extreme heat that arises directly from the fire passes off, which renders it equally as pleasant and as healthy as an open Franklin; with the addition of his patent oven. They are considered by those who have had them in use, superior to any stoves offered to the public.[31]

Although cookstoves were available during the early nineteenth century, it was the 1850s before they were in widespread use. Both Catharine Beecher's *Treatise on Domestic Economy* and her later supplement, *Miss Beecher's Domestic Receipt-Book,* which was published in 1846, offered recipes for hearth cooking. For example, in the supplement, under the heading of "Roasted Meats," Beecher advised that for roasted and baked meats, "be sure you have your spit and tin oven very clean and bright . . . Have a fire so large as to extend half a foot beyond the roaster each side. When meat is thin and tender, have a small, brisk fire. When your meat is large, and requires long roasting, have large solid wood, kindled with charcoal and small sticks. Set the meat, at first, some distance from the place where it is to roast, so as to have it heat through gradually, and then move it up to roast."[32]

Initially cookstoves and ranges were slow to catch on as women long skilled in hearth cooking were hesitant to foresake the reliable for what appeared to be a complicated contraption. As evidence of this, the March 1839 edition of the *Journal of the Franklin Institute of Philadelphia* included this observation: "The greatest objection to the kitchen ranges

The 1845 frontispiece from The New England Economical Housekeeper, and Family Receipt Book *by Mrs. A. E. Howland. Like other recipe books of this era, this one included instructions for hearth cooking. Note the image depicts two women working in a large kitchen with fresh meat and fowl hanging on the walls. A large roasting-kitchen sits before the hearth.*

Courtesy Prints and Photographs Division, Library of Congress.

devised by various ingenious projectors, is the want of simplicity. Cooks will not take the trouble of learning to use them, or, which is necessary, to keep in order the various novel articles by which they are accompanied."[33]

As previously discussed, there were differences between ranges and cookstoves, and from the 1830s on both were continually being changed and improved. However, many models remained inefficient or difficult to operate. In a popular monthly publication entitled *American Agriculturist*, published by Orange Judd & Company of New York City, the November 1847 issue reported "stoves are now so generally used all over the middle and Northern portions of the United States for cooking, that one is to be found in almost every dwelling. Common as they are, the mass of them are defective, and in many cases very poor." This was actually a prelude to a testimonial for the Granger's air-tight cooking stove which featured a brick-lined oven (reported to turn out baked goods as delicious as any baked in the hearth) and was simplified for easy operation.

Hundreds of iron-work foundries were turning out coal and/or wood-burning cooking appliances during the 1850s and 1860s and their wares were advertised in agricultural publications, city directories, trade catalogs and flyers. A small sampling includes the Tyson Furnace of Plymouth, Vermont, which was turning out box-like cookstoves in the 1830s; Moses Pond & Company of Boston, Massachusetts, whose "Union Range" won several noted awards during the 1850s; Vose & Company and Rathbone, Sard & Company, both of Albany, New York; and M.L. Filley of Troy, New York.

While the cast-iron cookstoves of the early Victorian period were small, fuel-efficient and portable, their size did place limits on the amount of cooking or baking that could be done at one time. Ranges, on the other hand, were quite large and numerous dishes could be prepared simultaneously. For example, the circa 1850s Metropolitan Cooking Range by Wilson, Richardson & Company, which was partially made of brick and commonly built within the old cooking hearth, included not only a bake oven but an area designated for roasting or broiling. A separate "hot closet" located below the oven would keep dishes warm and several range-top burners allowed water to heat and foods to cook. The large range heated the kitchen and either coal or wood served as the main source of fuel.

During the 1860s cookstoves made with a combination of cast iron and sheet metal grew in size to accommodate attached roasting ovens and water reservoirs and as we've already seen, it was such a stove that Catharine Beecher recommended in her 1869 *American Woman's Home.*

The importance of the shift from hearth cooking to use of the range or cookstove cannot be overstated. This development altered American cookery methods and meal planning, while at the same time relieving the housewife or cook of multiple backbreaking chores such as lifting and moving heavy iron cookware. Perhaps most importantly, the introduction of the stove brought technology into the kitchen and as the century progressed, a continuous stream of updated and improved appliances became available, leading to the eventual development of the coal/oil and gas stoves of the late 1800s.

Regarding the mass-production of cast-iron kitchen gadgetry (many of which were constructed with gears), the majority of apple parers, egg beaters and cherry stoners proved helpful in the kitchen. The factory-like operations of transforming raw materials into meals were still very time-consuming but some new gadgetry did give the cook or house-keeper short-cut methods that proved time-saving and more convenient than the "old-fashioned" way of doing things. For example, the excessive menus and deliberate display of opulence in the typical meal prepared for a dinner party of twelve guests created enormous amounts of work. Faye Dudden points out in *Serving Women,* a social history of domestic servitude, that " . . . the natural bounty of the American environment tended to encourage profusion at the table, while the influence of foreign example and expertise lent a concern for more careful preparation and artful combination. These changes did not operate with equal force in every kitchen, but both developments tended to increase the work of preparation, serving and cleaning up, simultaneously introducing a new range of cares in planning and choosing."[34] Simply put, at a time when cookery was becoming increasingly important and a major portion of any social event, both domestics and mistresses were no doubt receptive to any and all new gadgetry intended to ease the burdens in the kitchen.

Whereas gadgets or utensils had previously been hand-crafted or hand-forged, machinery could now turn them out in bulk, thus making them readily available when needed. For example, while the mortar and pestle had been a necessary household tool for years, pre-1850 examples were made by hand from wood or blown glass. The 1860s introduced machine-made cast-iron and wooden examples.

Fruit was an important part of the Victorian diet, and especially so during the mid-nineteenth-century focus on healthful eating. For example, apples were used in pie, cider, jelly, apple butter and fruit cheese. They were also dried, baked and used in preparing puddings, custards and fritters. Hand-crafted wooden apple parers with forged iron forks were slowly replaced during the 1850s and 1860s by several cast-iron examples patented and manufactured in the Northeast. These factory-produced parers were either designed to clamp onto the worktable, such as the "Climax" apple "segmenter," which was produced by D.H. Goodell of Antrim, New Hampshire, or existed on a wooden base like the model turned out by Sargent & Foster's of Shelburne Falls, Massachusetts. The mode of operation varied from examples with a plunger-action blade to those with turn-cranks and action gears.

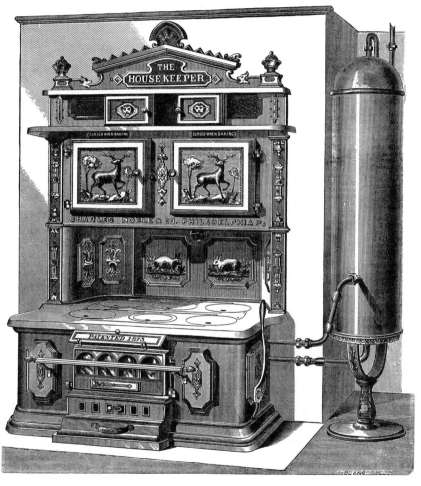

Although patented during the 1870s, this range, The Housekeeper, clearly illustrates how large and ornate such an appliance could be. With an attached hot water tank, dual baking ovens and six burners, the cook or housekeeper could prepare several dishes at once.

The Dover Stamping Company of Boston, Massachusetts produced a trade catalog during the 1860s that offered a variety of cast-iron kitchen tools. Along with the apple parer, cherry stoners were available in footed, tabletop models with hoppers or models attached to a wooden base. With the tedious work involved in preparing cherries for preserves, jellies and desserts, the cherry stoner was welcome relief from removing pits or stones by hand.

Cast-iron peach parers, lemon squeezers, nutcrackers and raisin seeders were also introduced during the mid-nineteenth century and proved be be an efficient means of preparing ingredients for pies, puddings, lemonade and so on. Large graters and small nutmeg graters with wooden handles and punched-tin surfaces were often replaced during the 1860s by cast-iron examples, and factory-made spice mills slowly gained favor over the mortar and pestle.

Novel contraptions were also introduced for working with meats and vegetables. The Athol Machine Company of Athol Depot, Massachusetts introduced an all-purpose food chopper during the 1860s. This cast-iron device with a crank mechanism to rotate a tin hopper (thus making the blade move up and down) was ideal for meats and smaller vegetables. Other meat choppers were constructed with a cast-iron frame housing a wooden tub. The crank handle would operate gears that caused the blade inside to "chop." Cast-iron sausage stuffers, pea shellers, bean slicers and potato slicers also became available.

The age-old method of mixing bread dough in a wooden bowl with a wooden spoon was intended to be simplified by the introduction of the dough mixer. Early examples were constructed of wood with cast-iron cranks, followed by a cast-iron and tin model offered by the Sparrow Kneader & Mixer Company of Boston, Massachusetts. These mixers were to be held in the crook of the arm or set on a tabletop and turning the crank was supposed to be less tiresome than constant stirring.

Several rotary egg beaters were patented during the 1860s and crank-action flour sifters were made available. Churning the butter with a plunger in a deep wooden "churn" was simplified with the advent of the tabletop cylinder churn with crank handles

In an ongoing effort to bring "system" to kitchen chores, many mistresses embraced every new piece of gadgetry that came along while others were content to adopt a "wait and see" attitude. Even though numerous new "inventions" had been around for several years, not all were deemed worthy of the high praise they received in advertisements or even considered necessary. In the 1871 publication of *Common Sense in the Household: A Manual of Practical Housewifery,* author Mary Virgina

Terhune offered readers a short list of practical necessities needed in every kitchen, including an egg-beater, raisin-seeder, potato peeler, apple corer, syllabub churn and farina kettle.[35]

Regarding cookware, the numerous foundries scattered across the country began turning out cast-iron pots, pans, kettles and so forth designed for use on ranges and cookstoves. In 1858 several patents were granted to Nathaniel Waterman of Boston, Massachusetts for various cast-iron "roll pans" with circular, oval and/or rectangular shaped cups. Waterman produced his own designs and they were also manufactured by the Russell & Erwin Manufacturing Company of New Britain, Connecticut.[36] It wasn't long before others followed suit and by 1869 housekeepers had a selection of cast-iron roll and muffin pans to choose from along with wafflers, pancake pans etc.

During the mid-nineteenth century ice cream became a fashionable dessert and favored dish at evening parties. It was commercially prepared and available in attractive molded forms but could also be prepared at home. In an effort to improve the equipment used in turning out homemade ice cream, Nancy Johnson invented a small ice cream freezer in 1864. Her freezer consisted of a wooden tub with tin lining and a churn-crank to mix ingredients. This was a welcome addition to most kitchens where ice cream was prepared on a regular basis.

Other household chores were altered by impacts of the industrial revolution. For example, carpeting was extremely popular in middle- and upper-class homes during the Victorian period, and "dusting" them with a broom accomplished little more than distributing the dirt around the room. Large carpet sweepers made of wooden boxes with a pulley system to rotate the encased brush were being advertised by the 1850s. During the 1860s Haley, Morse and Company of New York City offered "The Boston Carpet Sweeper," a smaller sweeper with rotary-action brushes in an attractive, stenciled walnut case. A circa 1863 ad proclaimed,

> . . . the annoyance of dust is entirely overcome, and the dirt is not sifted through the carpet by being driven across it, as in the old way. The long pivoted handle permits the operator to sweep under beds, sofas, tables and pianos without moving them, or constant stooping. A delicate lady, or a child, can thoroughly sweep a room without other exertion than is required to push the Sweeper before her across the carpet; and dusting is unnecessary. Carpets wear much longer when swept by a sweeper than when the common broom is used, and as The Boston Carpet Sweeper will last from five to ten years, doing its work perfectly all the time, it really is cheaper than a corn broom.[37]

The Doty washer, first invented during the early 1860s, was improved upon during the next several years, with sturdy legs, galvanized metal parts to prevent rust and a balance mechanism to make operation easier. This circa 1871 ad includes information on the latest model and testimonials.

Laundry had always been a dreaded task and continued to be so throughout the nineteenth century. Minor improvements may have eased the burden somewhat in certain households but that was determined by which new "washer" the mistress chose to buy. Several washing machines were patented and produced during the 1860s and their methods of operation varied considerably. For example, the "Metropolitan," first produced in the late 1850s, included two large "wings" that allowed "pounders" to be moved up and down in the wash tub, thus doing away with the need to scrub clothing on a washboard. A wringer could be attached to the side of the large tub so the entire operation was completed in one spot.

Another washing machine, turned out by Thomas J. Price of Illinois in the late 1850s, included a footed, wooden tub with a lever that caused washboard-like slats inside the tub to move back and forth.

The "Eagle" washer was manufactured by Oakley & Keating of New York City during the 1860s. This machine consisted of a table-top, round washtub with an attached cylinder, and crank handle that would roll the clothing or linens through an oscillating roller frame with guards.

While a few of the early washers may have proved a positive addition to the laundry room, others were discarded in favor of a return to old methods as they had a tendency either to stain or to rip clothing and linens.

For those who continued to do their wash the old-fashioned way, new washboards with wooden rollers or beaded bars replaced primitive, hand-crafted examples. Cast-iron models with well-defined corrugations were also factory-produced but didn't prove to be as convenient as lighter-weight wooden boards.

Various irons became available during the mid-nineteenth century, including fluting irons such as the "Geneva Hand Fluter," manufactured by W.H. Howell of Geneva, Illinois in the 1860s. In addition, improved box irons were advertised, such as the charcoal iron by Russell & Erwin Manufacturing Company of New Britain, Connecticut, which included a heat shield underneath the handle to protect the user.

The endless variety of gadgets and household tools patented and manufactured during the mid-nineteenth century ran the gamut from ingenious to ridiculous, but, collectively, they encouraged and inspired the continual advances that resulted in the explosion of kitchenware items produced during the last quarter of the nineteenth century.

Early Victorian
Household Hints and Recipes

❦HOUSEHOLD HINTS❦

That home is her appropriate and appointed sphere of action there cannot be a shadow of a doubt; for the dictates of nature are plain and imperative on this subject . . . Whenever she goes out of this sphere to mingle in any of the great public movements of the day, she is deserting the station which God and nature have assigned to her.

Woman in America: Being an Examination into the Moral and Intellectual Condition of American Female Society
—Mrs. A. J. Graves, 1841

Hot soup at the table is very vulgar; it either leads to an unseemly mode of taking it, or keeps people waiting too long whilst it cools. Soup should be brought to the table only moderately warm.

Hints on Etiquette
—Charles Day 1844

It is not elegant to gnaw Indian corn. The kernals should be scored with a knife, scraped off into the plate, and then eaten with a fork. Ladies should be particularly careful how they manage so ticklish a dainty, lest the exhibition rub of a little desirable romance.

Hints on Etiquette
—Charles Day, 1844

Excellence in housekeeping has come to be considered as incompatible with superior intellectual culture. But it is not so. The most elevated minds fulfill best the every-day duties of life.

The Young Housekeeper's Friend, or, A Guide to Domestic Economy and Comfort
—Mrs. Cornelius, 1846

FRIENDLY COUNSELS FOR DOMESTICS

My friends, you fill a very important and respectable station . . . On your faithfulness and kindness depends the comfort of a whole family . . . Whenever therefore, anything vexes, or troubles you, comfort yourselves by thinking that it is designed for your good, and reap at least one benefit, by bearing it with patience and cheerfulness. In all your dealings with those who employ you, try to follow "the golden rule," and do by them as you wish to have others do by you, when you are the mistress of a family, and hire others to help you.

Miss Beecher's Domestic Receipt-Book
—Catherine E. Beecher, 1846

WEIGHTS AND MEASURES

It is a good plan to have a particular measure cup kept for the purpose, and after once weighing all those receipts that are given by weight, to measure the quantity by this cup and then write the measures in your receipt book, and keep the cup only for this purpose. The following is some guide in judging of the relative proportion between measures and weights. A quart of flour, or of sifted loaf sugar, or of softened butter, each weigh about a pound. The flour, if sifted, must be heaped.

A pint equals eight ounces.
A half a pint equals four ounces.
One gill equals two ounces.
Half a gill equals one ounce.
A quart of brown sugar, or of Indian meal, equals a pound and two ounces of the same.

One great spoonful of flour, loaf sugar, or of melted butter, equals a quarter of an ounce of the same. It should be a little heaped.

Four spoonfuls equal an ounce, or half a gill.
Eight spoonfuls equal one gill.
Sixteen spoonfuls equal half a pint.
Spoons differ so much in size, this is an uncertain guide.
A medium-sized teaspoon holds sixty drops of water.
Ten eggs usually weigh a pound.
Four gills make a pint.
Two pints make a quart.
Four quarts make a gallon.
Eight quarts make a peck.
Four pecks make a bushel.

Miss Beecher's Domestic Receipt-Book
—Catharine E. Beecher, 1846

Clean house in the Fall instead of Spring, and you get rid of all the filth made by flies. But when you burn bituminous coal, Spring is the proper time for house cleaning.

Miss Beecher's Domestic Receipt-Book
—Catharine E. Beecher, 1846

Kitchens are the favorite resort of the common fly. In these a fly trap, as it is called, may be used to attract the fly to settle upon it rather than upon the walls or ceiling. Flies seem to incline to settle more on suspended objects than on any other; and thence the use of the "fly trap," which is usually formed of papers of various colours cut out fancifully in order to render them somewhat ornamental as well as useful.

An Encyclopedia of Domestic Economy
—Mrs. Parkes, 1848

Never oblige your servants to tell a falsehood for you, and they will not be so likely to tell a falsehood to you.

Godey's Lady's Book
August 1867

In our country, where every family wishes to appear respectable, it is essential to know how to make the most of small means. For this purpose, order is the first law, true economy being impossible without method; then good taste and moral refinement of mind, which can see the beautiful in the fitting, are requisite.

Godey's Lady's Book
August 1867

HABITS OF SYSTEM AND ORDER

Monday . . . is devoted to preparing for the labors of the week. Any extra cooking, the purchasing of articles to be used during the week, the assorting of clothes for the wash, and mending . . . these, and similar items, belong to this day. Tuesday is devoted to washing, and Wednesday to ironing. On Thursday, the ironing is finished off, the clothes are folded and put away, and all articles which need mending are put in the mending-basket, and attended to. Friday is devoted to sweeping and house-cleaning. On Saturday, and especially the last Saturday of every month, every department is put in order; the casters and table furniture are regulated, the pantry and cellar inspected, the trunks, drawers, and closets arranged, and everything about the house put in order for

Sunday. By this regular recurrence of a particular time for inspecting everything, nothing is forgotten till ruined by neglect.

American Woman's Home
—Catharine E. Beecher and Harriet Beecher Stowe, 1869

WHITEWASH FOR INSIDE WALLS

To a peck of slacked lime add a pound and a half of white vitriol, a pound of salt, and half a pound of dissolved glue. The effect of the salt and glue is to prevent rubbing off.

The Philosophy of Housekeeping
—Joseph & Laura Lyman, 1869

PRESERVATION OF MILK

As soon as milked, place in narrow, deep cans and set in a very cool place, being careful not to stir or jar it, and excluding air as much as possible, especially when it thunders. In this way, even in July, milk may be kept sweet three days.

The Philosophy of Housekeeping
—Joseph & Laura Lyman, 1869

MAKING OF CLOTHING

With the present facilities for sewing, it is practicable for every house-keeper to cut out and make up all the articles worn by the different members of her family, with the exception, perhaps, of dress-coats and overcoats. The saving which she will thus make will more than pay the wages of a domestic, who will perform all the drudgery of a household, such as washing, cleaning, ironing, sweeping, etc.

The Philosophy of Housekeeping
—Joseph & Laura Lyman, 1869

❧ RECIPES ❧

MAKING CAKE

When a pastry is to be made, take care not to make trouble for others by scattering materials, and soiling the table or floor, or by needless use of many dishes. Put on a large and clean apron, roll your sleves above the elbows, tie something over your head lest hair may fall, take care that your hands are clean, and have a basin of water and a clean towel on hand. Place everything you will need on the table, butter your pans, grate your nutmegs and squeeze your lemons. Then break your eggs, each in a cup by itself, lest adding a bad one should spoil the whole. Make your cake in wood or earthen, and not in tin.

The Young Housekeeper's Friend, or, A Guide to Domestic Economy and Comfort
—Mrs. Mary Hooker Cornelius, 1846

APPLE JAM

Weigh equal quantities of brown sugar and good sour apples. Pare and core them, and chop them fine. Make a syrup of the sugar, and clarify it very thoroughly; then add the apples, the grated peel of two or three lemons, and a few pieces of white ginger. Boil it until the apple looks clear and yellow. This resembles foreign sweetmeats. The ginger is essential to its peculiar excellence.

The Young Housekeeper's Friend
—Mrs. Mary Hooker Cornelius, 1846

TO BOIL A TURKEY

Make a stuffing for the craw, of chopped bread and butter, cream, oysters, and the yolks of eggs. Sew it in, and dredge flour over the turkey, and put it to boil in cold water, with a spoonful of salt in it, and enough water to cover it well. Let it simmer for two hours and a half, or if small, less time. Skim it while boiling. It looks nicer if wrapped in a cloth dredged with flour. Serve it with drawn butter, in which are put some oysters.

Miss Beecher's Domestic Receipt-Book
—Catharine E. Beecher, 1846

SOUTHERN GUMBO

This is a favorite dish at the South and West, and is made in a variety of ways. The following is a very fine receipt, furnished by a lady, who has had extensive opportunity for selection. Fry one chicken, when cut up, to a light brown, and also two slices of bacon. Pour onto them three quarts of boiling water. Add one onion and some sweet herbs, tied in a rag. Simmer them gently three hours and a half. Strain off the liquor, take off the fat, and then put the ham and chicken, cut into small pieces, into the liquor. Add half a tea-cup of ochra, cut up; if dry, the same quantity; also half a tea-cup of rice. Boil all half an hour, and just before serving add a glass of wine and a dozen oysters, with their juice. Ochra is a fine vegetable, especially for soups, and is easily cultivated. It is sliced and dried for soups in the winter.

Miss Beecher's Domestic Receipt-Book
—Catharine E. Beecher, 1846

CORN GRIDDLE CAKES WITH YEAST

Three coffee-cups of Indian meal, sifted. One coffee-cup of either rye meal, Graham flour, or fine flour. Two tablespoonfuls of yeast, and a salt spoonful of salt. Wet at night with sour milk or water . . . and in the morning add one teaspoonful of pearlash. Bake on a griddle. If Graham flour is used, add a very little molasses.

Miss Beecher's Domestic Receipt-Book
—Catharine E. Beecher, 1846

COMMON APPLE PIE

Pare your apples, and cut them from the core. Line your dishes with paste, and put in the apple; cover and bake until the fruit is tender. Then take them from the oven, remove the upper crust, and put in sugar and nutmeg, cinnamon or rose water to your taste; a bit of sweet butter improves them. Also, to put in a little orange peel before they are baked, makes a pleasant variety. Common apple pies are very good to stew, sweeten and flavor the apple before they are put into the oven. Many prefer the seasoning baked in. All apple pies are much nicer if the apple is grated and then seasoned.

Miss Beecher's Domestic Receipt-Book
—Catharine E. Beecher, 1846

SAMPLE MENU FOR A DINNER PARTY OF TWELVE

Soup. Fish. A boiled ham. A boiled turkey, with oyster sauce. Three roasted ducks, and a dish of scalloped oysters. Potatoes, Parsnips, Turnips, and Celery. For dessert, Pudding, Pastry, Fruit and Coffee.

Miss Beecher's Domestic Receipt-Book
—Catharine E. Beecher, 1846

TO MAKE AN ORNAMENTAL PYRAMID FOR A TABLE

Boil loaf of sugar as for candy, and rub it over a stiff form, made for the purpose, or stiff paper, which must be well buttered. Set it on a table, and begin at the bottom, and stick onto this frame, with the sugar, a row of macaroons, kisses, or other ornamental articles, and continue until the whole is covered. When cold, draw out the pasteboard form, and set the pyramid in the centre of the table with a small bit of wax candle burning with it, and it looks very beautiful.

Miss Beecher's Domestic Receipt-Book
—Catharine E. Beecher, 1846

POACHED EGGS

Have ready a kettle of boiling water, pour it in a pan . . . which is set on coals; have the eggs at hand; put a little salt in water, and break them in, one at a time. Let remain till white is set and take them out with an egg spoon.

Useful Receipts and Hints to Young Housekeepers
—Elizabeth E. Lea, 1859

SCRAPPLE

Take eight pounds of scraps of pork, that will not do for sausage, boil it in four gallons of water; when tender, chop it fine, strain the liquor and pour it back into the pot; put in the meat, season it with sage, summer savory, salt and pepper to taste, stir in a quart of corn meal; after simmering a few minutes, thicken it with buckwheat flour very thick; it requires very little cooking after it is thickened, but must be stirred constantly.

Godey's Lady's Book
September 1867

APPLE CHEESECAKE

Peel, core and boil some apples till they are quite soft, with a few cloves and some lemon-peel. The saucepan in which they are boiled will only require about a tablespoonful of water at the bottom to keep the apples from burning. When they are soft, remove the lemon-peel and cloves, and beat them up in the saucepan with moist sugar and a little piece of butter. Cut up some candied peel, and add to the apples with currants in the proportion of a quarter of a pound to one pound of apples. Mix well together, and let the mixture stand until quite cold. Line a dish . . . with light paste, fill with the apple and bake.

Godey's Lady's Book
November 1867

ARROW-ROOT CUSTARD

In Winter, when eggs are very dear, take two spoonfuls of arrow-root mixed in a teacup of cold milk; boil a quart of milk, beat up three eggs, and mix in the arrow-root. Pour in the boiling milk, stirring the eggs and arrow-root continually; put it in a pitcher, and boil as above directed.

The Philosophy of Housekeeping
—Joseph B. & Laura E. Lyman, 1869

BOILED INDIAN PUDDING

One pint sweet milk, one pint Indian meal, one-third of a pint of rye flour, one-third of a cup of molasses, one teaspoonful of soda. A little chopped suet improves it.

The Philosophy of Housekeeping
—Joseph B. & Laura E. Lyman, 1869

TO COOK MACARONI

Simmer a quarter pound of maccaroni in plenty of water, until it is tender. Strain off the water, and add a pint of milk or cream, an ounce of grated cheese, and a teaspoonful of salt. Mix well together, and strew over the top two ounces of grated cheese and crumbs of bread. Brown it well in baking, on the top. It will bake in half an hour.

The Philosophy of Housekeeping
—Joseph B. & Laura E. Lyman, 1869

GINGER BEER

Pound well one ounce of ginger-root, of which make one quart of strong tea. Add water to make four gallons. In this, dissolve four pounds of brown sugar, one ounce of cream tartar, add and thoroughly mix one pint of good yeast. After standing twenty-four hours, strain carefully, and bottle tightly, tying down the corks. In forty-eight hours from the time of bottling, it is fit for use, and makes a delightful drink in hot weather.

The Philosophy of Housekeeping
—Joseph B. & Laura E. Lyman, 1869

3

The Late Victorian Kitchen 1870–1899

"THE WAY TO A MAN'S HEART IS THROUGH HIS STOMACH"

This woodcut from an 1876 issue of The American Agriculturalist illustrates a rural kitchen with convenient "built-ins" such as those recommended by Catharine Beecher. This kitchen, with wainscoting and wood floor, includes an encased sink with hand pump, a shelf over the sink, storage cupboard next to the sink (with glass panes in top cupboard doors) and what appears to be a small pass-through between the kitchen and the pantry.

Home is the woman's kingdom, and there she reigns supreme. To embellish that home, to make happy the lives of her husband and the dear ones committed to her trust, is the honored task which it is the wife's province to perform. All praise be to her who so rules and governs in that kingdom, that those reared beneath her roof shall rise up and call her blessed.

Our Deportment, Compiled from the Latest Reliable Authorities
—John H. Young, A.M., 1882

*A*s the industrial revolution gained speed during the late nineteenth century and the middle-class woman's role in the home began to change with the decrease in domestic servants, architectural developments and then-popular styles or fashions in home decoration subtley influenced the kitchen's design, location and manner of decoration. In addition, new products, services and appliances continued to alter cooking methods and housekeeping in general.

Differences between the rural "country" kitchen and the urban kitchen continued to exist. During the 1870s popular books of architectural home designs still offered plans for city townhouses with basement kitchens but these became passé by the end of the decade with the introduction of gas lines to service light fixtures and gas stoves, and the advent of indoor plumbing. The early tinplate and lead pipes that had been used during the mid-1800s to transport water from the well to the kitchen sink were replaced by iron, and urban centers now boasted of a

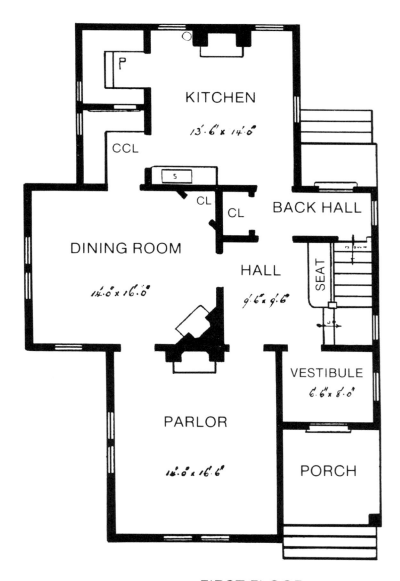

P

KITCHEN

13'·6" x 14'·0"

CCL

S

CL

CL

BACK HALL

DINING ROOM

14'·0" x 16'·0"

HALL

9'·6" x 9'·6"

SEAT

VESTIBULE

6'·6" x 8'·0"

PARLOR

14'·0" x 16'·6"

PORCH

FIRST FLOOR

The 1878 publication of Palliser's American Cottage Homes *included this first-floor plan for a modest seven-room house. Note the kitchen, which is 13 feet 6 inches by 14 feet, is at the rear of* the home and the plan indicates placement of the sink, pantry and a pass-through/closet area between the dining room and kitchen. The range would be placed against the back kitchen wall.

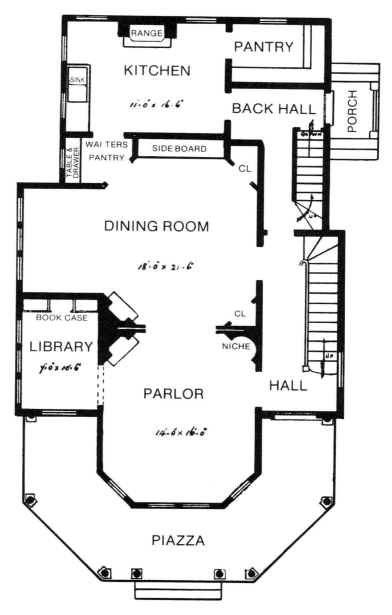

RANGE

PANTRY

KITCHEN

SINK

11·0" x 16·6"

BACK HALL

PORCH

TABLE & DRAWER.

WAITERS PANTRY

SIDE BOARD

CL

DINING ROOM

18·0" x 21·6"

UP

BOOK CASE

CL

LIBRARY

NICHE

9·0" x 10·6"

HALL

PARLOR

14·6" x 16·0"

UP

PIAZZA

This plan from Palliser's American Cottage Homes *offers greater detail in regard to the kitchen. Placement of the sink and range are clearly indicated* and the kitchen includes a large pantry as well as a "waiter's" or butler's pantry with space for a table with drawers.

THE LATE VICTORIAN KITCHEN 1870–1899 ❧ 87

city-wide distribution of water and organized service systems. Also, as the populations in the cities continued to increase, there was a shift towards building large apartment houses or buildings rather than townhouses and brownstones. As a result, the last quarter of the nineteenth century found the majority of kitchens built on the first floor, at the rear of the home (or the same floor the "apartment" was located on.)

The pantry continued to be an integral part of the kitchen and additional storage closets were not uncommon. In larger homes the passageway between the first-floor kitchen and dining room grew to accommodate not only a small sink but built-in cupboards for the good china. This became known as the "butler's pantry" and was a convenient location for last-minute preparations and transporting of hot dishes from the kitchen to the dining room for family meals, formal dinners or evening parties.

The laundry facilities and "cold-spot" storage areas were usually located in the basement, often divided into a series of separate rooms.

Architectural pattern books, which proved quite popular from the 1870s on, illustrated basic kitchen floor plans that indicated placement of the range and sink but little else. More elaborate plans might also indicate the location of an icebox, built-in china closet and a butler's pantry. *Palliser's American Cottage Homes,* published in 1878 by Palliser, Palliser & Co. proved to be a very successful pattern book that offered an extensive selection of small to large "cottages" for middle-class Americans. In the book's preface the company told readers,

> it is an erroneous idea, that it is necessary to enclose convenience and comfort in the internal arrangements with ugliness, or that it is impossible to obtain a pleasing and effective design with a good plan and a modern construction. We have seen buildings which, externally, were perfect, but their plans of interior arrangement were absolute failures, being without a closet or pantry . . . The first and main object of consideration should be the plan, the design being of a pliant nature and easily adapted to the ever-varying forms of comfortable and convenient plans.[1]

The popularity of pattern books encouraged other publishers in offering house plans and they soon began to appear in national publications targeting women and family life. For example, the March 1897 issue of the *Ladies' Home Journal* included an article entitled, "A MODEL $2000. HOUSE," by Walter F. Keith. The author described in detail a "house

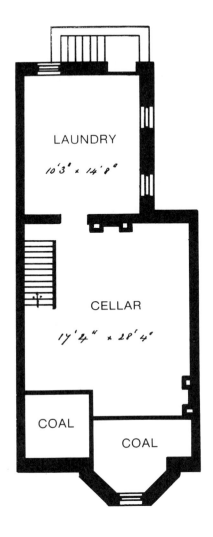

LAUNDRY

10'3" x 14'8"

CELLAR

17'4" x 28'4"

COAL

COAL

CELLAR PLAN

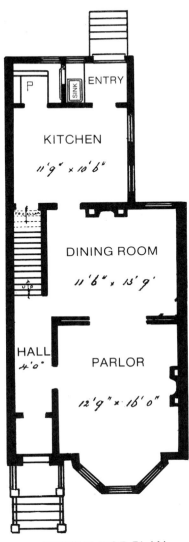

P

SINK

ENTRY

KITCHEN

11'9" x 10'6"

DINING ROOM

11'6" x 15'9'

HALL

4'0"

PARLOR

12'9" x 16'0"

FIRST FLOOR PLAN

From the 1878 Palliser's American Cottage Homes, *this cellar and first-floor plan is for a brick Queen Anne–style city home or row house. The cellar* contains a separate laundry area and the first-floor kitchen includes a small pantry and indicates placement of the sink and back entrance way.

of ten rooms, beside bathroom, toilet-room, halls and pantries." Of the kitchen area he wrote,

> Back of the Reception-Room is placed the dining room, to which access is had from the kitchen through the butler's pantry, which, being properly arranged, is the delight of the housekeeper. So large is this pantry that it is possible to have the mixing-board, flour-bins, etc., placed in one end near the window, so that good light is insured for the work which must be done there. The kitchen also has the recommendation of size, especially so as the room is made more available by places having been provided for the necessary furniture. There is a space in the entry for the refrigerator, so that the ice man, by his muddy boots, need not soil the kitchen floor each morning, as he will have no occasion to enter. Under the refrigerator is provided a drain to carry off the drip, thus avoiding a constantly overflowing ice pan. The kitchen, it will be noticed, is in every way separated from the main part of the house by two doors, and not only that, but through the servants' hall, access to the front door may be had by the servant without passing through any of the other apartments. The servants also go directly to their rooms by the back stairway without at anytime entering the main part of the house.[2]

While convenience in the kitchen during the early Victorian period had been proposed by authors of domestic science manuals and home guides (although they referred to convenience as "economy" and "system"), the later part of the century saw interest spread to architects and builders in response to both technological developments and the growing servant problem. As indicated in the passages above, kitchens were being given as much thought as the rest of the home in regard to convenience (of special interest to the wife who had to assume a greater portion of household chores) and/or they included back stairways and the like to keep the servants as removed from the family as possible. This of course appealed to those who looked unfavorably upon their immigrant girls.

Furnishings in the kitchen continued to be a series of freestanding cupboards, dressers and worktables. Large dressers (cupboards) with upper doors sliding one in front of the other or opening on hinges were used to store pots, pans, tableware and so on. A small table located next to the sink was ideal for preparing vegetables and meats and a marble-top, or later, zinc-top, table was often included for baking. By the 1890s a baker's table, usually made of pine or oak with a zinc work-top and upper section full of small spice drawers and/or cupboards was introduced and these proved to be the forerunner of the twentieth-century all-purpose hoosier cabinet.

During the 1870s the cast-iron coal and/or woodburning stove grew quite large and many were embellished with decorative nickel-plated features. Most now included hot water reservoirs, either within the stove or in an attached tank, and stoves were set upon brick or tile flooring to avoid the danger of fire.

Operating the cookstove in the most economic manner possible continued to be a source of concern for housekeepers. In the March 1897 *Ladies' Home Journal*, Sarah Tyson Rorer, author of the column "Markets and the Household," advised readers that "An ordinary range or stove should not consume over half a ton of hard coal in a month; more than this cannot be used for cooking purposes. Every housewife should study

A typical middle-class kitchen of the 1870s. Note the large cast-iron range with hot water tank, the storage closet or pantry for staples and dishware, worktable and converted dry sink with faucets. The all-important kitchen clock can be seen on the wall above the dry sink.

the draughts, and the particular construction of the range she uses, so that she may be able to direct the cook how best to get good results from the amount of coal burned. The direct damper should be closed, save when the ashes are being taken down and out—a task which should always be performed with great care and neatness, or the appearance of the kitchen will suffer." The column continued, instructing readers on the proper way to regulate the stove fire and arrange the draughts.[3] The introduction of the gas stove in the late 1800s, while met with skepticism by some, was no doubt a relief for many a housekeeper or cook weary of continually fussing over the coal or woodburning stove.

With the introduction of indoor plumbing, the wood-encased kitchen "dry sink" with a soapstone, granite or cast-iron insert was

In the 1888 Mott's Plumbing catalog this ornate kitchen sink was featured. The do-it-yourself homeowner was told he or she could construct such a sink with either wooden or nickle-plated hollow brass legs as seen here, a porcelain or stainless-steel basin, a marble back and wood trim. Decorated metal tiles or ceramic tiles could be used on the sides and across the front of the sink.

slowly replaced by an all-metal or cast-iron sink on legs. These were either quite plain and functional or unusually elaborate with fancy hot and cold water taps.

Although iceboxes had been available since the 1860s, it was the 1880s before they were widely used. Once the majority of households took advantage of indoor refrigeration, the icebox was delegated space on the back porch, in the pantry or kitchen proper. A large block of ice was placed inside the icebox (which was lined and had shelves), and the resulting cool air would circulate among the perishables. In the 1891 publication, *Palatable Dishes: A Practical Guide to Good Living*, Sarah J. Cutter advised readers on the care of a refrigerator. She wrote that "People who live in the city, and especially those living in flats, are so dependent upon keeping their food fresh in a refrigerator. Two of the most important things is to have a good refrigerator and to keep it sweet and perfectly clean . . . keep upon one of the top shelves a saucer of powdered charcoal . . . It is a good absorbant of strong odors . . . keep on the top shelf vegetables and fruits that have strong odors, and put on the lower shelves . . . delicate foods, such as butter, milk, cream, etc., salad dressings, and sauces. The delicate foods should be well covered. Do not leave raw meat in a brown paper, but remove directly to an earthen dish . . . and watch closely that the meat is not tainted."[4]

In 1873 when Catharine Beecher's *The New Housekeeper's Manual* became available, the noted authority on all matters pertaining to domestic science was recommending whitewashed kitchen walls "to promote a neat look and pure air."[5] She also continued to advise in this updated version on her 1869 *American Woman's Home* that kitchen floors be painted or covered with oilcloth. In order to "procure a kitchen oilcloth as cheaply as possible," Miss Beecher suggested "buy cheap tow cloth, and fit it to the size and shape of the kitchen. Then have it stretched, and nailed to the south side of the barn, and, with a brush, cover it with a coat of thin rye paste. When this is dry, put on a coat of yellow paint, and let it dry a fortnight. It is safest to first try the paint, and see if it dries well, as some paint never will dry. Then put on a second coat, and at the end of another fortnight, a third coat. Then let it hang two months, and it will last, uninjured, for many years. The longer the paint is left to dry, the better. If varnished, it will last much longer."[6]

Another popular alternative for kitchen flooring during the late Victorian period was linoleum. First created in 1863 by British inventor, Federick Walton, linoleum was available in the United States by the 1870s when Walton founded the American Linoleum Manufacturing Company in New York City. This machine-made flooring consisted of linseed oil, fillers and ground-cork on a burlap backing and was produced as a total floor covering or in "rug" form. Linoleum proved to be especially desirable by the late 1890s since it was stronger and more durable than oilcloth and less expensive than tile. If properly taken care of, linoleum could last for thirty or more years and housekeepers were pleased it didn't require the same constant scrubbing demanded of a wood floor. The most popular Victorian-era patterns were a geometric tile-like design or linoleum sporting the look of wooden flooring. During the 1890s linoleum was often found in middle-class kitchens while the upper middle class or wealthy preferred tile or brick kitchen flooring.

As women in middle-class homes began spending more time in the kitchen doing light chores or baking, there was a tendency to try and make the kitchen light and airy—even comfortable. Household manuals recommended kitchens be built with windows to provide good light and ventilation, and while the kitchen was not yet viewed in terms of "decoration," it did undergo a series of "treatments" before the arrival of the new century. For example, when *The Household Cyclopaedia of Practical Receipts and Daily Wants* by Alexander V. Hamilton was published in 1873, the author proposed the kitchen should be papered "in varnished staircase paper, as the soils can be easily washed off." As an alternative Hamilton offered, "in many houses kitchens are wood-panelled, or the walls covered with tiles, after the good old fashion common in Germany and Holland."[7]

Wallpaper was an uncommon wall treatment in the kitchen during the nineteenth century and of the small number of homes that employed such a covering, it was no doubt a "sanitary" or washable paper.

The 1876 centennial ushered in a period of nostalgic Colonialism and some kitchens were outfitted (decorated) with fireplaces, hearth utensils hanging on the walls, colorful curtains and tablecloths, primitive containers etc.

During the late 1800s the popularity of the dado and frieze as a wall treatment in the parlor, dining room and so on inspired a similar treatment in the kitchen via wooden wainscoting and functional plate rails. In addition, attractive pressed tin ceilings were employed in the kitchen, in imitation of the fancy carved plaster ceilings found elsewhere throughout the house. Tin ceilings were viewed favorably since they were easy to wipe clean and didn't harbor insects and germs. This typical late-Victorian, middle-class kitchen was quite common in cities and found as well throughout rural areas where following fashions and styles was becoming easier thanks to the availability of goods, mail-order catalogs and increasing numbers of magazines.

This kitchen in the President Calvin Coolidge home interprets the late 1870s period when the Coolidge family purchased the home. The kitchen changed very little over the years and remains as it was when Coolidge became president in 1923. A large cast-iron stove, converted dry sink and drying rack behind the stove can be seen. The kitchen floor is wood planks and kitchen walls are papered, which was unusual during the late nineteenth century. Cookware sits atop the stove along with a sadiron and other kitchen necessities are on the shelf over the sink. A cast-iron match safe hangs on the door frame to the right of the sink.

Courtesy Vermont Division for Historic Preservation/President Calvin Coolidge Birthplace.

The circa 1880s John Muir House kitchen in Martinez, California includes the original stove installed in the early 1880s. The stove is cast-iron with a double door oven and two fire boxes and the entire unit sits atop a brick platform. An oak icebox can be seen under the window but was most likely kept on a lattice-enclosed back porch when the Muir family was in residence. A pan pantry or storage cupboard and a food pantry are located off the kitchen. Wood flooring and wainscoting are used in the kitchen and as the Muir family employed a Chinese chef, this kitchen was a "workroom" with few frills or decorative touches.

Courtesy U.S. Dept. of the Interior, National Park Service.

Throughout the period 1870–1899 color in the kitchen reflected first the popular opinion of domestic science experts and then decorating styles—albeit on a limited scale. After *Hints on Household Taste* by Charles L. Eastlake was published in England in 1868, it achieved huge success in the United States and went through several printings by the early 1880s. Eastlake proposed simplicity in furnishings, decorating and household accessories, and his advice, coinciding with the early development of the Arts and Crafts movement, shifted the Victorian household from excess and opulence in decorating to scaled-down, naturalistic simplicity. He wrote, "In an age of debased design at least, the simplest style will be the best."[8] Regarding the kitchen, colors employed were muted tones inspired by nature such as tan, soft green or light gold, and while they may have been fashionable colors, they no doubt suited the kitchen because they were serviceable and easy to maintain.

As further evidence that the kitchen was being given increased attention, the 1891 publication of *Manners, Culture and Dress of the Best American Society,* by Richard A. Wells, A.M., noted that "While speaking of the different rooms we must not forget the kitchen. There should be a pleasant window or two through which fresh air and sunlight may come, a few plants on the window sill, a small stand for a work basket, an easy chair, the walls painted or calcimined with some beautiful and cheerful tint, the woodwork grained instead of painted in some dingy color, and a general air of comfort pervade the whole room."[9]

There was a tendency during the late 1800s to build houses with smaller kitchens that would require less "help" and to locate cooking and household necessities centrally. Kitchens and pantries were outfitted with tall, built-in cupboards that featured glass-front doors. Not only did they provide storage areas but they aided the housekeeper in practicing "system" in her kitchen since items could be located at a glance.

The gate-leg and drop-leaf tables that serviced the kitchen during the 1860s and 1870s were replaced during the late nineteenth century by factory-made oak furniture that could be purchased through mail-order catalogs as well as in home furnishing stores.

During the last decade of the century, emphasis in the kitchen shifted from airy and light to sanitary, sparkling and laboratory-like. In 1898, *Smiley's Cook Book and New and Complete Guide for Housekeepers* advised women that "upon the kitchen and its management the comfort of the whole house largely depends . . . all its *sanitary* arrangements should be most carefully examined and attended to, since negligence here will affect the whole household." The editors also proposed kitchen walls should be painted or white-washed—never papered—and hardwood floors should be varnished—never painted—as "white floors are too suggestive of aching backs and tired arms." They were of the opinion that an oilcloth floor was too cold and a tile floor too hard on the feet. Linoleum, however, was noiseless, impervious to dampness and not as cold as oilcloth.[10]

The focus on sanitation shifted the kitchen from a factory-like center of operations to a laboratory-like, sterile workplace. This concept (the kitchen as a laboratory) would persist through the 1920s.

Kitchen equipment during the late nineteenth century was constantly changing as industries turned out new and/or improved gadgets, utensils, appliances etc. New, more convenient cookware was introduced and both packaged and canned food products lessened the factory-like operations in the kitchen where everything was made from scratch.

A circa 1890s kitchen with a coal/wood-burning stove, oak china cupboard, table and chairs and wainscoting on the walls. A string hangs on the wall behind the stove to dry towels, and lace on the back wall shelf and in the china cupboard adds a decorative touch to this late Victorian kitchen.

Courtesy GE Appliance Archives.

FRYING PAN.

DRIPPING PAN.

GRIDIRON.

REVOLVING GRIDIRON.

WIRE VEGETABLE STRAINER.

WIRE DISH COVER.

BREAD GRATER.

KNIFE BASKET.

COLLANDER.

KITCHEN UTENSILS.

*A selection of kitchen utensils illus-
trated in the 1873 book* The Household Cyclopaedia of Practical Receipts
by Alexander V. Hamilton.

In Mrs. F. L. Gillette's and Hugo Ziemann's 1887 book, *The White House CookBook*, the authors included the following list to assure every housekeeper of a properly equipped kitchen:

2 Sweeping Brooms and 1 Dust Pan
1 Whisk Broom
1 Bread Box
2 Cake Boxes
1 large Flour Box
1 Dredging Box
1 large-sized tin Pepper Box
1 Spice Box containing smaller Spice
    Boxes
2 Cake Pans, two sizes
4 Bread Pans
2 square Biscuit Pans
1 Apple Corer
1 Lemon Squeezer
1 Meat Cleaver
3 Kitchen Knives & Forks, 1 large
    Kitchen Fork, 4 Kitchen Spoons,
    two sizes
1 Wooden Spoon for Cake Making
1 Large Bread Knife
1 Griddle cake turner, also 1 Griddle
1 Potato Masher
1 Meat Board
1 dozen Patty Pans, and the same
    number of Tartlet Pans
1 large Tin Pail and 1 Wooden Pail
2 small Tin Pails
1 set of Tin Basins
1 set of Tin Measures
1 Wooden Butter Ladle
1 Tin Skimmer
1 Tin Steamer
1 Dippers, two sizes
2 Funnels, two sizes
1 set of Jelly Cake Tins
4 Milk Pans, one strainer
1 dozen iron Gem Pans or Muffin Rings
1 course Gravy Strainer, one fine
1 Colander
1 Flour Sifter
2 Scoops, one for flour, one for sugar
2 Jelly Molds, two sizes
1 Can Opener
1 Eggbeater
1 Corkscrew

1 Chopping Knife
2 Wooden Chopping Bowls, two sizes
1 Meat Saw
2 large Earthen Bowls
4 Stone Jars
1 Coffee Mill
1 Candlestick
2 Market Baskets, two sizes
1 Clock
1 Ash Bucket
1 Gridiron
2 Frying Pans, two sizes
4 Flat-irons, two #8, two #6 (Pounds)
2 Dripping Pans, two sizes
3 Iron Kettles, Porcelain-lined if possible
1 Corn Beef or Fish Pan
1 Tea-Kettle
2 Granite-ware Stewpans, two sizes
1 Wire Toaster
1 Double Kettle for cooking custards,
    grains, etc.
2 Sugar Boxes, one for course, one for fine
1 Waffle Iron
1 Step Ladder
1 Stove, one coal shovel
1 Pair Scales
4 Pie Pans
3 Pudding Molds, one for boiling, two
    for baking, two sizes
2 Dish Pans, two sizes
2 Cake or Biscuit Cutters, two sizes
2 Graters, one large, one small
1 Coffee Canister
1 Tea Canister
1 Tin or Granite-ware Teapot
1 Tin or Granite-ware Coffeepot
2 Coal hods or buckets
1 Kitchen Table, two kitchen chairs
1 large Clothes Basket
1 Wash Boiler, one wash board
8 dozen Clothes Pins
1 large Nail Hammer & one small
    Tack Hammer
1 Bean Pot
1 Clothes Wringer

The *White House CookBook* explained that "an ingenious housewife will manage to do with less conveniences, but these articles, if they can be purchased in the commencement of housekeeping, will save time and labor, making the preparation of food more easy—and it is always economy in the end to get the best material in all wares . . ."[11]

Included in the above listing are numerous pieces of cookware. While cast-iron and tin pots, pans etc., had been readily available for some time, the introduction of graniteware (generic term) kitchen and household items was a significant, "modern" advancement in regard to convenience and sanitation. Not only was this enamel over sheet-steel product lightweight compared to cast iron, but it was also easier to

The Wm. Frankfurth Hardware Company of Milwaukee, Wisconsin offered this Gold Medal Apple Parer in a late nineteenth-century catalog. Considered a kitchen necessity, merchants could purchase these in bulk at $8 for one dozen.

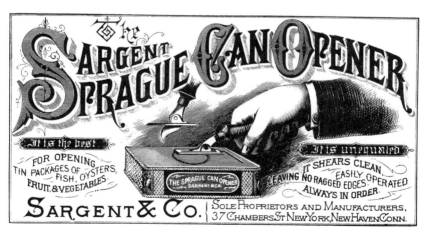

A late nineteenth-century advertisement for the Sargent Sprague Can Opener. The can opener had become an important kitchen tool with the introduction of new canned food products.

·:ᐧ❅Wm. Frankfurth Hardware Co.❅ᐧ·

COPPER WARE.

TEA KETTLES, SPUN COPPER.

PLANISHED COPPER.   NICKEL PLATED.

Pit Bottoms.

Nos.	-	-	7	8	9	Nos.	-	-	7	8	9
Per Dozen,	-		$27 00	30 00	33 00	Per Dozen,	-		$36 00	39 00	42 00

The Wm. Frankfurth Hardware Company offered an extensive selection of tea kettles during the late 1800s, including planished copper and nickle-plated models. The tea kettle was an important kitchen item and could usually be found warming atop the stove.

This advertisement for the Home Comfort Range appeared in the September 1897 issue of Ladies' Home Journal. *The recipient of several awards, the Home Comfort was sold throughout the United States and Canada from the back of salesmen's wagons.*

clean and maintain. The process of enameling to create graniteware originated in Germany during the eighteenth century and by the mid-1800s several European countries were exporting these wares to the United States. With the 1870s came the American manufacture of enamel-coated iron and then sheet-steel cookware by the Jacob J. Vollrath Manufacturing Company of Sheboygan, Wisconsin. The Vollrath Company is considered the first in the U.S. to produce iron with an enameled coating (1874), followed by the production of enameled sheet steel in 1892. "Vollrath Ware" enameled kitchenware was initially double-coated with speckled or mottled blue, black, brown or gray enamel.

Lalance and Grosjean of Brooklyn (and later, Long Island), New York was founded by Frenchmen Charles Lalance and Florian Grosjean. They too began producing enameled goods in the 1870s and became well known for the high quality of their mottled "Agate Ware," which was produced with three coatings of enamel.

The St. Louis Stamping Company of St. Louis, Missouri, founded by the Niedringhaus brothers in the 1860s was also a prolific manufacturer

An 1886 Wm. Frankfurth Hardware catalog included a variety of graniteware goods such as this teapot and coffeepot, which were both kitchen necessities during the late nineteenth century according to the authors of The White House Cookbook.

An ad in an 1896 issue of Ladies' Home Journal *told readers Iron-Clad Manufacturing Company's Salamander Ware would not scorch. With a double bottom, the gray enameled ware reportedly would not chip and the contents in the pan would cook without burning.*

of enameled wares. This company went on to become part of a multi-company merger in 1899, which resulted in the formation of the National Enameling & Stamping Company, which turned out the "Nesco Royal Granite Enameled Ware" line.

Numerous smaller manufacturers also produced enameled wares and European imports maintained a stronghold on the U.S. market until the early 1900s. Enameled or graniteware items could easily be purchased at hardware stores, local emporiums, department stores (where household items were usually delegated a small space in the basement) or through mail-order catalogs. For example, the 1895 Spring and Summer Montgomery Ward & Co. catalog included an assortment of enameled goods. They offered wares "known as Granite and Agate Ware," and proclaimed, "We are now prepared to offer this justly celebrated kitchenware at unheard of prices. It is guaranteed to be absolutely pure and safe to use and is the most durable ware in the world. It is especially desirable, as it is so easily cleaned." Montgomery Ward offered a selection of water pails, covered buckets, milk pans, saucepans, tubed cake pans, pudding pans, bake pans, dishpans, pie plates, dinner plates, jelly cake plates, preserve kettles, stockpots, rice boilers, water pitchers, dippers, measuring cups, wash basins, teapots, coffee pots and so on.[12] Enameled wares remained popular well into the twentieth century until aluminum cookware sales increased in the 1930s.

In regard to kitchen "furnishings," an article by Sarah Tyson Rorer that appeared in the September 1897 issue of *Ladies' Home Journal* told readers,

> One of the greatest economies is the furnishing of the kitchen with non-breakable utensils. In my twenty-five years experience I find it thoroughly pays to furnish well the kitchen. Insist upon good care, and see that each utensil is used for the purpose intended. Granite iron plates may be used instead of stone china for the refrigerator. If they happen to fall they will not break. Ordinary iron bowls, lined with white enamel, may be used for mixing purposes.

Cups for measuring should be of tin, glass or granite ware. Boards for kneading may be of ordinary metal. They are easily kept clean and do not require scrubbing.[13]

The explosion of factory-made, cast-iron kitchen gadgetry that began during the 1850s and 1860s continued on through the remainder of the century and numerous new "conveniences" were introduced to aid in preparing elaborate meals, cut down on time-consuming tasks and increase productivity in the kitchen. While items such as the apple parer, cherry stoner and lemon squeezer had become commonplace in the kitchen, during the 1870s–1890s the housekeeper was encouraged to employ potato chippers, revolving slicers, rotary flour sifters, tabletop milkshake machines, wire-mesh corn poppers and other kitchen-ware items. Necessity was no longer the predominant catalyst for invention—"economy," or convenience was taking center-stage. House-keepers were becoming increasingly vocal about their displeasure in assuming a greater hands-on role in the kitchen due to the shortage of domestic help and industry responded by offering them an ever-increasing number of tools to provide shortcut or "modern" ways of completing household tasks. In fact, new products were often referred to as the new "servants" for the home or kitchen. Unfortunately not all new gadgetry was easy to operate, achieved successful results or was deserving of the praise it received. In her 1875 recipe book, *Breakfast, Luncheon and Tea,* author Marion Harland recounted her introduction to the Dover egg-beater. She wrote, "Four years ago, without prevision that one of the blessings of my life was coming upon me, I paid a visit

To promote their product, this circa 1897 advertisement by Lalance & Grosjean Mfg. Co. assured readers that their cookware was safe, containing no arsenic or lead. Their Agate Ware was double coated for long service and the "strongest enamel ware made."

to my house-furnisher. He had a new egg-beater for sale." Mrs. Harland went on to tell readers she was skeptical, given her great disappointment in other new gadgetry she'd tried over the years but she took the Dover home, agreeing to try it out and report back to the merchant regarding its worthiness. She then told readers,

> I beg you to believe that I am not in league with the patentee of my favorite. I do not know whether "Dover" stands for his name, that of the manufacturing company, or the place in which it was made. "Dover Egg-beater, Patented 1870" is stamped upon the circumference of the iron wheel. I know nothing more of its antecedents. But if I could not get another I would not sell mine for fifty dollars—nor a hundred. Egg-whipping ceased to be a bugbear to me from the day of which I speak. Light, portable, rapid, easy, and comparatively noiseless, my pet implement works like a benevolent

This advertising trade card entitled "The Attack," told potential customers on the reverse, "The picture upon the other side of this card is very properly named. The young man is blessed with a good appetite, and will soon dispose of the contents on the dish set before him. No attack however can be successful that is made upon The Granite Iron Ware. If you would be upon good terms with Health, Economy and Happiness, use and use only The Granite Iron Ware."

The March 1987 Ladies' Home Journal included this small ad for the New Triumph Meat Cutter. A handy kitchen tool during the late 1800s and the early twentieth century, the meat cutter or grinder could be clamped onto a work-table or baker's cupboard for convenience.

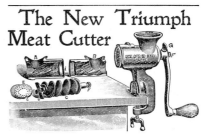

The New Triumph Meat Cutter

Expressly for family use. **Cutting parts of forged steel; easily cleaned;** pays for itself every 6 months. Receipt book of numerous dishes made with cutter, free to any address.

Box B

The Peck, Stow & Wilcox Co., Southington, Conn.

(Right) This 1891 advertisement intro-duces a convenient and sanitary way to store flour in the kitchen. Promoted as a kitchen "luxury," the tin flour receptacle would hold 50 pounds of flour and included a sifter attachment with a turn-handle.

(Below) From the March 1890 The Housewife magazine, the advertisement illustrates the "new" way of wringing out the kitchen mop and the "old" way done by hand. This self-wringing mop was, according to the ad, "The greatest labor-saving invention in years."

A KITCHEN LUXURY!

Tyler's Flour Receptacle

holding 50 lbs. with sifter attached.
   Most convenient method for keeping flour ever invented! No waste or litter such as you must make in dipping your flour from the sack.
   Agents wanted in every city and town.
   —Address—

Ben'j. Waterman,

General Agent No. 518 Kirk Blk., Syracuse, N. Y.

Agents Can Make 150%

by selling what every lady wants; our **Patent Broom Holder.** Sure sale for two or three in every house. Send 15c for sample. Special price for quantities. **VOLZ & CO, .La Crosse, Wis.**

THE NEW WAY

REWELL RATCHET MOP

THE OLD WAY

LATEST AND BEST SELF-WRINGING MOP.

Valuable improvements over all others. Perfect ratchet device for holding cloth when wrong. This feature alone worth the price. Heavy twine cloths knit by a patent process. Outwear all other cloths, yet easy to wring, and absorb water like a sponge. Malleable castings. Steel wire. Bright finish. Cannot rust. Hard wood handles. **Only perfect self-wringing mop.** Agents just started report tremendous sales and success beyond their expectations. The greatest labor-saving invention in years. No experience necessary. Our methods, and merits of the mop, assure success. Best terms. We allow for freights. Energetic men and women investigate this. NO FOR-TUNE TO OFFER TO YOU, BUT SPLENDID RE-TURNS FOR HONEST LABOR. Illustrated circulars free.

CEO. M. REWELL,
223 Public Square, Cleveland, O.

This late nineteenth-century advertising trade card was typical of the appealing images used to advertise everyday household items or chores such as black-ening or polishing the cast-iron stove. The flood of packaged products during the late 1800s were supposed to make such tasks easier to perform.

brownie. With it I turn out a meringue in five minutes . . . make the formidable "snow-custard" in less than half an hour, with no after tremulousness of nerve or tendon . . . Winter and summer, it has served me with invariable fidelity, and it is to all appearance, stanch as when it first passed into my reluctant hands . . . I hope the . . . unknown patentee will live as many years as he has saved hours of labor to American housewives and cooks.[14]

Along with the various kitchen tools and cookware needed to maintain "system" and order within the kitchen, an assortment of cleaning and laundry supplies were on hand for the daily and weekly chores and annual or semiannual cleaning events. Brushes and brooms for dusting, sweeping, scrubbing, cleaning clothes and clearing the table were required. Wire or rattan rug beaters with wooden handles were employed to "beat" the dust from carpets and rugs.

For laundry work, copper boilers replaced the wooden washtub and washboards made with a wooden frame and zinc or brass insert evolved from the earlier all-wood models with spools or ridges. Even though

The Mrs. Pott's sadiron with convenient removable handle was widely used during the late nineteenth century until the introduction of gas irons, which may have been more convenient but also posed a threat of fire or explosion.

washing machines were available, many housekeepers continued to find them hard on the clothing, tearing them or leaving stains that were impossible to remove. For the most part, old methods of doing the wash continued through the turn of the century.

Several sadirons of different weights were on hand for ironing but by the end of the nineteenth century, gasoline models had been introduced. Rather than iron on a board placed between two chairs, many housekeepers opted to invest in one of the new "ironing tables" introduced during the 1890s. With a compartment underneath, the new table proved a handy storage area as well as a more convenient (and portable) tool for ironing.

By the dawn of the twentieth century the kitchen had achieved status as the great laboratory of the household. Improvements in kitchenware, appliances and cookware, along with increased availability of packaged and prepared foods, shifted the focus from "system" in performing manual labor to sanitary measures and "economy" of time and use of goods. Although the housewife had, in most middle-class homes, been responsible for the marketing, she was no longer simply choosing raw materials to be transformed into family meals, she was slowly evolving into a full-fledged consumer of factory-made goods. The kitchen itself, while still considered a workroom, was no longer the domain of the domestic servant.

Madam Returns to Her Kitchen

Woman was originally the inventor, the manufacturer, the provider. She has allowed one office after another gradually to slip from her hand until she retains, with loose grasp, only the so called housekeeping . . . she rightly feels that what is left is mere deadening drudgery, and that escape from this condition is essential to her well being as an individual.

The Outlook (Magazine)
—Essay by Ellen Swallow, 1897

By 1870, just a few short years after the end of the Civil War, the shortage of good "domestics" was becoming an ongoing problem, especially in large cities where the demand for them was greatest. Expansion and opportunity in industry and new service professions were attracting young women at the same time many middle-class familes were suffering the effects of the economic depression that lasted from 1873 until 1878.

While the early Victorian period generally found an energetic and skilled young woman opting among positions as a seamstress, teacher, mill worker or domestic, during the last quarter of the century opportunities for employment increased and choosing a household service position was often considered a last resort. For example, the 1889 publication of *The Home Manual,* compiled by Mrs. John A. Logan, offered detailed information on the areas of work available to women. Logan reported that for the working woman " . . . every year the world is opening more avenues by which she can increase her store of knowledge, either for the sake of education itself or for the increased facilities it will afford her of successfully entering the ranks of breadwinners."[15] A list of positions included:

Attendants in Asylums—These include all grades of Service—nurses, cooks, waitresses, laundresses, seamstresses, etc.

Bookbinding and Folding—This trade is now mostly given up to women, and girls can begin as early as thirteen or fourteen. The work is generally paid by the "piece," and can be satisfactorily performed by uneducated persons.

Bookkeeping—The chief requisites in this branch are accuracy in figures, correctness in spelling and a good handwriting.

China Painting—A girl can begin work as soon as she leaves school. Her first work is to cut out the printed paper patterns, next she learns to transfer these to the ware, and gradually rises to the higher grades of the work. There are also merely menial positions that can be filled by the uneducated.

Christmas Card Making—This industry gives employment to many ladies, is pleasant and remunerative. Much of it is mechanical, and consists in copying from designs.

Clerkships—In many departments of commercial work, women are superseding men. The requirements differ according to the line of business needing a clerk, but short-hand and book-keeping, with quickness and accuracy in changing money are always desirable.

Cutlery—Women are employed as scourers and dressers, and their work is the scouring of goods with sand-paper.

Electro-Plating—Here is a clean and healthy business, in which about one-sixth of the labor is performed by women.

Embroidery—Machine work has so far superseded that done by hand that this means of earning one's living is not so remunerative as formerly; it is work too that is very trying to the eyes and wearying to the back. A skillful needlewoman may however, obtain employment with ecclesiastical furnishers, robe-makers, and art needlework establishments.

Factory Hands—The hours, wages, and requirements differ with the kind of work produced by each establishment, and must be learned by application at the particular factory from which employment is sought.

Feather Making—Like artificial flower making, the demand in this branch of trade fluctuates with the fashions, but it is an easy, as well as pleasant employment for young girls.

Glove Making—Workers at this trade are employed either in their own homes or at a factory, work is paid for by the dozen, and is done both by hand and with a machine.

Hair-Dressing—The time required to learn this business, which should include hair-cutting and shaving the head for the sick, varies from nine months to a year. Gentleness and pleasant manners are important characteristics.

Indexing—Patience, system, exactness, and punctuality are required for success in this occupation. Of a kindred nature is the arranging of literary matter for compilation, much of which is now entrusted to ladies.

Laundry Work—Only strong young women, able to labor for ten or twelve hours per day, should engage in this work. In steam laundries, besides the workers, women are also employed as superintendents and clerks.

Literary Work—Women may now be found in every department of literature, and for such as possess real ability there is always employment and fair remuneration.

Lithographing—This is another of the artistic branches in which women could do good work, as it is employed in producing fashion-plates and is not over-crowded.

Medical Drawings—Though not a pleasant occupation, it has fallen almost exclusively to women, because they are said to be more painstaking and accurate.

Nursing—There is a growing demand for trained nurses, and every facility for those designing to adopt this profession to fit themselves for the noble work.

Mrs. Logan's list was extensive and also mentioned work available for women as proofreaders, piano tuners, teachers, telegraph and telephone operators, tobacco sorters, typists, waitresses and librarians. Of employment as a "Household Servant," she noted, "In no industry is there such constant demand as for reliable, competent household servants, and many girls seeking employment in the over-crowded, underpaid trades would do well to turn their attention to domestic service, where they would be sure of finding comfortable homes, wholesome food and high wages."[16]

Given the stiff competition to obtain—and then retain—good domestic help during the last quarter of the nineteenth century, those middle-class households that could still afford domestic servants did indeed find it necessary to offer competitive wages. While the wealthy continued to employ a staff of domestics, the majority of homes that had two or three servants in their employment prior to the Civil War now found they had to make do with one or perhaps two. During the 1880s and 1890s many middle-class homes were fortunate if they could obtain one maid-of-all-work and hire additional help as needed for seasonal cleanings or entertaining. In a 1904 article entitled "The Planning and Furnishing of the Kitchen in the Modern Residence," the author notes that in 1870, 1 out of every 8 families had a domestic servant but by the year 1900 it was only 1 in 15 families.[17]

Nineteenth-century household manuals were constantly reminding the mistress of the proper way to treat her help, indicating she may often have been the source of her *own* "domestic problem." Newly arriving immigrants in search of freedom and equal status were skeptical of employment that would infer they were of a lower class. In addition, the centennial celebrations in 1876 reinforced and renewed for many the American spirit of independence and cast an unfavorable light on domestic service. In *Manners, Culture and Dress . . .,* author Richard A. Wells, A.M., points out, "For fear of being suspected of that mean and ungenerous sentiment of desiring to make others feel that the difference which fortune has, and perhaps too undeservedly made between us, I am more upon my guard, as to my behavior to my servants and to others who are called my inferiors than I am towards my equals."[18]

It was therefore recommended that mistresses treat their servants with respect and as though simply conducting business; not with a noticeably superior attitude or obvious distaste for their ethnic differences or religious affiliations.

Even if a mistress displayed the best of intentions toward domestic employees, it was increasingly difficult to find women to fill such positions. Among immigrant families facing economic uncertainty from the moment of their arrival in America, it was necessary for the majority of women to work in order to help pay the rent and buy food. They usually opted for factory work despite the long hours and reputedly low pay. Domestic service was noted as being difficult for a woman with a family or a young single girl that desired a social life or the opportunity to meet eligible young men. *Harper's Bazar* pointed out the realities of the servant's life in an 1874 article entitled simply, "Domestic Service." The piece presented the grim truth by telling readers, "A servant's work, it is said, is never done potentially if ever actually; she is liable to be rung up at all hours; her very meals are not secure from interruption, and even her sleep is not sacred. All this sounds very dreadful but it really only comes to this, that a servant who is engaged to answer the bell is expected to come when it rings."[19]

Not only did a domestic have little free time to call her own, but she was virtually isolated from others in her solitary work and often experienced extreme loneliness. It's no wonder the factory appeared more appealing; at least she would be with others throughout the day and even though the hours may be long, at the end of her shift, her time was her own. In addition, there was always the hope of work well done being rewarded with a promotion and increase in pay.

In those middle-class households fortunate enough to have more than one domestic, daily rituals were performed by the cook and the housemaid. They went about their business according to a weekly schedule and the mistress could maintain her position as manager. While the cook was engaged in the kitchen during the early morning hours, receiving the ice man, milk man and possibly the bread man, and preparing the family breakfast, the housemaid was airing rooms, making fires, disposing of ashes and making herself ready to serve the first meal of the day. After the family finished breakfast the housemaid cleared the table, washed the dishes and silverware. From there she would proceed to her chamber work and then clean and dust the other rooms in the house. The cook and housemaid shared laundry chores and the housemaid was frequently interrupted to answer the doorbell. She also served afternoon tea and waited on the family at their evening meal. Her daily routine came to a close after she took hot water up to the bedrooms in the evening and turned down the beds. Certain tasks, such as scrubbing the floors, polishing furniture and washing windows were assigned to a certain day of the week.

The majority of middle-class women could afford to hire only one domestic during the late nineteenth century and as a result were presented with new difficulties. As Faye E. Dudden points out in her book *Serving Women: Household Service in Nineteenth-Century America,* "The standards of elite homes demanded painfully difficult emulation by more modest families. The woman who could afford to hire only one domestic was caught in awkward compromises; unwilling to share household drudgery with her domestic, she was also unable to delegate that work as fully as the advice literature tended to suppose. Even with technolog-

THE WELCOME ANSWER
(FROM OLD IRELAND.)

This advertising trade card by a department store was meant to appeal to the
large immigrant population. The card
depicts an Irish maid or servant who
undoubtedly did not have an easy life
as a "domestic."

HOME COMFORT.

An illustration from the 1890 book The Home Manual *by Mrs. John A. Logan shows the lady of the house well dressed and relaxing with a book. Clearly this mistress had servants performing her household chores.*

ical advances, there was still more menial work than one domestic could assume completely."[20] The Victorian housewife faced a dilemma—her financial position was moving her into a role she had no desire to assume while at the same time she was painfully aware that to present anything less than an ideal home to the outside world would diminish her family's standing within the community. As Harvey Green points out in his 1983 work, *The Light of the Home,* "A woman was measured by the state of her home. It was the prevailing orthodoxy that if the yard and garden were untended, the house unpainted, and the rooms neglected and unkempt, the family would be less moral and less successful than one residing in a carefully maintained home."[21]

Reluctantly, middle-class women returned to their kitchens and engaged in routine chores. Women's magazines and household manuals of the 1890s recognized this trend and offered advice accordingly. For example, in *Home Comfort* Mrs. Logan targets the one-servant household and includes a sample "arrangement" of tasks performed by the servant and mistress. Of the weekly schedule, and beginning with Monday, she wrote,

> The one maid must rise early enough to accomplish part of the washing before breakfast. By rising at five, there will be two hours before it is time to lay the table and prepare the first meal . . . after having cooked the breakfast and waited the table, the girl sets before her mistress a neat dish-pan, a mop, and two clean towels; then takes the heavy dishes, knives and forks into the kitchen, while the lady washes the glass, silver, and china. Having accomplished this task and put the glass and china away, the lady shakes and folds the table-cloth, sweeps the dining room with a light broom, and dusts it carefully, opening the windows to air the apartment, and then proceeds to set the parlor in order. Meanwhile, the servant should go to the chambers, turn the mattresses, make the beds, and then go back to the kitchen, clean the pots and kettles used in preparing the breakfast, and then devote her undivided attention to the heavy work of washing. Care should be taken to choose a plain dinner—steaks or chops, potatoes, and some ready-made dessert. The afternoon is occupied by finishing the washing, hanging out the clothes, and getting the tea, which must be a meal easily cooked; for the tidying up of the kitchen is yet to be done before the girl can rest. It will be of great assistance, in places where the visiting is sufficiently informal to permit it, if some member of the family opens the door on busy days. Tuesday by general consent, is assigned to the work of ironing; and here it will usually be necessary for the mistress to lend a hand, and aid in clear-starching and ironing the fine clothing. Wednesday is devoted to baking

This 1887 sketch from Harper's Young People shows the mistress of the house visiting the kitchen to inspect the surroundings and converse with the cook working at the stove. Note the cast-iron stove with coal hod nearby to replenish the fire.

From the 1886 Girl's Own Annual, *this sketch illustrates the one-servant household were madam carefully washed the good china and glassware herself after the maid or servant had filled the washtub for her.*

part of the cake, bread and pies that will be needed during the week. In this work the mistress helps by washing the currants, stoning the raisins, beating the eggs, and making the light pastry. Often a lady who has a taste for cooking makes all the desserts, cakes, and pies. She should never consider it extravagant to supply herself with the best cooking utensils—egg-beaters, sugar-sifters, double-boilers, etc., and, if a good housekeeper, she will find both pride and pleasure in her jars of home-made pickles and preserves. Thursday the maid must sweep the house thoroughly, for this work, if the carpets are heavy, requires strength. The mistress then dusts room after room, and, last of all, the servant follows with a step-ladder to wipe off mirrors and windows. Friday is commonly occupied in general house-cleaning: scrubbing the floors, cleaning the brasses and silver, scouring the knives, and putting linen-closets and drawers in order. Saturday is filled with baking bread and cake, preparing the Sunday dinner so that the servant may have her Sunday afternoon out, and the toil of the week closes with a thoroughly swept and orderly house, a clean kitchen, and all the cooking done except the meat and vegetables for the Sunday dinner.[22]

The lower middle-class mistress that could not afford a live-in servant or the woman who could not find someone to fill the position hired part-time workers to come in to do the washing or large projects such as spring and/or fall cleaning. The remainder of the work was done by madam herself, perhaps with the assistance of a daughter or two. The bulk of their daily work was conducted in the morning, with the afternoon given over to routine weekly chores or sewing.

With "spring cleaning," housekeepers were encouraged to keep the process as "systematic" as possible to avoid disturbing the master of the house or causing him any inconvenience. At the end of each day's work during this week-long ordeal, the house was to be restored to perfect order and all cleaning supplies put away until work began again the next day. Many domestic authorities recommended that cleaning start at the top of the house, or the garret, and proceed downward. Others proposed starting with the cellar before going to the garret as a clean basement was imperative to the good health of the family. In whatever manner the housekeeper wished to proceed, spring cleaning involved literally tearing apart each and every room to dust, wash, and disinfect the walls, floors, windows, furnishings and so on. Kitchen walls and floors were painted or white-washed, rugs throughout the house were removed for cleaning, winter stoves in the parlor and other rooms were removed from the house for the summer and heavy clothing was packed away. Heavy drapes were often removed in favor of light lace panels for the coming months and furnishings were polished, repaired or reupholstered if needed, or slip-covered for the summer.

The massive amount of furnishings and decorative accessories routinely found in the late-Victorian home were subject to an accumulation of film or dust from the oil-burning and/or gas lamps and soot from coal and/or wood-burning stoves. In addition, the mere fact that city streets were unpaved contributed a good amount of dust and dirt to the ordinary household. It's therefore not surprising that the Victorians introduced this ritualistic cleaning into their household schedules.

Regarding the family meals, the housekeeper, or cook (with the assistance of the housekeeper), strove to prepare tasty and attractive dishes. While it was both fashionable and practical for the urban household to serve dinner, the large meal of the day, in the early evening hours, rural communities continued to have dinner around midday. A typical daily menu might include a hot cereal, mush, pancakes or ham and eggs with fruit and coffee for breakfast; a cold or hot dish with bread and butter, fruit or cake and tea for the mid-day meal; and a soup, meat or fish, selection of vegetables, cheeses, cakes or pie with fruit and coffee or tea for the evening dinner. By the 1890s urban dwellers commonly referred to the midday meal as "luncheon," and dinner was generally served at 6 or 7 P.M.

In order to turn out good meals and promote economy in the kitchen, it was important that the housekeeper and servant understand the best means of operating the stove or range, otherwise the household budget would end up diverting extra funds toward the cost of fuel. Detailed directions offered by Helen Campbell in *The Easiest Way in Housekeeping and Cooking* guided readers in building a fire. The housekeeper was to remove the covers on the stove and put ashes and cinders into the grate. Covers were then replaced, all doors and draughts closed, and the contents of the grate placed into the pan below. Paper shavings and small sticks laid in crisscross fashion were arranged in the grate, draughts opened and the paper set on fire. Once the sticks caught fire, they were to be covered with several inches of small coals and as the coals began to burn, dampers were closed except for the slide in front of the grate. This method was suggested for building a fire that would last for several hours. If the housekeeper or cook was careless and allowed the coal to rise up above the edge of the firebox (or lining), ashes and cinders would clog the oven flues and stove covers resting on hot coals would soon burn out. This of course resulted in extra cleaning and replacement of covers. For those using wood in the kitchen stove the same directions were recommended; however, the wood stove required a more frequent addition of fuel.[23]

White Soap

An absolutely pure, snow-white, floating soap. For toilet, bath, nursery and fine laundry work. Cleanses thoroughly and leaves the skin soft as velvet.

Made in two sizes—a 5-cent cake, which is most suitable for nursery and toilet, and a larger cake for laundry and bathroom use.

The growing concern over sanitary measures in the kitchen during the late nineteenth century focused on the importance of the proper way to wash dishes. Two pans (or a single large pan with a partition) were needed and one was to be filled with hot water and soap suds while the other was filled half-way with water as hot as the mistress could tolerate. Glasses and silverware were to be washed first, but if possible, they were to be washed in hot water with ammonia. Many housekeepers preferred this method and chose to wash these items themselves. A small dish-mop tied to a handle was used to wash cups, saucers and plates, and the cookware was washed last.

This 1897 advertisement offers an example of the new pre-packaged cleaning supplies that were available as sanitation in the kitchen and throughout the home became increasingly important to guard against disease.

From an 1890 issue of The Housewife *magazine, this small illustration depicts the housekeeper in her role as mother. Targeting the middle-class mistress, this periodical devoted the major portion of its editorial content to recipes, household advice, needlework instructions and child-rearing advice.*

Pots and pans were then placed in a warm spot by the stove to dry while the tableware was carefully hand-dried with a clean dishtowel. A half-cup of milk was often added to hard dishwater to keep hands soft and promote sparkling dishes.

Disinfectants, antiseptics and deodorizers became increasingly important household necessities during the 1890s due to the outbreak of diseases such as cholera and smallpox, and ever-present bacteria and disagreeable odors. Housekeepers, however, were reminded in home manuals and magazines that sunlight, fresh air, soap and water and a watchful eye in the kitchen were their first line of defense against germs.

The majority of households had a locked cupboard or high shelf on which to store their weaponry against germs and dirt. Popular solutions included a mixture of carbolic acid (made from coal tar) and water, chloride of lime, chloride of zinc, corrosive sublimate, sulfate of iron, sulfate of zinc (known as white vitriol) or chloride of lead to clean, disinfect or deodorize sinks, drains, water closets (bathrooms) and cellars. The housekeeper of the 1890s was not only a nurse to sick children and other family members, but also the household chemist, mixing and preparing the above for routine tasks and annual cleaning marathons.

In those households employing a domestic servant, the laundry was her responsibility but the ironing required a helping hand from the mistress. In an 1889 publication entitled *The Home Manual, Or the Economical Cook and House Book: Hints on the Daily Duties of a Housekeeper,* readers were told that

> Ironing . . . has, through all time, been a wearisome, worrying process, at times, in the experience of all. The day has, I hope, nearly gone by, when "good fires" will be kindled and kept up—perhaps through a whole day, while the thermometer ranges at 90 degrees—just that a family ironing may be accomplished. In cities, where we have gas, an elastic tube is introduced into a flat-iron made for the purpose; and at a cost of about four cents an hour, we have a perpetually heated

flat-iron. For those who have not gas, an equally pleasant spirit iron, with a wick lit by alcohol, performs the labour.[24]

With added responsibilities throughout the house, and children and a husband to be cared for, many housekeepers began to simplify their life-styles out of necessity. By the late nineteenth century, excess was being viewed unfavorably and simplicity was the new darling of the etiquette manuals.

In home entertaining the dinner party was still quite fashionable during the late nineteenth century but an ostentatious display of adornments or excessive table setting was now considered vulgar. Any attempt to impress guests with a show of wealth was taboo. A fine white table cloth with a lace embroidery was acceptable, with a low dish of slightly fragrant flowers as a centerpiece. Place settings included a plate, array of silverware and a water goblet. The serving of several courses, such as those presented at the early Victorian period dinner party, was determined by the size of the household staff. A comparatively simple dinner was acceptable. In the 1898 book *Smiley's Cook Book and New and Complete Guide for Housekeepers,* the editors advised, on the subject of serving dinner, that

the first course will be oysters . . . when the oysters are eaten the plates are removed, and soup is brought on by the servant who places it, together with soup plates, before the hostess . . . The hostess then ladles out the soup . . . and the servant places it before the guest . . . After the soup comes fish, which is carved by the host . . . The servant passes each plate as the host hands it to her, and the servant should always pass the plates in at the left-hand side of the guest. After the fish comes the meat or game which is carved by the host, and passed by the servant in the same way. The vegetables go with the meat . . . The hostess serves the salad. Then the table is brushed and the dessert brought in and placed before the hostess who serves the pastry or pudding. The usual order for dessert is pastry or pudding, ices, fruit, nuts and raisins, and bon-bons. Coffee follows fruit . . . At the close of the meal, when the hostess sees that all have finished, she looks at the lady seated at the right of the host, and the guests rise, and they retire to the drawing room in the order in which they are seated. The above described method of serving dinner is appropriate for a family of moderate means with one or two servants. In cases where more expensive establishments are maintained, with many servants, the fish and meat would be carved by the butler, and the different courses would all be served from the sideboard by the servants, instead of being placed on the table as described above and served by the host and hostess.[25]

With limited household help the afternoon tea became a popular means of entertaining during the 1890s and required much less preparation.

As more emphasis was placed on "economy" towards the end of the century and many middle-class families struggled depending upon economic conditions, the housekeeper was repeatedly encouraged to keep careful record of household expenses. In her role as the home "book-keeper," she was to devote an hour each morning to maintaining a careful record of expenses for food, coal, domestic service and linens used in the kitchen and dining room. In this way she'd have greater control over her household budget or allowance. For example, the *Ladies' Home Journal* for March 1897 told readers,

From the 1898 Smiley's Cook Book and New and Complete Guide for Housekeepers, *this illustration offers the latest in simple table settings for the* middle-class household. As women assumed responsibility for more work within their homes, family meals and entertaining became less formal.

... there should be kept in the kitchen a small book containing menus for one week in advance, and another book, to contain a list of marketing for each day ... This book should be taken to the market and the price of each article registered when purchased ... Then at the end of each month she can readily balance her cash, and will know from day to day the exact cost of the table. With regard to fuel, have the coal for heating purposes in one bin, and the coal for the kitchen in another, so that the prices may be registered and the cost of the fuel calculated ... Regular housekeeping, with regular accounts, need not interfere with the arrangements and pleasures of the housewife. On the contrary, it gives her more leisure because all work done systematically is easily done.[26]

The concept of the middle-class Victorian mistress as a "virtuous woman" commanding a "Christian home" from which moral and patriotic children were sent forth and in which men sought refuge at night from the industrialized world was reinforced in popular advice manuals through the 1870s. After that point a number of factors combined to decrease the influence and importance of the domestic sphere and the period 1880 through the turn-of-the-century was marked by conflict between the sexes, new theories about women and increasing technological advances that helped reduce or eliminate the need for domestics while at the same time creating the self-sufficient housekeeper who was plagued by drudgery.

As "virtuous women," middle-class wives and mothers often felt compelled to become involved in charitable works for the less-fortunate and civic organizations that would enhance their communities. This increasing involvement with matters outside the domestic realm were met with disapproval by many.[27] For example, as women took an increasingly active role outside the home there was concern that straying from the domestic sphere would compromise their family's well-being and injure their own health. An editorial in the January 1899 issue of *Ladies' Home Journal* cautioned readers, "There is no denying the all too apparent fact that our women have drifted away from much of the simplicity of living, and instead have complicated their lives by trying to crowd too much into them ... Organizations have taken by far too great a hold upon the lives of our women ... It is high time that our women should lead calmer lives and get away from the notion that what we call 'progress' in these days demands that they shall fill their thoughts and lives with matters at the cost of their health and peace of mind."[28]

Regarding this conflict between the sexes during the late 1800s, Glenna Matthews summarized it well when she wrote, "Simply put, the epic style of domesticity empowered women both inside and outside the home. Yet to speak of empowerment suggests a corollary to this generalization: domesticity would become more controversial as the century wore on because power won by one group may well entail the loss of power and privilege by another . . . after the sectional crisis ended, some of the political issues galvanizing the nation resolved themselves into the politics of gender, pitting men against women."[29]

In addition to the ongoing struggle between men and women that resulted from women venturing out of the home in increasing numbers to campaign for suffrage and equal opportunities and to conduct charitable works, woman's role—in fact her very being—was reduced to purely physical elements by Charles Darwin and his evolutionary followers. In 1859 Darwin's *On the Origin of Species* was published, followed in 1871 by his work, *The Descent of Man*. Darwin not only subscribed to the theory that women were biologically inferior to men, but that their ability to reproduce was their most noteworthy attribution.

The conflicts between men and women, combined with the publication of Darwin's work, impacted on Victorian concepts of wife, motherhood and housekeeper. The sanctity of both women and the home were now in question.[30]

A third factor that altered the manner in which domesticity was viewed points to the last quarter of the nineteenth century as a period

VOL. 5.—No. 11.   NEW YORK, MARCH, 1890.   50 CENTS A YEAR.

From the title page of the March 1890 issue of The Housewife *magazine, the slogan "The housewife makes the home and the Home makes the nation" echoes old-fashioned sentiment at a time when the housewife's role was in question and home was no longer considered a safe haven from the outside world.*

of economic instability with our industrialized society being plagued by railroad riots, labor strikes, civil unrest and so forth. Home no longer served as a safe haven from the outside world. In addition, technology was changing the manner in which housework was conducted. As a result, by the turn of the century, "scientific technique" was to be employed in the kitchen and throughout the house; to be a loving, nurturing housekeeper was no longer sufficient.

In short, increasing technology reduced the significance of the housekeeper's role and "home" was viewed simply as a place where the family lived. The broader concept of "home" with its political overtones had ceased to exist.[31]

By the dawn of the new century urban housekeepers could purchase fresh meat from the local butcher and fresh baked goods from the bakery. Packaged foods were available at the market and neighborhood "laundries" took in wash and even did the ironing. In *Woman's Proper Place,* author Sheila M. Rothman notes that families were now spending more on durable goods and less on the services of domestics.[32]

To cope with the day-to-day "drudgery" housekeepers were experiencing in the late 1890s, a small book entitled *Life's Gateways or How to Win Real Success,* which was published in 1897 concluded that everyone, especially housekeepers, experienced weariness regarding daily routine, but that this "drudgery" should be viewed as character-building. Women were advised that the accomplishment of steady, rhythmic tasks would carry them forward and provide a successful life.[33] This was typical of the type of encouragement they received from books, magazines and even the Sunday sermon.

The Popularity of the Cookbook and Home Manual

I certainly feel that the time is not far distant when a knowledge of the principles of diet will be an essential part of one's education. Then mankind will eat to live, be able to do better mental and physical work, and disease will be less frequent.

> *The Boston Cooking-School Cook Book*
> —Fannie Farmer, 1896

The introduction of an American cookery book during the eighteenth century and the proliferation of etiquette books during the early nineteenth century was followed by the popularity of the household manual during the period 1870–1899. Cookbooks continued to enjoy strong success but were often incorporated into household manuals that included lengthy advice on numerous household topics. The use at first of woodburning, and then coal, oil and gas, stoves, combined with the introduction of baking powder and new kitchen gadgetry provided an ongoing need for guidance and instruction. Recipes were provided, as well as the advice middle-class housekeepers sought, on caring for the ill, raising children, decorating and cleaning the home, sanitation and ventilation, sewing, table etiquette, furnishing the kitchen, care and instruction of servants and home economy.

Cookbooks and/or household manuals were sold by door-to-door salesmen, by subscription and by booksellers and mail-order catalogs.

It was not unusual for men to author domestic guides, just as they did etiquette manuals during the Victorian period. For example, *The Household Cyclopaedia of Practical Receipts and Daily Wants* by Alexander V. Hamilton was published in 1873 and contained chapters devoted to the following:

Directions for Household Management
Receipts for Domestic Cookery
Sick Room Cookery
The Detection of Adulterations in Food
Practical Family Receipts
Domestic Medicine and Surgery
Clothing; How to Choose and Care for
Forms of Contracts, Wills, and other Legal Papers
How to Obtain Patents and Copyrights
The Rules and Principles of Business
Tables of Weights and Measures
Useful Social and Scientific Facts
Indoor and Outdoor Games and Amusements
Domestic Pets and Their Management in Health and Disease
Domestic Pests and How to Destroy Them
The Etiquette and Manners of Modern Society
Ladies' Ornamental Work
The Nursing of the Sick
Counsel and Information for Mothers
The Diseases of Childhood, Their Prevention & Treatment
Veterinary Medicine, Hygiene and Diseases of Domestic Animals
Hints on Correct Speaking and Writing
Something For Everybody, Etc., Etc.

Hamilton's publication was promoted as a book for every home and was an especially valuable resource for the rural community because of advice pertaining to domestic animals and pests.

The book included countless recipes, many of British origin, and the author defined the "Art of Cookery" as "the best and most efficient ways of preparing raw food so as to preserve its natural qualities unimpaired and render it most palatable and nutritious."[34]

On the subject of "Conduct in the Kitchen," the author advised,

A small illustration from The Housewife *magazine in 1890 depicts a housewife hard at work in her own kitchen. Wearing an apron she prepares a pie to be put in the cast-iron stove.*

"Cleanliness is the most essential ingredient in the art of cooking; a dirty kitchen being a disgrace both to mistress and maid. Be clean in your person, paying particular attention to the hands, which should always be clean. Do not go about slipshod. Provide yourself with well-fitting shoes. You will find them less fatiguing in a warm kitchen than loose untidy slippers. Provide yourself with at least a dozen good-sized serviceable bibs . . . When you are in the midst of cooking operations, dress suitably . . . the modern crinoline is absurd, dangerous, out of place and extravagant."[35]

Marion Harland, author of the popular *Common Sense in the Household* series published during the 1870s included a "Familiar Talk with the Reader," in her works. In her cookbook, *Breakfast, Luncheon and Tea,* published in 1875, she devoted her "familiar talk" to responding to a letter she'd received. A young woman wrote Mrs. Harland,

I wish you could set me right on one point that often perplexes me. Is housekeeping worth while? I do not despise the necessary work. On the contrary, I hold that anything well done is worth doing . . . Is it worth while for a woman to neglect the talents she has, and can use to her own and her friends' advantage, in order to have a perfectly appointed house? To wear herself out chasing around after servants and children that things may always be done well, and at the started time? I have seen so many women of brains wear out and die in harness, trying to do their self-imposed duty . . . And these women could have been so happy and enjoyed the life they threw away, if they'd only known how *not* to keep house. While on

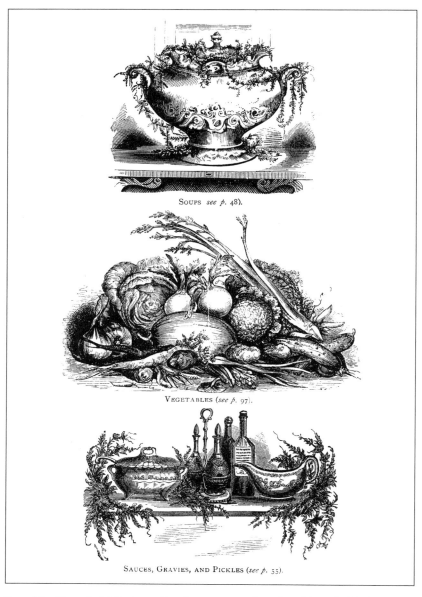

SOUPS *see p. 48).*

VEGETABLES *(see p. 97).*

SAUCES, GRAVIES, AND PICKLES *(see p. 55).*

From The Household Cyclopaedia of Practical Receipts *by Alexander V. Hamilton, this 1873 illustration found in the recipe section is presented with typical Victorian flourish. Hamilton's manual combined household advice with recipes, etiquette, legal matters and so on, making it a popular all-purpose household guide.*

the other hand, with a small income and one servant the matter is so much worse. I should not mind if one could ever say "it is a well-finished thing!" But you only finish one thing to begin over again, and so on, until you die and have nothing to show for your life's work. It looks hopeless to me, I confess. I wish you would show me the wisdom—or the folly of it all.

In responding to the above, the author pointed out to her readers that nothing worth doing is ever completed—not the artisan's ongoing stuggle to create nor the teacher's efforts to educate young children year after year. After all, she proposed, aren't the kitchen and dining room of great importance in determining the character of the home? On the subject of utilizing talents, Harland believed a woman could cultivate and practice such gifts even while operating her household. Although she strongly believed wider avenues of opportunity for employment should be open to women, she urged that this was not because "the duties of the housewife are overburdensome or degrading," but rather, "so that if left bereft of fortune during uncertain economic times," a woman would be able to support herself and her children. The author was also convinced that every woman and daughter should be educated and have knowledge of performing and supervising household chores in order to better train servants, and then be able to cope should they up and leave her. Harland had little respect for "Mrs. Nouveau Riche," who habitually "dawdles all the forenoon over a piece of tasteless embroidery, and gives the afternoon to gossip; while Bridget or Dinah prepares dinner, and serves it in accordance with her peculiar ideas of right and fitness."[36] In the tradition of Catharine Beecher and others, Harland clearly used her cookbooks and home manuals as a vehicle for expressing her convictions and standing on the issues of the day.

The Everyday Cook-Book and Family Compendium by Miss E. Neil, circa 1880s, offered extensive information on all manner of cooking, including invalid cookery and putting up preserves, and also included hints on house cleaning, family illness and injury, home decoration, dressmaking and how to be a handsome woman. On the subject of "Girls Learn to Cook," Miss Neil wrote,

> Yes, yes, learn how to cook girls; and learn how to cook well . . . Let all girls have a share in housekeeping at home before they marry; let each superintend some department by turns. It need not occupy half the time to see that the house has been properly swept, dusted, and put in order, to prepare puddings and make dishes, that many young ladies spend in reading novels which enervate

both mind and body and unfit them for every-day life. Women do not, as a general rule, get pale faces doing housework. Their sedentary habits, in overheated rooms, combined with ill-chosen food, are to blame for ill health. Our mothers used to pride themselves on their housekeeping and fine needlework. Let the present generation add to its list of real accomplishments the art of properly preparing food for the human body.[37]

In an attempt to keep readers abreast of changing, "modern" methods in the kitchen, the author provided information regarding the use of ammonia in baking powders. She remarked,

The recent discoveries in science and chemistry are fast revolutionizing our daily domestic economies. Old methods are giving way to the light of modern investigation, and the habits and methods of our fathers and mothers are stepping down and out, to be succeeded by the new ideas, with marvelous rapidity. In no department of science, however, have more rapid strides been made than its relations to the preparation and preservation of human food . . . Among the recent discoveries in this direction, none is more important than the uses to which common ammonia can be properly put as a leavening agent, and which indicate that this familiar salt is hereafter to perform an active part in the preparation of our daily food . . . The bakers and baking-powder manufacturers producing the finest goods have been quick to avail themselves of this useful discovery, and the handsomest and best bread and cake are now largely risen by the aid of ammonia, combined of course, with other leavening material.[38]

Other popular household manuals published during the 1880s included *The Successful Housekeeper—A Manual of Universal Application, Especially Adapted to the Every Day Wants of American Housewives: Embracing Several Thousand Thoroughly Tested and Approved Recipes,* by M. W. Ellsworth and F. B. Dickerson (published by the Pennsylvania Publishing Co., Harrisburg, Pa. 1883). Like other all-purpose manuals published at that time, *The Successful Housekeeper* . . . offered advice on multiple daily concerns. Over six hundred pages were devoted to recipes and household hints etc.

The White House Cook Book, by Mrs. F. L. Gillette and Hugo Ziemann, was first published in 1887 and went through several revised editions. This manual proved to be so popular that it was published in German for immigrant domestic servants to refer to.

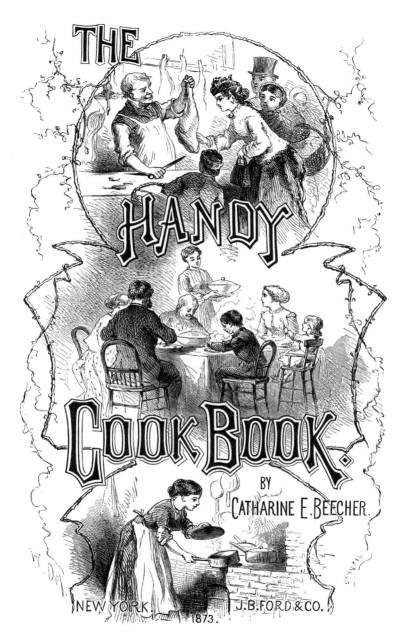

The frontispiece of the cookbook section found in Catharine E. Beecher's 1873 book, The New Housekeeper's Manual.

This illustration depicts the lady of the house visiting the butcher, the family meal and the cook working at the stove.

All pastry-cooks of note use ROYAL BAKING POWDER. Their employers and their reputations demand the production of the finest, lightest, sweetest bread, cake and pastry. For this they declare ROYAL BAKING POWDER is indispensable.

Included in Munsey's Magazine of February 1896, this ad for Royal Baking Powder was quite timely since baking powder was revolutionizing the *way women baked cakes and bread. Baking powder, a leavening agent, was a great time-saver and brought convenience to baking.*

Two movements were taking place during the last quarter of the nineteenth century that ultimately impacted on eating habits and cooking methods. In 1876 the Western Health Reform Institute of Battle Creek, Michigan became the Battle Creek Sanatarium operated by Dr. John Harvey Kellogg. The doctor's wife, Ella Eaton Kellogg, had charge of the kitchen at the sanatarium and her ongoing interest in healthful foods and experimentation in preparation of same resulted in the 1892 publication of her book *Science in the Kitchen,* followed in 1898 by *Every-Day Dishes.* Mrs. Kellogg developed a strong following of believers who advocated moderate eating with an emphasis on the use of fruits, grains and cornmeal in cooking. Her books elevated the importance of diet and offered valuable information on the nutritional value (and lack of value) regarding certain foods.

With the pace at which new and improved cookstoves, kitchen tools and prepared foods were being introduced during the late nineteenth century, it's no wonder the middle-class housekeeper was often perplexed by change. In an effort to ease her burden and increase her skill in the kitchen, cooking schools became a popular institution during the 1870s.

Miss Juliet Corson, who opened the first cooking school in New York in 1876, authored the popular *Cooking Manual,* which was published the following year.

In Boston, Massachusetts, Maria Parloa, author of the 1872 *Appledore Cook Book,* taught classes in the cooking school founded by Mrs. Mary Lincoln. In 1880 Parloa published another work, entitled *Miss Parloa's New Cookbook and Marketing Guide.*

Mrs. Lincoln, founder of the school in Boston, also put recipes in book form, based on teachings at the school. The 1887 publication of the *Boston School Kitchen Text-Book* differed from the majority of cookbooks available in that the author listed ingredients at the start of each recipe rather than simply including them within the body of instructions.

Several years later, a graduate of the Boston Cooking School (who later served as director at the school), Fannie Farmer, achieved huge success with her publication of *The Boston Cooking-School Cook Book,* first released in 1896. Miss Farmer's recipe book called for exact measurements of ingredients to assure reliable results in cooking. She viewed cooking as both an exact science and as an art, and her cookbook proved to be such a valuable tool that it went through numerous revised editions and became an all-time favorite. *The Boston Cooking-School Cook Book* became synonymous with the author's name and was often simply referred to as "Fannie Farmer's."

In 1881 a little book entitled *The Easiest Way in Housekeeping and Cooking* was written by Helen Campbell. The author told readers in her introduction that she had taught cooking classes in a large school in Raleigh, North Carolina and had also instructed women for several months at an institute for the deaf and dumb. Her work was intended as a practical, no-nonsense guide for families of moderate means living in towns and villages removed from large urban centers, and as a teacher's manual for those instructing cooking classes. Campbell made available detailed instructions in regard to "The Day's Work," geared especially for those women having just one servant, or none at all. Her recipes were not for fancy dishes but the plain, every-day meals most families were in the habit of eating.[39]

While the majority of household manuals published were quite large, consisting of hundreds of pages, smaller cookbooks were also available that offered valuable tidbits of advice rather than lengthy, detailed instructions regarding household concerns. For example, the 1889 *Economical Cook Book and House Book: Hints on the Daily Duties of a Housekeeper,* by Elizabeth Nicholson, was a small, 160-page recipe book with straightforward advice on select, timely topics. Although the urban Victorian mistress no longer had to concern herself with keeping a vegetable garden or tending the chickens, this publication did offer advice on making an attractive city garden full of annuals, roses, climbers, grapevines and rock work. Instructions were included for knitting, crochet, leather work, making shoes, building cottage furniture and constructing picture frames. Hints were offered for washing and ironing days and the reader was even advised how to paper a wall, preserve pencil drawings and mix an economical paint.

By the 1890s it was popular practice to combine recipes and household advice with the rules of etiquette and laws of conducting business, the result being a massive, all-purpose family manual that would serve every purpose. For example, in *The Home Manual—Everybody's Guide in Social, Domestic, and Business Life,* prepared by Mrs. John A. Logan, the introduction told readers,

> This volume is dedicated to the millons of busy people in this country who have no leisure to ransack libraries and peruse books, to glean the valuable knowledge here presented in condensed form. The mother bending anxiously over her sick child . . . the toilers in factories injured by accident; the housekeeper to whom economy of time means additional strength and leisure for improvement; the wife anxious to make home beautiful for her husband;

the gay young girl who desires to know the rules that govern the social world, the best means of enhancing her charms, or the latest dainty device in fancy work; the woman whom misfortune has suddenly forced into the crowded ranks of the breadwinners . . . the writer uncertain how to prepare manuscripts; the little ones longing for some new game—all will find the *Home Manual* a guide, counsellor, and friend, ever ready to aid. Who can tell from what hours of activity its timely assistance may guard many a household?[40]

In the majority of manuals women were reminded that the family's good health was determined by the type of foods prepared; their bodily comfort dependent upon heat from fire, clothing, nourishment and exercise; cleanliness of the body and home was imperative; rest essential; and self-control of great importance. To make her home pleasant the housekeeper was to begin her day with a smile for each member of the household and offer words of praise to servants and children alike, celebrate holidays as festive occasions, have music in the home, expose children to books and share recreational activities with them.

Toward the end of the century the importance of sanitation in the household was clearly conveyed in household manuals and/or cookbooks as they took an increasingly "scientific" approach to cooking and housekeeping. *Smiley's Cook Book and New and Complete Guide for Housekeepers,* published by the Smiley Publishing Company in 1898, endeavored to explain not just the processes in cooking and cleaning, but the reasons for doing them in a particular way as well as the underlying principles, in order to assure good results. The editors noted the average housekeeper was overworked and many household problems harassed her on a daily basis. To help increase her efficiency at the cookstove, *Smiley's* included extensive "Time Tables for Cooking," something not generally found in earlier manuals.

Regarding household chores, this same publication reported that,

In housekeeping, as in everything else, system is of the utmost importance . . . not only should there be a place for everything, and everything put in its place, the importance of which is often insisted on, though none too often, but there should also be a time for everything. Have certain days of the week for doing certain things, and also arrange the work of the day, as far as possible, allotting time for every duty . . . Use your head in your work, and keep cool and self-possessed . . . Plan your work carefully and work systematically . . . Never rely on servants, but oversee everything . . .

MAY IT BRING
HELPFULNESS AND PLEASURE
INTO YOUR LIFE
AND HOME.

FOR _____

FROM _____

_____ 18 ____

A charming frontispiece from the 1890 Home Manual by Mrs. John Logan. It was hoped that the gift of this book full of household advice would be a great help to the owner and bring pleasure to her life. In typical Victorian fashion, a practical tool such as this guide was embellished with attractive artwork.

Avoid both extravagance and waste . . . Keep an accurate account of both receipts and expenditures . . . Pay cash, and avoid debts as you would a pestilence . . . It may be safely said that the housewife is called upon to display an amount and variety of knowledge and skill such as is required of few men.[41]

By the end of the nineteenth century small, regional cookbooks had become a popular means of raising funds for charitable causes. In addition, businesses and manufacturers were distributing advertising recipe leaflets free of charge or as product premiums to their many customers. Both became commonplace during the early 1900s and ever-increasing numbers of recipe booklets spread across the country.

Notable Changes: Mass-production of Packaged Goods, Widespread Use of the Ice-Box and the Introduction of the Gas Stove

. . . the woman who attempts to do her work well, should try and secure the best utensils and the most conveniences she can, and should aim to obtain improved and labor-saving devices as they appear from time to time. A trifling outlay for a new article will often save a great deal of work.

Smiley's New and Complete Guide for Housekeepers
—Smiley Publishing Co., 1898

The last quarter of the nineteenth century brought sweeping changes to the American middle-class kitchen and the concept of domestic science. By the year 1900 the housekeeper was no longer the primary producer of food and clothing; she'd advanced to the position of consumer, bringing home a variety of store-bought foodstuffs that slowly began to reduce the amount of time spent cooking. Necessities such as milk, butter, cream and ice could be delivered directly to her back door and the corner bakery afforded her the option of purchasing fresh-baked breads, cakes and so on, rather than laboring in her own kitchen to produce the same goods.

Indoor plumbing allowed for the convenient first-floor location of the kitchen with hot and cold running taps and widespread use of the icebox meant perishables could be kept close at hand.

By the turn of the century the introduction of the gas stove had taken much of the mystery and confusion out of cooking and did away with the soot and ashes associated with the coal and/or wood-burning stove.

To introduce the housekeeper to the flood of new goods and services available during the late nineteenth century, first handbills, limited advertisements in papers and then trade cards became a popular means of conveying testimonials and increasing product awareness. The advertising trade card was an especially effective means of reaching the middle-class household. These colorful, chromolithographed cards were distributed free of charge to consumers via the postal service, by merchants, door-to-door salesmen or youngsters stationed on busy

This large dual-image advertising trade card illustrates the woman on the left suffering from the heat in her kitchen while the housekeeper and mother on the right enjoys *a carefree moment with her children thanks to the convenience and comfort of a Florence Kerosene Stove.*

USE ACORN SOAP.

It will please you.

This whimsical advertising trade card for Acorn Soap depicts a child playing the role of an adult. Consumers were enticed on the reverse side to "mail 25 Acorn Soap wrappers with full address to receive 'The Snow Boy'—our newest picture." Trade cards proved a successful advertising tool and were often collected and saved by middle-class women and children who stored them safely away in scrap albums.

This 1889 trade card for "soothing syrup" depicts a charming mother and child. The reverse side includes an 1889 calendar and advice to mothers in English, German and French. The advertiser proclaims "Mrs. Winslow's Soothing Syrup should always be used for children teething. It soothes the child, softens the gums, allays all pain . . ."

street corners. While one side of the card presented a charming, often whimsical image, the reverse was devoted to slogans, product information, household hints etc. Some trade cards depicted the item they were promoting while others relied on the sentiment attached to adorable puppies and kittens, the heart-tugging cherub faces of children or the charms of an attractive woman to draw attention to their product. These cards were a successful advertising tool designed to appeal especially to middle-class women—the housekeepers of American homes. They accomplished the goal of spreading the word while at the same time becoming a popular Victorian collectible that was frequently saved in scrap albums by women and children alike. Trade cards chronicled the birth of many nineteenth-century products and reflected late Victorian styles, customs and home comforts.

By the early 1900s advertising trade cards had become obsolete as both new and established magazines flourished and dramatically in-

HUCKINS' SOUPS

Tomato,	Mock Turtle,	Terrapin,
Ox Tail,	Okra or Gumbo,	Macaroni,
Pea,	Green Turtle,	Consommé,
Beef,	Julienne,	Soup and Bouilli,
Vermicelli,	Chicken,	Mullagatawny.

RICH and PERFECTLY SEASONED.

Require only to be heated, and are then ready to serve. | Prepared with great care from only the best materials. | Have enjoyed the highest reputation for more than 32 years.

Send us 20 cents, to help pay express, and receive, prepaid, two sample cans of these Soups, your choice.

TEST FREE

SOLD BY ALL LEADING GROCERS.

J. H. W. HUCKINS & CO.

Sole Manufacturers, Boston, Mass.

With the availability of packaged and canned goods during the late nineteenth century, variety in the kitchen became commonplace. This 1889 advertisement shows a wide, albeit unusual, selection of canned soups available from J.H.W. Huckins & Co. of Boston, Massachusetts.

A "Triumph in Cookery," Van Camp's Boston Baked Pork and Beans were advertised in the September 1896 Ladies' Home Journal. The housekeeper is serving them directly from the pan to the table as a "hasty meal." As more and more canned goods became available, the housekeeper became a full-fledged consumer.

creased their advertising space. However, from the 1870s through the end of the century, women across the country were introduced to new appliances, kitchen tools, canned or boxed goods, cleaning supplies, tonics and remedies, beauty aides and so on courtesy of the trade card.

In considering the mass-production of packaged foodstuffs, Englishman Thomas Kensett was presented a patent for food-preserving tin vessels by President Monroe in 1825. Thereafter, commercially prepared meats, fruits and vegetables were produced in America on a limited basis prior to the Civil War. The war, however, created a significant need for portable foods to feed the troops and as a result, the canning industry rapidly expanded. Noted manufacturers such as Borden, Heinz, Campbell, Van Camp and Libby began canning by mechanized means in the 1860s and 1870s and others soon followed. Canneries sprung up in growing industrial centers near railways and companies such as the American Stopper Company, Somers Brothers and S.A. Ilsley & Company of Brooklyn, New York; Ginna and Company of New York City; and Hasker and Marcus Manufacturing Company of Richmond, Virginia were turning out tin containers to meet the increasing demand by food, coffee, tea and spice manufacturers.

The initial response to canned foods was one of skepticism and the age-old practice of "putting up" preserves, fruits and vegetables at home continued in many middle-class kitchens. By the time the new century had arrived, hundreds of food products were being commercially prepared and sales began to indicate the American housekeeper was embracing the convenient new products. Not only did packaged goods bring economy to the kitchen in terms of time and effort, but the increased availability of fruits and vegetables all year round meant the family no longer had to dine according to what was in season.

While the majority of prepared foods were preserved in tin cans and containers, boxes proved ideal for cereal, salt, powdered gelatin, soaps and so on. Shredded Wheat, Postum Cereal Company's Grape Nuts and Quaker Oats were being marketed by the 1890s and boxed Jell-O dessert gelatin became a huge success just after the turn of the century. The scouring powder Sapolio was also sold in cardboard packaging and commercially prepared soap such as Procter & Gamble's Ivory (available as early as 1879) was sold with a paper wrapper.

As packaged foods and other household items began to fill the pantry of the late nineteenth-century kitchen, perishables such as meat, milk and butter took up residence in the icebox. First introduced in the 1860s, the icebox had become a necessity by the 1890s as urban populations increased, and one could be found in the great majority of middle-class homes. Combining a means of insulation with the theory of circulation

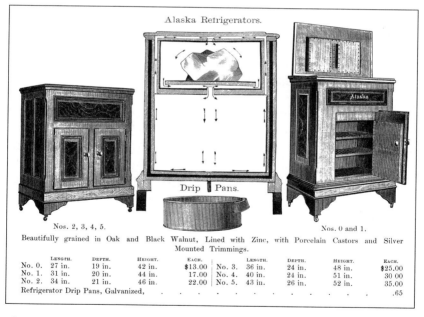

Alaska Refrigerators.

Drip Pans.

Nos. 2, 3, 4, 5. Nos. 0 and 1.

Beautifully grained in Oak and Black Walnut, Lined with Zinc, with Porcelain Castors and Silver Mounted Trimmings.

	LENGTH.	DEPTH.	HEIGHT.	EACH.		LENGTH.	DEPTH.	HEIGHT.	EACH.
No. 0.	27 in.	19 in.	42 in.	$13.00	No. 3.	36 in.	24 in.	48 in.	$25.00
No. 1.	31 in.	20 in.	44 in.	17.00	No. 4.	40 in.	24 in.	51 in.	30 00
No. 2.	34 in.	21 in.	46 in.	22.00	No. 5.	43 in.	26 in.	52 in.	35.00
Refrigerator Drip Pans, Galvanized,				.	.	.	.	.	.65

The Simmons Hardware Company advertised many iceboxes during the late nineteenth century, including these two Alaska "refrigerators." The illustration *shows placement of the drip pan to catch the runoff from melting ice and the assortment of sizes each model was available in.*

(warm air will rise to the top, sending cool air down into the food compartment), numerous competitors manufacturing iceboxes actively campaigned to increase the sale of their product. Each proclaimed their appliance was more sanitary and economical than the next. Toward this end, the hardwood iceboxes were first lined with metal or zinc and then later porcelain, which was considered more "sanitary" as it did not rust or corrode. Many manufacturers turned out these golden oak, elm, ash or occasionally pine "boxes," including Baldwin Manufacturing of Burlington, Vermont; Eureka Refrigerator Company of Indianapolis, Indiana; John C. Jewett Manufacturing Company of Buffalo, New York; Monroe Refrigerator Company, Lockland, Ohio; Northern Refrigerator Company, Grand Rapids, Michigan; and White Enamel Refrigerator Company of St. Paul, Minnesota.

An icebox could be purchased from a home furnishing store or through mail-order catalogs. For example, Montgomery Ward & Company's 1895 spring and summer catalog offered several models priced between $7 and $22. Their factory was turning out over 200 iceboxes per day and proclaimed the superiority of their "Dry Cold Air Refrigerators" lay in scientific insulation. Between the outside wooden box and the zinc lining inside, were several layers of wool felt, followed by a dead air space and layers of charcoal sheathing. These iceboxes were available in single or double door models.[42]

Depending upon the size of the household or establishment the icebox would serve, they were available in various sizes ranging from a 25-pound to a 100-pound capacity and numerous styles were offered from plain and functional to very ornate. The iceman made routine deliveries of ice to keep the appliance in working order and a drainage pipe carried melting water either outdoors or into a pan the ever-watchful housekeeper would empty before an overflow. A large cardboard card

This small advertisement published in 1897 proclaims Leonard's refrigerators are "scientific" and "cleanable," which was very important in maintaining a sanitary kitchen during the late nineteenth century. A small, basic icebox could be purchased for $9.50 while a large, ornate model was priced $28.50.

Majestic

You can cook and heat water for the entire house, with either coal or gas, or both at the same time, with the MAJESTIC Combination Coal and Gas Range.

The Highest Economy

of fuel using of either kind. Economy of kitchen space, compared to two separate stoves. One plumbing connection.

When gas ranges were introduced during the late nineteenth century many manufacturers began turning out combination coal/gas-burning stoves such as this Majestic. The dual-fuel stoves were advertised as cost-effective and more convenient than simply owning a coal or gas stove.

with various numbers on it was often placed in the window so the iceman would know how much ice was needed for the icebox on any given day.

The icebox remained a primary fixture in kitchens across America until the electric refrigerator became commonplace in the 1930s.

Although the icebox was a significant addition to the late Victorian kitchen, the gas-burning stove upstaged it by removing the distaste long associated with coal, soot, uneven cooking temperatures and the general confusion that surrounded dampers, flues and fire grates on coal- and/or wood-burning stoves.

Wm. W. Goodwin & Company of Philadelphia, Pennsylvania manufactured what is considered the first gas stove in 1879. Their "Sundial Range" in various models included two to four cooking burners and an oven and open broiler below. This early gas stove was plain but functional and as the middle-class housekeeper became increasingly aware of the convenience and cleanliness of the gas stove, early fears that gas would taint the food fell by the wayside.

By the 1890s use of the gas stove had increased dramatically in urban areas. The merits of cooking with gas became common knowledge and it cost no more than keeping a steady supply of coal or wood on hand. With water, sewer and gas lines now feeding into city homes, increasing numbers of kitchens could take advantage of the new appliance.

The gas stoves of the late nineteenth century were constructed of sheet steel rather than cast iron and were often embellished with attractive nickel plating just as large coal- and/or wood-burners were. Water tanks were available for many models and some gas stoves boasted a special small burner for slow simmering. By the turn of the century the rectangular, box-like design of the gas stove had changed very little from the first examples manufactured in the late 1870s but advances in technology allowed for numerous options such as various size ovens, extension burners and swing-out or drop-down oven doors.

Whereas the 1895 Montgomery Ward & Company catalog devoted three-quarters of a page to iceboxes, seven full pages depicted then-popular stoves and ranges. Albeit the majority advertised were coal- and/or wood-burners, gas ranges were featured, including the Windsor model, which retailed for $18 and the Process stove, which was listed at $22.31.[43]

Improvements upon all of the above and the introduction of electric appliances during the early 1900s would advance the kitchen into the "modern" age and significantly alter the manner in which "housewifery" was performed.

Late Victorian Household Hints and Recipes

❦HOUSEHOLD HINTS❦

MARKETING

A good and thrifty housekeeper will, if possible, go to market herself, in order to select the best pieces, and get them at the lowest price. A housewife will vary the kinds of meat which she buys, not only as they may be suitable to the seasons, but as calculated to promote the health of the family.

The Household Cyclopaedia of Practical Receipts
—Alexander V. Hamilton, 1873

BEST MODES OF PRESERVING FOOD

Meat should be carefully examined every day in summer, wiped dry, and such parts are beginning or seem liable to taint, particularly kernals, removed . . . fruit should be gathered just before it is ripe; the floor and shelves of the room on which the fruit is placed should be strewn with straw, and the fruit should be laid on this without being suffered to come into contact with each other. Poultry and game must be hung in a cool place, covered with a muslin net to keep off flies and dust.

The Household Cyclopaedia of Practical Receipts
—Alexander V. Hamilton, 1873

DOMESTIC MEDICINE: BURNS & SCALDS

For all simple burns coat the place well with common flour, or, which is better, powdered whiting, or scraped potato, or cotton-wool with flour thickly dusted over it, or gum water, or sweet oil and bind a cloth over. Even plunging in cold water will do good, as it answers the first necessity, keeping the injury from the air.

The Household Cyclopaedia of Practical Receipts
—Alexander V. Hamilton, 1873

TO MAKE FURNITURE POLISH

Equal proportions of linseed-oil, turpentine, vinegar and spirits of wine. When used, shake the mixture well, and rub on furniture with a piece of linen rag, and polish with a clean duster.

Everyday Cookbook and Family Compendium
—Miss E. Neil, circa 1880s

STOVE POLISH

Stove lustre, when mixed with turpentine and applied in the usual manner, is blacker, more glossy, and more durable than when mixed with any other liquid. The turpentine prevents rust, and when put on a rusty stove will make it look as well as new.

Everyday Cookbook and Family Compendium
—Miss E. Neil, circa 1880s

HOW TO CLEAN THE KITCHEN

First—Dust down the ceiling and side walls with a feather duster, or a clean cloth tied over a broom.

Second—Sweep the floor, setting the broom evenly upon the floor, and moving it with long, regular strokes, being careful not to fling the refuse about the room, or raise much dust.

Third—Wash the paint with a piece of clean flannel dipped in hot water, in which borax has been disolved in the proportion of one tablespoonful to a gallon of water; if the spots are not easily rubbed off, use a little soap, rinsing it off thoroughly, and wiping the paint with the flannel wrung out of clean water.

Fourth—Wash the window glass with a soft cloth which does not shed lint, dipped in clean water and wrung out; polish the glass with a clean, dry cloth, or newspaper.

Fifth—Scrub the tables with hot water, in which a little washing-soda and soap have been dissolved, using a stiff brush; then rinse them with a cloth wrung out of clean, hot water, and wipe them dry as possible.

Sixth—Scrub the floor in the same manner, and wipe it quite dry.

Seventh—Wash all the scrubbing brushes and cloths in hot water containing a little soda and soap.

Eighth—Wash all the dish cloths, and kitchen towels in hot water, with soap and soda, or borax, every time they are used, and keep a clean, dry stock of them on hand.

Cooking School Text-Book and Housekeeper's Guide
—Miss Juliet Corson, 1880

WEIGHTS AND MEASURES

As many families have no scales for weighing, a table of measures is given which can be used instead. Weighing is always best, but not always convenient.

The cup used is the ordinary coffee or kitchen cup, holding half a pint. A set of tin measures, from a gill up to a quart, is very useful in all cooking operations.

One quart of sifted flour is one pound.
One pint of granulated sugar is one pound.
Two cups of butter packed are one pound.
Ten eggs are one pound.
Five cupfuls of sifted flour are one pound.
A wine-glassful is half a gill.
Eight even tablespoonfuls are a gill.
Four even saltspoonfuls make a teaspoonful.
A saltspoonful is a good measure of salt for all custards, puddings, blancmanges, etc.
One teaspoonful of soda to a quart of flour.
Two teaspoonfuls of soda to one of cream of tartar.
The teaspoonful given in all these receipts is just rounded full, not heaped.
Two heaping teaspoonfuls of baking powder to one quart of flour.
One cup of sweet or sour milk as wetting for one quart of flour.

The Easiest Way in Housekeeping & Cooking
—Helen Campbell, 1881

A HOUSEHOLD ABC

As soon as you are up, shake blankets and sheet.
Better be without shoes than sit with wet feet;
Children, if healthy, are active, not still;
Damp sheet and damp clothes will both make you ill;
Eat slowly, and always chew your food well;
Freshen the air in the house where you dwell;
Garments must never be made to be tight;
Homes will be healthy if airy and light;
If you wish to be well, as you do, I've no doubt,
Just open the windows before you go out;
Keep your rooms always neat, and tidy and clean,
Let dust on furniture never be seen;
Much illness is caused by the want of pure air;
Now to open your windows be ever your care;
Old rags and old rubbish should never be kept;

People should see that their floors are well swept;
Quick movements in children are healthy and right;
Remember the young cannot thrive without light;
See that the cistern is clean to the brim;
Take care that your new dress is all tidy and trim;
Use your nose to find out if there be a bad drain,
Very sad are the fevers that come in its train;
Walk as much as you can without feeling fatigue—
Xerxes could walk full many a league;
Your health is your wealth, which your wisdom must keep,
Zeal will help a good cause, and the good you will reap.

Peterson's (Magazine), June 1888

TO WASH OIL CLOTH

Oil cloth may be made to have a fresh, new appearance, by washing it every month with a solution of sweet milk with the white of one beaten egg. Soap, in time, injures oil cloth. A very little "boiled oil" freshens up an oil cloth: very little must be used, and rubbed in with a rag.

Economical Cookbook & Housekeeper's Treasury
—Elizabeth Nicholson, 1889

SOFT SOAP

To 1 pound of the Saponifier add 3 gallons of rain or soft water: set it boiling, and then put in 4 pounds of soap-fat or tallow. When the solution is clear and the fat all combined, which is seen by the disappearance of all fatty eyes or spots on the liquid, add 12 gallons of soft or rain water; when cold, your soap is ready for use.

Economical Cookbook & Housekeeper's Treasury
—Elizabeth Nicholson, 1889

TABLE ETIQUETTE FOR CHILDREN

Teach the child to take its seat quietly; to use its napkin properly; to wait patiently to be served; to answer promptly; to say "thank you;" if asked to leave the table for a forgotten article or for any purpose, to do so at once; never to interrupt and never to contradict; never to make remarks about the food; teach the child to keep his plate in order; not to handle the bread or to drop food on the cloth or floor; to always say "Excuse me, please," to the mother when at home or to the lady or hostess when visiting; if leaving the table before the rest of the party, to fold its napkin and to put back its chair or push it close to the table before leaving; and after leaving the table not to return.

Good Housekeeping (Magazine), May 1889

In a recent number of a household journal, a housewife states that she always devotes Monday to the picking up, brushing and putting away of the clothing worn on Sunday by her husband and children. Wouldn't it be just as well if some of the Mondays were spent in teaching those children to attend to their own clothing? We won't say anything about the husband, perhaps he is too old to learn. Evidently his mother did not bring him up right. Many a wife has to suffer the foolish indulgence of her husband in his youthful days by his mother. Mothers owe it to their boys, as well as to their girls, to teach them to be helpful and to take care of their own possessions instead of throwing off that care upon a sister or wife.

The Housewife (Magazine)
—Editorial by Lizzie Sanderson, March 1890

TO KEEP GLASSWARE SHINING

When using eggs, save your egg shells, crush them into small bits, put them into your decanters three-parts filled with cold water, then thoroughly shake them, and rinse. The glass will look like new. All kinds of glass washed in the same water will look equally well.

Palitable Dishes
—Sarah Cutter, 1891

REGULATING THE DAY'S HOUSEWORK

The ordinary daily labor of the household is made difficult and hard by lack of thought and method. If economy of time is duly considered, and a regular routine for the servant laid down each day, a tremendous amount of work may be done without worry, flurry or fatigue. In preparing a dish think first of all the materials needed. Bring those from the cellar at a single journey; from the pantry and refrigerator the same; then stand perfectly still and prepare the dish, thus saving both your time and strength . . . Articles not liable to perish may be purchased in large quantities. They should be kept under lock and key.

"Small Leakages of a Household," *Ladies' Home Journal*
—Sarah Tyson Rorer, September 1897

SAVING IN KINDLING, COAL AND LIGHT

The trimming of lamps should not be left until the very moment they are needed. Nothing is more unsightly or vexatious than an untrimmed, crooked lamp-wick. As the oil is apt to spoil a good pair of scissors, keep a special pair with your lamp cloths, also a few new wicks, and a goodly supply of cotton waste, in one of the bags on the back of the pantry door. Always keep a supply of lamp-chimneys on hand. The best oil is the cheapest.

"Small Leakages of a Household," *Ladies' Home Journal*
—Sarah Tyson Rorer, September 1897

TAKING CARE OF KITCHEN BELONGINGS

A little water in the tubs or buckets will prevent them from
falling to pieces.
Twine taken from the bundles sent home from both dry goods
and grocery stores should have the ends neatly tied and be
wound at once on a ball.
Pieces of brown paper should be folded and put into your little
wall pocket on the back of the pantry door.
A quart of fine sand at two cents will do the work of three
pounds of scouring soap costing five cents each.
Brooms should be rested on the handle or hung, in order that
the bristles may remain perfectly straight; they should never be
used for scrubbing. Brushes are made for this purpose.
Scrubbing brushes, hair-brushes and small vegetable brushes
should be rested on the bristles to dry; otherwise the water will
destroy the brush.
Pastry-brushes should be washed as soon as used, and put in a
warm place to dry. Old table-cloths may be cut into squares and
hemmed, to use over the screen on which you turn your cakes
and buns to cool. They will also serve as silver cloths.

"Small Leakages of a Household" *Ladies' Home Journal*
—Sarah Tyson Rorer, September 1897

Flat-irons which are rough or rusty can be cleaned by putting a little salt on a piece of brown paper and rubbing the hot iron in it, then rub the bottom of the iron with a little piece of beeswax tied in a piece of muslin and it will make it smooth.

Smiley's New and Complete Guide for Housekeepers
—Smiley Publishing Co., 1898

❦ RECIPES ❦

BAKED OYSTERS

Chop fine, and pound in a mortar with crumb of bread dipped in cream; a little parsley and chives, or a very small onion, a shred of anchovy, butter, salt, and pepper. When well pounded, add white of egg beaten up, in the proportion of one egg to two dozen oysters; mix all well together, put into scallop shells, and bake brown.

The Household Cyclopaedia of Practical Receipts
—Alexander V. Hamilton, 1873

SPRING SOUP

Take a quart of young green peas and a quantity of lettuce, sorrel, chervil, parsley, chives, spinach, and young spring onions—all thoroughly cleaned and cut into small pieces. Put them into your stewpan with a pint of stock, a couple ounces of fresh butter, pepper and salt. Stew gently, turning them over occasionally, until all are quite tender. Then pass them through a hair sieve, and add two or three quarts more stock, according as you like your soup thick or thin; throw in a little boiled rice or bread crumbs, simmer twenty minutes, skimming and stirring and serve.

The Household Cyclopaedia of Practical Receipts
—Alexander V. Hamilton, 1873

BEEF OR MUTTON PUDDING

Boil some good potatoes until they are ready to fall to pieces; drain well in a sieve, clear them of all impurities and specks, mash, and make into a smooth batter, with two eggs and a little milk. Then place a layer or rather thick slices of cold roast beef or mutton, seasoned with pepper and salt, at the bottom of a baking dish, cover them with the batter, and so on until the dish is full, adding a thin layer of butter at the top. Bake it till well browned.

The Household Cyclopaedia of Practical Receipts
—Alexander V. Hamilton, 1873

SICK ROOM COOKERY: CAUDLE

Make a smooth gruel of good grits, and when well boiled, strain, stirring occasionally till cold; add sugar, wine, lemon peel, and nutmeg. A spoonful of brandy may be added, and also lemon juice.

The Household Cyclopaedia of Practical Receipts
—Alexander V. Hamilton, 1873

JENNY LIND'S PUDDING

Take the half of a stale loaf, and grate the crumb; butter a pie-dish well and put in a thick layer of the crumbs; pare and slice ten or twelve apples, and put a layer of them and sugar; then crumbs alternately, until the dish is full; put a bit of butter on the top, and bake it in a slow oven.

The Household Cyclopaedia of Practical Receipts
—Alexander V. Hamilton, 1873

TO CURE HAMS

Rub the legs of pork with salt, and leave them for three days to drain; throw away the brine. For hams of from fifteen to eighteen pounds weight, mix together two ounces of saltpetre, one pound of course sugar, and one pound of salt; rub with this, lay in deep pans with the rind down, and keep for three days well covered; then pour over a pint and a half of vinegar, turn them in the brine, and baste with it daily for a month; drain well, rub with bran, and hang for a month high in a chimney, or a smoking house, over a wood fire to smoke.

The Household Cyclopaedia of Practical Receipts
—Alexander V. Hamilton, 1873

FRITTERS OF CANNED CORN

1 can sweet corn, drained in a cullender; 3 eggs very light; 1 cup of milk; pepper and salt; 1 table-spoonful butter; flour for thin batter; dripping for frying; a pinch of soda. Beat up the batter well, stir in the corn and drop the mixture in spoonfuls into the boiling fat. Drain off all the grease in a cullender.

Breakfast, Luncheon and Tea
—Marion Harland, 1875

GRAHAM BREAKFAST CAKES

Two cups of Graham flour, one cup of wheat flour, two eggs well beaten; mix with sweet milk, to make a very thin batter; bake in gem irons; have the irons hot, then set them on the upper grate in the oven; will bake in fifteen minutes.

Everyday Cookbook and Family Compendium
—Miss E. Neil, circa 1880s

ICE CREAM

One quart of new milk, two eggs, two tablespoons of corn starch; heat the milk in a dish set in hot water, then stir in the corn-starch mixed smooth in a little of the milk; let it boil for one or two minutes, then remove from stove and cool, and stir in the egg and a half-pound of sugar. If to be extra nice, add a pint of rich cream, and one-fourth pound of sugar, strain the mixture, and when cool, add the flavoring, and freeze as follows: Prepare freezer in the usual manner, turn the crank one hundred times, then pour upon the ice and salt a quart of boiling water from the kettle. Fill up again with ice and salt, turn the crank fifty times one way and twenty-five the other (which serves to scrape the cream from sides of freezer); by this time it will turn very hard, indicating that the cream is frozen sufficiently.

Everyday Cookbook and Family Compendium
—Miss E. Neil, circa 1880s

TOMATO CATSUP

Wash and boil one bushel tomatoes. When soft, pass the whole through a colander, mashing the mass till it has ceased to drip. There will be about 11 quarts of juice. Put this in a china-lined kettle, and add 4 tablespoonsful salt, 2 do. allspice, 3 do. ground mustard, 1½ teaspoonful ground black pepper, 1 do. cayenne. Boil this two hours at least: if you wish it thick, 3 or 4 hours. Bottle, putting a little sweet oil on the top of each, to exclude air. Seal, and it is ready for use in 2 weeks—is better in two years.

Economical Cook Book and Housekeeper's Treasury
—Elizabeth Nicholson, 1889

BUTTER

In each pan of milk put enough of sour milk to make it very sour and thick in 36 hours: in moderate weather 2 or 3 tablespoonsful will answer; in cold weather it should be kept in a room at summer heat. Skim it every night and morning, in a pot, and before putting it into the churn, scrape off the top with a knife, as it will make the butter strong. Work most of the buttermilk out—then salt it—then work it well with a cloth,

THE LATE VICTORIAN KITCHEN 1870–1899 ❦ *157*

till there is no more milk in it—print it—throw it in water a while, and set away in a cool place.*

* In making butter, once the churning process worked out most of the buttermilk, cheesecloth was often used to squeeze any remaining liquid from the butter. It was then "printed" or placed in decorative wooden butter molds to form shapes and cooled.

Economical Cook Book and Housekeeper's Treasury
—Elizabeth Nicholson, 1889

A PLEASANT WINE

2 quarts morel cherry juice, 1 quart water, and 2 pounds sugar: boil and skim it, and when cool add 1 pint brandy.

Economical Cook Book and Housekeeper's Treasury
—Elizabeth Nicholson, 1889

LOBSTER SANDWICHES

Take as much firm meat from a can of lobster as required, with some of the coral [mature ovaries] . . . mince both meat and coral or mash them with the back of a fork, as you find best . . . Add butter enough to make a paste that will spread, season, and then cut neat, thin slices of stale bread, butter them, and spread one with lobster, then if you choose, sprinkle a little vinegar over it, or shred a small pickle very fine; cover each sandwich with another slice of bread and butter, and then divide into convenient size. Sometimes a slice of bread cut into four fingers makes a more convenient sandwich to eat than larger ones.

The Home Manual
—Mrs. John A. Logan, 1890

SARATOGA POTATOES

Shave them thin, soak in cold or ice water 20 or 30 minutes, drain them, dry on a towel, and fry in boiling fat to a light brown; when done, drop them on blotting or unglazed paper to absorb the extra fat; sprinkle on salt and serve hot. Enough can be done at one time, if desired, for several meals; they keep well, are easily warmed by setting them in the oven a few minutes, and are nearly as good as fresh.

Smiley's New and Complete Guide for Housekeepers
—Smiley Publishing Co., 1898

BAKING-POWDER BISCUITS

Have the oven hot to begin with, then rub a piece of butter the size of an English walnut into a cup of flour and butter your baking tins. Next put a level teaspoon of salt, and two heaping teaspoons of baking powder in the flour and stir it well. Up to this time you can work leisurely, but from this onward, work as fast as you can "fly." Add a cup of sweet milk, stir it, and add enough more flour to make a soft dough; take it out onto the molding board, and form it quickly into a round mass; cut it in 2 parts, then 4, then 8; give the pieces just a roll in the floured hands, put it in the tin, and bake 8 to 10 minutes. The oven should brown them top and bottom in that time. Everybody likes them.

Smiley's New and Complete Guide for Housekeepers
—Smiley Publishing Co., 1898

RICE PUDDING

Use 1 pint of milk, 1 tablespoon washed rice, ½ cup raisins, ½ cup sugar, a little salt and nutmeg. Mix and put to bake; stir 4 times to keep rice and raisins mixed; let it bake about one hour, or until rice is done. Serve cold with cream and sugar.

Smiley's New and Complete Guide for Housekeepers
—Smiley Publishing Co., 1898

4

The Post-Victorian Kitchen 1900–1919

"CLEANLINESS IS, INDEED, NEXT TO GODLINESS"

A typical turn-of-the-century Idaho kitchen including a cast-iron stove, step-back storage cupboard, porcelain sink with taps and a drainboard. An oak table and chairs, child's high chair and worktable are among the kitchen furnishings.

Courtesy Idaho State Historical Museum.

Kitchen convenience is the key-stone in the arch of domestic economy which has come in large measure to spell human progress.

The Complete Housekeeper
—Emily Holt, 1917

*B*y the year 1900, three key words best described the focus for kitchens of the new century—convenient, economical and sanitary.

Firmly established on the first or ground floor of the home, the kitchen was located at the rear, and both preexisting and newly built houses during this period included a pantry off the kitchen. The fortunate housekeeper also had a separate laundry room close by the kitchen, but this was the exception rather than common practice. Most laundry areas were located in the basement. By no means spacious, the kitchen of the early 1900s was most often square in shape and accommodated a range, built-in sink and very often, a china closet. It was the housekeeper's ingenuity that determined the best possible placement of her icebox, worktable or kitchen cabinet, and assorted household necessities. The room itself changed little during the move from one century into the next, but appliances were updated, "work areas" gained recognition and both floor and wall treatments were made "sanitary."

The late nineteenth-century industrial revolution had ushered in invention for convenience sake, necessity no longer being the primary catalyst for labor-saving devices. The shortage of available domestic help during the late 1800s was even more pronounced during the early years of the new century and housewives readily embraced any new gadgetry that would cut down on the amount of time spent in the kitchen.

Economy referred not only to wise use of household funds, but also to economy of time spent performing kitchen chores, and economy of steps and energy in completing the multitude of household and kitchen-related tasks.

The emphasis on sanitation, cleanliness and antiseptic measures in the kitchen accompanied the growing awareness of germs, spread of disease and the constant need to maintain proper hygienic conditions when cooking and cleaning.

With these three concerns in mind (that the kitchen be a convenient, economical and sanitary place in which to work), the ideal middle-class kitchen of the early 1900s had a tile floor and tile or vitrified brick walls. Tile was considered the best possible material in terms of cleanliness. It was easy to clean, the crisp white tiles favored as a wall treatment did not harbor unwanted germs, insects or dust, and tile flooring was thought the ultimate surface in regards to the cook's comfort. This "ideal" kitchen was, however, costly to create and was generally found only in the homes of the upper middle class or the wealthy. For those who could not afford tile, a linoleum floor was the next best choice, along with walls having a smooth, hard-finished plaster and painted surface or tile wainscoting. Wooden wainscoting, a common wall treatment during the 1880s and early 1890s, was no longer considered a desirable addition to the kitchen since the modern housekeeper realized wood absorbed odors and dampness, and attracted dust and insects. Plaster walls, on the other hand, could be kept clean with regular washing and a yearly coat of whitewash or fresh paint, never suffering the ill effects of dampness and odor. In the 1909 book *Household Discoveries: An Encyclopaedia of Practical Recipes and Processes*, author Sidney Morse advised

> kitchen walls should be covered with washable materials . . . If the walls are new and smooth, tint them in waterproof cement or paint them with water colors and coat with soluble glass . . . or washable paper is excellent. It can be washed and kept perfectly clean, and does not absorb grease or moisture. Or paint the walls with common oil paint of a good quality and finish with a coat of enamel paint . . . so they can be mopped the same as the floor . . . Try to make the kitchen a room in harmonizing tints by painting or tinting the walls in light greens and the floor in dark green. Or a clear, light yellow is a good color for the kitchen walls, with the floor in brown.[1]

This advertisement for Florence Cook Stoves illustrates a "sanitary" kitchen where plastered walls have been whitewashed and the hanging porcelain sink is left open underneath so germs and dirt cannot collect in hidden areas. Exposed water pipes and the lack of color add to the laboratory-like appearance of this room.

During the early 1900s The Congoleum Company offered "rugs" for the kitchen floor that were made of a waterproof, sanitary material. These "rugs" were a popular alternative to oilcloth floor coverings and were available in assorted patterns and colors. This 1919 advertisement illustrates a kitchen with pale blue walls and a blue-and-white checkered Congoleum kitchen "rug." Note the gas stove, worktables and kitchen cabinet in this illustration.

Pity the poor housekeeper who could neither afford tile or linoleum in her kitchen. She was left to choose between oilcloth or cocoa-fiber matting to protect her old-fashioned wooden floor. She was not alone, as the majority of older homes retained wooden flooring in the kitchen and even a large number of new homes were built with a wood floor to contain costs. Oak or ash were recommended for their longevity and natural beauty, but well-seasoned pine was also suitable, and less costly than hardwoods. During the early 1900s it was popular practice to maintain wooden flooring in a natural state. It was scrubbed often, and unlike the wood kitchen floor of the 1860s, painting was not recommended by all household authorities. For example, Sidney Morse offered,

> A tight, smooth floor of unpainted wood, hard enough not to splinter and to admit of being scrubbed, is perhaps the best floor for a kitchen . . . Or the floor may be covered with linoleum, which is perhaps, all things considered, the most satisfactory floor covering . . . Or oilcloth may be substituted for linoleum . . . This is inexpensive, and with proper care will last a long time.[2]

With both economy and convenience in mind, the housekeeper was encouraged to carefully consider location of her kitchen appliances and furnishings and also learn to "make do" with the oftentimes inefficient placement of "built-ins." For example, the icebox was often located on the back porch, in a hall near the kitchen or sometimes in the pantry if it was large enough. Both the apartment dweller and the woman living in a rural area may have had a fresh-air closet outdoors—a mini pie safe of sorts, made of a frame and wire mesh with shelving inside. The fresh-air closet was attached to the outside of the house or building, up off the ground (a north wall was preferable) to store staples in the cooler months, thus saving on the cost of ice for the icebox.

The ideal kitchen sink of the early 1900s was cast iron or porcelain-lined. The old-fashioned soapstone or wood and zinc-lined sinks were considered unsanitary and therefore unacceptable. The kitchen sink stood on either two or four straight legs and was fixed to the wall. The underside of the sink and exposed pipes were frequently painted the same color as the kitchen walls. A splashback and drainboard were a part of the sink and the space beneath the fixture was best left open to allow air to circulate about it. In this way, unwanted moisture and decay would not be allowed to breed germs and disease.

Fastened to the wall above the sink, a wireware tray or basket held soap, sponges and so on. A hook nearby was for the washcloth and a

By 1900 an icebox was considered a necessity in the middle-class kitchen. The Leonard Refrigerator was one of many popular brands available and with the emphasis on sanitation in the kitchen, customers were assured the porcelain lining in this appliance would keep the icebox fresh and clean.

This Wonderful Range With Two Ovens

Bakes Bread, Pies, Biscuits Broils, Roasts, and Cooks Nine Different Vegetables All At One Time.

Although it is less than four feet long it can do every kind of cooking for any ordinary family by gas in warm weather, or by coal or wood when the kitchen needs heating.

The Coal section and the Gas section are just as separate as though you had two ranges in your kitchen.

Gold Medal
Glenwood

Note the two gas ovens above—one for baking, glass paneled and one for broiling, with white enamel door.

The large oven below has the indicator and is heated by coal or wood.

See the cooking surface when you want to rush things—five burners for gas and four covers for coal.

When in a hurry both coal and gas ovens can be operated at the same time, using one for baking bread or roasting meats and the other for pastry baking—It

"Makes Cooking Easy"

Write for handsome free booklet 168 that tells all about it.

Weir Stove Co., Taunton, Mass.

Many manufacturers offered stoves that could be fueled by either gas or coal, such as this Glenwood Range by the Weir Stove Company in Massachusetts. The advantage of having both fuels allowed the housekeeper to use coal during the cold months when the heat was appreciated throughout the house and gas in the summer to keep the kitchen from becoming too warm.

roller-towel rack was recommended for drying hands. Dish towels were usually hung on wooden pegs or a metal contraption with "arms" that could accommodate several towels at once. These dish towels were to be hung by a window to benefit from both fresh air and sunlight, nature's disinfectants.

The kitchen stove or range of the early 1900s burned coal, oil or gas. The coal range, while a reliable heat source, made the kitchen unbearably hot in the summer months. Gas ranges were popular due to their effectiveness and minimal operating costs. Oil stoves, once the cause of unpleasant odors, advanced to the rank of acceptable with continued improvements in operation. In *The Complete Housekeeper,* author Emily Holt commented that

> Fifty years back the most part of these United States did their cooking and much of their heating with wood. The wood-stove, in capable hands, unquestionably turned out miraculously good things. Still, eternal vigilance was the price of them—it was impossible to count certainly upon more than ten minutes of steady and equal heat from the best of them. So it is a matter for rejoicing that the coal-range abounds, the gas-range is cheap, plenty and effectual, and the oil-stove has ceased from smelling vilely, and gone regularly into business. As to choice betwixt the three, for a medium or large family, with laundry work done at home, a coal-range is best throughout eight months of a year. Throughout the other four it is a refinement of cruelty to keep the kitchen and the cook's temper at simmering heat . . . A very little money will provide an oil or gas range which anybody can learn to manage in half an hour. Comfort wholly aside, either will save its cost in fuel the first season . . .[3]

In older homes the range took up residence in front of the fireplace or a brick wall closing off the fireplace while in newer homes it was placed a safe distance from the wall with the stove-pipe running up toward the ceiling. Metal range hoods or vent hoods were used to eliminate cooking odors and help keep the kitchen clean. The efficient housekeeper would often make use of the valuable wall space behind the stove by having her husband make shelves to hold assorted small items such as the kitchen clock or matchsafe (a metal box which held matches to light the stove), two items no kitchen could do without.

If the kitchen lacked a closet for storing pots and pans, these were stacked in the pantry or in a movable dresser (freestanding cupboard) that could be located near the stove as a step-saver.

McDougall Kitchen Cabinets

Every mother wants her daughters to have economical housekeeping ideas. Your children will appreciate the object lesson in kitchen economy that is taught by the McDougall Kitchen Cabinet. The McDougall Idea is to lighten the work of the housewife and to make the kitchen more attractive. This idea is the foundation upon which McDougall Kitchen Cabinets are built.

30 Days' Trial in Your Own Home

You can only appreciate the immense saving in time, energy and food supplies that a McDougall Kitchen Cabinet will effect for you, by putting it to the actual test in your kitchen. Any dealer is authorized to place a McDougall Kitchen Cabinet in your home on this plan.

Ask Your Dealer To Show You The McDougall Kitchen Cabinets

or write for handsomely illustrated catalogue, showing styles ranging in price from $14.90 to $90.00.

Look for the name-plate "*McDougall, Indianapolis.*" It is the maker's guarantee of quality, your protection against imitation.

G. P. McDougall & Son, 527 Terminal Building, Indianapolis, Ind.

This circa 1905 advertisement for McDougall Kitchen Cabinets illustrates the convenience of these all-purpose "work centers." This large cabinet is equipped with cupboards for pots, pans and dishware, small bin-type drawers for flour and sugar and an aluminum extension-top work surface on which to roll dough, prepare a meal and so on. Designed to save steps and add convenience to kitchen work, these cabinets, later known simply as "hoosiers," were the forerunner of built-in cupboards with a continuous countertop.

A linen-press could still be found in larger kitchens for storing aprons, dish towels and assorted cloths. In addition, and according to Emily Holt, "Whatever else it may lack, a kitchen should have one comfortable chair, and a smallish solid-standing table with one or two drawers . . . The table is for cookbooks, account books, receipt books, a work box, shears, tape and binding twine. Fasten a small slate to the wall just above the table, and hang a bit of pencil to the frame underneath. The slate is a kitchen record—for things to be bought, things in need of special attention . . . indeed it has uses too numerous to specify, and is as much help to the mistress as the maid."[4]

No turn-of-the-century kitchen was complete without a center of operation or a work station. This may have been a simple wooden chopping table, a baker's table with bins for flour and cornmeal, or one of the "all-purpose" kitchen cupboards introduced during the late 1890s. These kitchen cupboards, early on known as baker's cupboards and then as klearfronts or hoosier cabinets, were undoubtedly one of the most significant kitchen developments. The efficiency and mass production associated with the industrial revolution spilled over into the kitchen and this concentrated "work center" was designed to save energy, time and steps, thereby increasing household productivity. The aluminum extension top found on early kitchen cupboards was considered a sanitary surface on which to work, the metal flour and sugar bins kept baking ingredients close at hand, and the enclosed overhead cupboards and drawers protected assorted spices, packaged goods, utensils, dishware and so on from germs and dust. (See Notable Changes.)

The china closet or cupboard was a built-in feature in both preexisting and new homes during the early 1900s. In those older houses that included a butler's pantry between the kitchen and dining room, built-in china cupboards could be found there. In homes without a butler's pantry, the china cupboard was often located in the wall between the kitchen and dining room, and was accessible from either room. A builder or architect with vision sometimes placed the china closet in the kitchen, close by the sink. A useful china closet had a large number of sturdy shelves for dishes, glassware and earthenware bowls, along with hooks for cups.

While white or very pale shades of gray or green dominated the sanitary kitchen and in fact made it appear "laboratory-like," the china closet allowed the housekeeper an opportunity to create an attractive and colorful display of her possessions. With glass-front doors, the contents of the closet were open to scrutiny and household manuals encouraged a careful, color-coordinated display within. For example, *The Complete Housekeeper* recommended

In filling them [china closets] study colours as much as possible . . . leave the shelf-surfaces plain, and cover them with linen cut to fit, and ornamented with a line of drawn work . . . Use judgement and an eye for colour in all places. A small, clear yellow bit against a background of dull blue illumines everything around it. Almost any green so situated would be ghastly, though one particular tone of green goes beautifully with old blue.[5]

The kitchen pantry, which had been included in architectural designs throughout the nineteenth century, continued to be an important part of the kitchen during the early 1900s. As an all-purpose storeroom, the ideal pantry included a window so it could also serve as a "cold spot" in the cooler months. Fruits, vegetables, cooked and salted meats, cheese, pots and pans, utensils and cleaning supplies could all be kept in the pantry. Enclosed cupboards were preferred over open shelves as a sanitary measure and to store those items best hidden from light, such as preserves and pickles. The proper pantry was painted white or given a coat of whitewash so that mold, insects or rodents would be easily spotted, and it was absolutely necessary to keep it sparkling clean. Pantry shelves were either enameled, covered with white oilcloth or "papered" with a washable covering.

Lastly, if the kitchen was large enough to accommodate a table and chairs (most kitchens were), these were usually the golden oak sets so popular at the turn of the century. While many families continued to enjoy dinner in the dining room, breakfast and lunch were usually served in the kitchen.

Decorative touches in the kitchen during this 20-year period were few. The Victorian-era concept of the kitchen as simply a "workroom" lingered, and the concern with sanitation left little need for creative measures. Windows were dressed with rod-pocket panels of muslin or dotted Swiss sheers and if there was any color in the kitchen at all, it was found in the flooring. Red quarry titles or checkered linoleum (either black and white or blue and white) were the most popular among those who could afford it. Other bits and pieces of color were found in enameled cookware, decorative packaged tins and the herbs that could be found growing on a sunny windowsill.

During the period 1900–1919, changes slowly began to alter the design of the kitchen. Domestic science, now every woman's concern, was being studied by home economists, cooking schools and colleges across the country to develop improved convenience, and their recommendations were acted upon. Whereas the turn-of-the-century builder was concerned with placing a sink, range and hot water tank in the kitchen, by 1920 he was also considering a place for the icebox and hoosier cabinet, and was including built-in broom closets, a drop-down ironing board and limited built-in cupboards in the kitchen.

Gustav Stickley, pioneer of the Craftsman-style homes so popular during the early 1900s, recognized the need for built-in cupboard space in the kitchen, incorporating them into many of his designs. In addition, Stickley noted the need for greater convenience in the kitchen and remarked in one of his architectural plan books

> . . . it is essential . . . that we simplify most of our present compli-cated ideals of cooking, ornament, apparel and furnishing; that we construct more convenient and comfortable homes; that we em-ploy labor-saving devices for the house . . . especially is this needed for the woman who now turns in disgust from the overwork and isolation of the country to the city with its artificial amusements. By the use of labor-saving devices, by more scientific methods of housekeeping, by the simplifying of ways of living and thinking, what is now heartbreaking DRUDGERY can be made a source of JOY and PRIDE.[6]

The "Science of Housewifery"

Woman power is the dominant force of today. It is making more stir and question than anything else. It is moving like a thunder-storm.

Ladies' Home Journal, 1900

While the middle-class woman of the mid-nineteenth-century home was manager of daily activities, overseeing a staff of domestic servants, the housewife of the early 1900s was, in the majority of homes, manager as well as work force. The late Victorian-era conflict over the concept of "home" in relation to the outside world, and more specifically, the role of the housekeeper, continued into the new century.

During the early 1900s a woman was governed by a strict code of acceptable behavior. It was generally thought that she should be pure in mind and spirit and above reproach. She was to be loving towards her family, and especially children. At the same time she was to remain distant where strangers were concerned. Her world could include edu-cation and employment before marriage (however, opportunities outside a narrowly defined list of acceptable positions were few), and after marriage she was free to participate in social clubs, charity work etc.[7]

How then was the housekeeper of the early 1900s perceived? Her home was no longer a sacred haven from industrialism and the problems of urban blight, and her servantless kitchen was equipped with new conveniences and packaged foods that were designed to free her from numerous time-consuming domestic tasks. Sheila M. Rothman notes in *Woman's Proper Place,* "Beginning in the twentieth century, with the coming of Progressivism, a new definition of proper womanhood emerged, a model of educated motherhood. Focusing with a new intensity on the needs of the child, the ideal looked to train women to the tasks of motherhood."[8]

While it was acceptable that women seek a higher education and then employment during the late 1800s and early 1900s, it was common practice for the majority of middle-class women to forsake a job in favor of home life upon marrying. Those women who sought a professional career, especially in the area of science, were limited to applying their talents and training to the domestic sphere. As a result, those who were determined to pursue such advanced work found Home Economics the only field readily accessible to them.[9] In effect, three notable women did much to advance the study of domestic science during this period. Between 1899 and 1908, Ellen Richards, Isabel Bevier and Marion Talbot attended and participated in several conferences held in Lake Placid, New York. The outcome of these conferences was the formation of the American Home Economics Association, which focused importance on applying "technique" in all household tasks and increasing awareness of nutrition in meal planning. Consequently, the American kitchen was assuming identity as an industry where "scientific" methods were to be employed and the housewife had little choice but to track the latest available information on how to best conduct her work.

In urban centers where apartments were home to many middle-class families, the down-sized kitchen with stove, icebox, built-in china cupboard and sanitary walls and floors reduced the importance of the servant problem since women were able to manage the home on their own.

To assist those women living in remote or rural areas of the country, the Smith-Lever Act of 1914 established a Cooperative Extension program that brought home-related classes and instructional literature to state colleges, in addition to the courses already offered via the domestic science departments operating at numerous agricultural schools.

If the early twentieth-century housewife experienced feelings of confusion, dread, isolation or mindless drudgery, she was encouraged

It Takes the Best Wheat to Make the Best Bread

THOUGH you are the *best* bread-maker in your neighborhood — you must have the right flour for *perfect* bread —

The Guaranteed OCCIDENT FLOUR

Costs More — Worth It

The best bread-making qualities must be *in the flour* — in the *wheat* the flour is made from.

The hard, glutinous Spring Wheats of North Dakota are the finest bread-making wheats grown. They come from the richest wheat lands in the world.

The Guaranteed OCCIDENT Flour is made *exclusively* of *First Choice* from these Hard Northern Wheats. This accounts for the peerless OCCIDENT Quality.

Try one sack. It costs but a trifle more than ordinary flour and if you decide that OCCIDENT does *not* give you whiter, lighter, tastier, more nutritious bread, and *more* loaves to the sack, your grocer will refund the purchase price without argument.

Every housewife should have our *Free* Booklet *"Better Baking."*

In every sack is our written money-back guarantee.

RUSSELL-MILLER MILLING CO.
Minneapolis, U. S. A.

The housekeeper that did her own baking was accustomed to buying flour in 50-pound sacks such as that illustrated here. Buying in bulk often meant saving money even though packaged foods could be more convenient and time-saving.

to be satisfied with her lot in life, do the best she could with what she had and be cheerful about it. For example, an article in a 1914 issue of *Woman's World* magazine presented the following scenario:

> Suppose you are a housewife. Your home is small. Your means are limited. Your "things to do with" are meager. Your children are trying. Your work is hard and monotonous . . . There you have a stream of events bearing you down. If you yield you become nervous, irritable, discontented, perhaps eventually careless and slovenly, a physical wreck and spiritual misery. And now, suppose you make up your mind not to yield. Suppose you say to yourself, "I will think beautiful thoughts. I will make my surroundings cheerful. I will be happy and strong and brave and make my husband and children even as I am." That you reply, is easier said than done. It is very hard. Wait! . . . it is not so hard as you imagine. Cease pitying yourself. Say, when you awake in the morning, "The world is beautiful. There are many great, noble, unconquerable souls. I am one of them . . . I shall make this house glow with peace and good will.[10]

Domestic science of the nineteenth century was commonly referred to as the "science of housewifery" by the early 1900s as the majority of women took up residence in their own kitchens. This "science" included the four branches of housework—cooking, cleaning, laundry and chamber work. In the homes of the wealthy, a cook and two or three servants or maids were still employed to perform these tasks. Many middle- or upper middle-class families retained one or two domestic workers with the wife acting as overseer or perhaps as the cook. In most homes however, it was the wife and mother who labored from morning until night, cooking, cleaning, tending to the children and caring for her home. She may have had help "come in" certain hours or days to do the laundry or heavy cleaning, but the bulk of the work was hers.

The same three words that described the trends in kitchens of the new century—sanitary, convenient and economical—were also applied to the practical aspects of the "science of housewifery." Young brides and housewives previously unacquainted with carrying out the multitude of laborious tasks in the kitchen could turn to household manuals, magazines and recipe books for guidance. They were instructed that in cooking, the emphasis on careful thought and variety in meal planning would help prepare wholesome, body-building foods that would fight off everything from disease to nervousness. The conscientious housekeeper had one or more trusted cookbooks toward this end.

Although the many food products that could be bought packaged in 1900 were considered sanitary, time-saving and compact in regard to storage, housewives were often advised to buy in "bulk" to cut costs. Food preparation was still quite involved, especially for the rural house-keeper who preferred to bake her own breads and put up preserves. Her sister in the city, however, frequented the bakery shops and often took advantage of short-cut measures in regard to the use of packaged products.

Thanks to the explosion of kitchenware items mass-produced during the late 1800s, most sanitary kitchens of the new century were equipped with the following labor-saving devices: food choppers, coffee mills, fruit presses, ice-cream makers, ice shredders, spice mills, assorted egg beaters, can openers, graters, juicers, nutcrackers, corkscrews, lemon squeezers, flour sifters, rolling pins, mashers and small kitchen scales.

As apartment living became the norm in cities, a 1912 issue of *Ladies' Home Journal* offered a list of kitchen items needed in furnishing a small flat. For the "kitchenette," the author recommended the following:

A two-burner gas stove
Adjustable oven for one burner
Sheet of zinc under the stove
Small size ironing board
Small glass washboard
Clothes line and pins
Two irons, holder and stand
Galvanized iron scrub-pail
Small covered garbage-pail
Scrubbing brush
Brooms and brushes
Two-gallon kerosene can
One quart ice-cream freezer
Small bread-board
Roller for towel
Rack for dish towels
Bread box
Six large canisters
Four small canisters
Wooden salt-box
Two sheet-iron pans to use as a
    roasting pan
One iron skillet
One double boiler
Dishpan

Dish-drainer
Plate-scraper
Two dishmops
Soap-shaker
Wire bottle washer
Vegetable brush
Small rolling pin
Muffin-tins
Chopping machine
Large saucepan
Three graduated small saucepans
Three graduated copper, enamel or
    nickel-handled dishes
Glass butter-jar
Two covered earthenware or enamel
    casseroles
Six popover or custard cups
Two pie plates, enameled
Soapdish
Alarm clock
Ice chest
Knives, forks, eggbeater, corkscrew,
    lemon-squeezer, etc.
Pot holders[11]

Regarding cookware, enameled pots and pans continued to be favored over cast iron as they were easier to clean, and as an additional

When you want
whipped cream
in a hurry
use the

Dunlap
Silver Blade
Cream Whip

Whips Cream in 30 Seconds
Makes Mayonnaise in 4 Minutes
Beats Eggs in 1 Minute
Mixes Omelettes
Whips Gelatine
Mixes Ice Cream
Mixes Custards

Will even whip the cream from the top of a milk bottle, in two minutes. So superior to long, tedious, old-fashioned methods of whipping.

The perforated blade works at the bottom of the bowl and can't slip. No spatter or waste. Cleaned in an instant.

If your dealer can't supply you, send his name and $1 ($1.25 western states) and we will send one prepaid.

and can be used for a hundred other purposes

Perforated blade (a) works at bottom of special non-slip bowl (b), which GOES WITH THE WHIP. Handle (c) set at handy angle.

CASEY HUDSON COMPANY
363 E. Ohio Street   Chicago, Ill.
BRANCH OFFICES
339 Phelan Building, San Francisco, Cal.
207 W. 76th Street, New York City, N. Y.
628 Plymouth Bldg., Minneapolis, Minn.

Buy advertised Goods — Do not accept substitutes

Kitchen gadgets and utensils were important in the home where the housekeeper did her own cooking and baking. New gadgetry, such as the Dunlap Cream Whip, were welcome relief from the old-fashioned ways of performing kitchen chores.

bonus, the availability of these items in speckled and mottled shades of blue, gray, red or green added a cheerful dash of color to an otherwise drab environment.

While enameled ware maintained popularity for many years (well into the 1930s), aluminumware and glass oven-to-table Pyrex cookware were also being used before 1920. Stove-top glass cookware was not introduced until 1936.

Aluminum cookware was actually first introduced during the 1890s but it was costly and inferior to enameled ware (graniteware) at that time. By 1910 manufacturers had improved their product and priced it competitively. As a result, the sale of aluminumware began steadily to increase. The Aluminum Cooking Utensil Company of New Kensington, Pennsylvania turned out the Wear-Ever line and the Wagner Manufacturing Company of Sidney, Ohio produced Wagner aluminumware.

Corning Glass Works of Corning, New York introduced Pyrex Ovenware in 1915. The glass baking dishes became popular because of

An ice-cream freezer was an important item in the turn-of-the-century kitchen and The Genesee Pure Food Company offered a Jell-O Ice Cream Powder to make homemade ice cream more conve- *nient to prepare. Rather than mixing eggs, flavoring, and sugar with milk and ice, this powder added to milk and ice in the ice cream freezer would turn out two quarts of delicious dessert.*

A Selection of Choice Recipes

RUMFORD BAKING POWDER

This charming recipe leaflet was given free of charge with the purchase of Rumford Baking Powder and included recipes for Rumford Muffins, Biscuits, Raisin Cookies and Cake.

The illustration on the cover is entitled "Playing Cook," and was designed to appeal to middle-class wives and mothers.

This cover from "The Enterprising Housekeeper" recipe booklet depicts a woman using her Enterprise meat grinder with easy one-hand operation.

This booklet included 200 recipes, numerous household hints and testimonials about the convenience and dependability of Enterprise kitchen tools.

their "purity" and economy (baking could be done at lower temperatures, thus saving on fuel).

Many of the manufacturers that produced new kitchen gadgetry, food products and cookware offered women advertising cookbooks or recipe booklets (either free of charge, as a product premium, or for a small fee) that included detailed information on their products and instructions for use and care. Many recipe booklets also included meal-planning and household advice, as well as a variety of recipes and menus. In addition, several of the so-called "medical companies" that produced spices and extracts issued yearly almanacs that also included recipes, advice and numerous advertisements for their assorted home remedies and other goods. For example, *Herrick's Almanac* for 1906 included a recipe for "Good Cakes Of Moderate Cost." Readers were told that "To be a successful cake baker it is necessary to follow closely a few rules laid down by those who know whereof they speak. Until practice makes perfect and you understand the principles of cake making, do not experiment with a good recipe, changing the proportions to suit your idea of economy, and expect your cake to be anything but a failure . . . Get one good reliable recipe that you know will not fail you and you can make a variety of cakes from it."[12]

Efforts to improve the quality of American family meals were enhanced with the passage of the Pure Food and Drug Act, and Meat Inspection Act of 1906. Once again, the growing awareness of illnesses and spread of disease, combined with false or outlandish advertising by unscrupulous merchants, prompted regulations to safeguard the public. By 1914 the importance of planning simple, economical meals was heightened by the outbreak of World War I. With food supplies being shipped overseas to our Allies, the housewife was to help the cause by using less meat, sugar, flour and so on. This became even more crucial when the United States declared war on Germany in 1917 and food supplies were also needed for our own troops. As evidence of this, the Woman's Committee of the Council of National Defense made available the following recipe leaflets which were advertised in the April 1918 issue of *Ladies' Home Journal:*

1. Start the Day Right With a Good Breakfast
2. Do You Know Cornmeal?
3. A Whole Dinner in One Dish
4. Choose Your Food Wisely
5. Make a Little Meat Go a Long Way
6. Do You Know Oatmeal?

7. Food for Your Children
8. Instead of Meat
9. Vegetables for Winter
10. Plenty of Potatoes

Women were advised "Get these yourself and tell your neighbor about them."[13]

In regard to cooking, the housewife continued the transition from producer to consumer as increasing numbers of packaged and ready-made goods became available. Popular magazines kept her informed of the latest products and a walk through the pages of national periodicals reveals a wide variety of familiar canned and boxed items. For example, 1912 issues of *Ladies' Home Journal* included advertisements for Underwood Deviled Ham, Campbell's Soup (which mentioned twenty-one different kinds of soup available for 10¢ a can), Welch's Grape Juice, Crisco Shortening, Postum Cereals, Heinz Baked Beans, National Biscuit Company Cookies and Crackers, Knox Gelatine, Steero Bouillon Cubes, Hormel's Hams and Bacon, Quaker Oats Cereals and Beech-Nut Peanut Butter. In addition to the above, 1919 magazines featured ads for Libby's Evaporated Milk, Diamond Crystal Shaker Salt, Log Cabin Maple Syrup, Royal Baking Powder, Armour Beverages (coffee, cocoa, grape juice, evaporated milk), Golden Age Macaroni, Borden's Condensed Milk, Quaker Oats Flour, Heinz products (vinegar, spaghetti, ketchup, baked beans), VanCamp's Pork and Beans, Sunkist Orange Marmalade, Karo Syrup, Junket, Jell-O, Wesson Oil and Kellogg's Bran.

An advertisement for Libby's Canned Meats pointed to the time-saving convenience of prepared foods by proclaiming,

> Left at home while the family plays, so many mothers never have time for fun—and yet those long hours in the kitchen are so unnecessary! Every stay-at-home mother has that big capacity for joy if she would only realize it herself and break the habit chains that bind her to monotony . . . the habit of service is so strong on her that she has ceased to distinguish between necessary and unnecessary services. The foolish sacrifice of her own good times and her family's companionship is so needless![14]

The growing list of convenience foods during the period 1900–1919 significantly altered the kitchen-related chores of the middle-class housewife. If she chose to do so, she could serve boxed cereal for

The Big Dessert *and* the Little Price

THE fine desserts and salads shown here are made from recipes in the 1918 Jell-O Book. The pictures are exact reproductions of the Jell-O dishes and give a good idea of their beauty and variety.

The popular plain Jell-O dessert, made by dissolving a package of Jell-O in a pint of boiling water, is not included for the reason that every housewife makes it, knows how beautiful it is, and doesn't need to be told anything about it. Such a dessert, big enough for six persons, costs 10 cents.

The more elaborate dishes can be made by any woman almost as easily as the simple, plain ones, and they cost little more. Not one requires the addition of whipped cream.

Jell-O can be whipped with an egg beater, just as cream is whipped, and whipped Jell-O is taking the place of cream and eggs in many Jell-O desserts.

The Strawberry Bavarian Cream at the left and the Glorified Rice at the right are made of whipped Jell-O. Bavarian Creams and Glorified Rice dishes can be made without Jell-O, but they cannot be made to taste so good, look so good, and so satisfactorily meet every requirement, including cost, as when made of Jell-O.

The same may be said of the Beauty Salad, the Neapolitan Jell-O and all other Jell-O salads and desserts. It is absolutely impossible to produce the same results with anything but Jell-O.

The Jell-O Book referred to above will be sent free to any woman who will send us her name and address. It is a beautiful book, printed in ten colors.

Pure Fruit Flavors

Jell-O is put up in seven pure fruit flavors: Strawberry, Raspberry, Lemon, Orange, Cherry, Peach, Chocolate.

The pure fruit flavors are preserved in full strength by the air-tight waxed paper safety bags enclosing Jell-O inside the package.

The price of Jell-O is **10** cents a package at any grocer's or any general store.

THE GENESEE PURE FOOD COMPANY
Le Roy, N.Y., and Bridgeburg, Ont.

JELL-O GRAPEFRUIT SALAD

BEAUTY SALAD

ORANGE JELL-O DESSERT

STRAWBERRY BAVARIAN CREAM

JELL-O SPANISH SALAD

NEAPOLITAN JELL-O

GLORIFIED RICE

The March 1918 issue of Ladies' Home Journal *included this full-page advertisement for Jell-O. The darling of the early 1900s, this boxed dessert* *was successful because it was so convenient to prepare and could be used in so many different ways.*

She Has Leisure

to read because she uses the work saver, C. C. Parsons' Household Ammonia, to clean the bath-room, the roughest woodwork or most delicate fabrics. Does it so quickly. Nothing harmful. Used by millions.

C.C. Parsons' Household Ammonia

TRADE MARK

Different Sizes—at Grocers

Beautiful Balancing Bird MAILED FREE

Instructive, interesting toy for children, sent with our book describing dozens of ways to lessen labor. Address

COLUMBIA CHEMICAL WORKS 46 Sedgwick St., Brooklyn, N. Y.

Typical of many advertisements published during the early 1900s, this ad for household ammonia promoted the product as both time-saving and labor-saving. Rather than mixing cleaning solutions at home, C.C. Parson's Ammonia would clean everything from the bathroom to delicate fabrics.

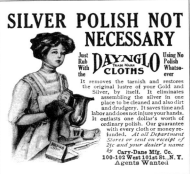

SILVER POLISH NOT NECESSARY

Just Rub With the **DAYNGLO CLOTHS** Using No Polish Whatsoever

It removes the tarnish and restores the original lustre of your Gold and Silver, by itself. It eliminates assembling the silver in one place to be cleaned and also dirt and drudgery. It saves time and labor and does not injure your hands. It outlasts one dollar's worth of ordinary polish. Our guarantee with every cloth or money refunded. *At all Department Stores or sent on receipt of 25c and your dealer's name* by **Cary-Dane Mfg. Co. 100-102 West 101st St., N. Y.** Agents Wanted

This 1912 advertisement offered an easy way to polish the family silver. Polish was no longer necessary and the housekeeper didn't have to go to the trouble of "assembling the silver in one place to be cleaned." With Daynglo cloths the drudgery and dirt associated with polishing would be eliminated.

breakfast, heat canned soup for lunch and prepare a pre-cooked ham and canned beans for dinner.

Cooking consumed a great deal of time and energy but was by no means the housekeeper's only concern. The other branches of the "science of housewifery," chamber work, general cleaning and laundry, required her careful attention as well.

Chamber work was a daily ritual performed after the family breakfast had been prepared, served and the morning dishes done. While urban brownstones, apartment buildings and new homes included a "bathroom" as we know it today, there were homes that had yet to convert a space for the "water closet" or bathroom, and chamber work included the unpleasant but necessary task of washing the toilet-ware. Commodes and slop-jars were filled with boiling hot soda-water and allowed to soak several hours in the fresh air. Toothbrush holders and soap dishes were also cleaned to disinfect and the washstand was wiped first with a damp cloth, and then gone over with a cloth soaked in alcohol. A piece of dry flannel was then used to dry the stand. Chairs, bedside tables and dressers were also dusted and wiped with a rag lightly moistened with kerosene. In addition, beds needed airing. According to Sidney Morse's 1909 book, *Household Discoveries . . .*,

> Emanations from the body are absorbed by the sheets and through these contaminate the other bedding. Moreover, at times the air in unheated rooms contains a good deal of moisture, and this penetrates all parts of the bedding. When the weather changes, the surface of the bed will dry much more quickly than other parts; hence the object of airing a bed is to purify it and to dry it by giving the moisture a good chance to evaporate. Open the bed first thing in the morning, remove the covers, and expose the mattress and sheets separately to the air. If the weather is clear, open the windows if possible, but not if the outer air is damp from fog or rain . . . The ideal way, from a sanitary point of view, is to leave the bed stripped all day and spread it up just before retiring. But as this is not always convenient, the next best course is to put off bed making until the last thing in the morning.[15]

General cleaning continued to be done regularly, following daily, weekly, monthly and seasonal schedules. To perform this branch of the "science," a multitude of tools was required and kept on hand, including soap, borax, washing-soda, ammonia, scouring-sand, cloth pads, alcohol, turpentine, kerosene, dust brushes, brooms, mops, pails and clean paint brushes. While the housewife of the early 1900s mixed her own cleaning solutions from among these various supplies, by 1920 she could purchase packaged soaps, polishes, disinfectants and so on, allowing her to do away with her large inventory of ingredients.

In the kitchen, floors were scrubbed at least every two weeks if the family was small and the housewife observant about preventing grease and flour from falling to the floor while cooking. For larger families, a weekly scrubbing was called for. Warm soapy water was used to wash, clear warm water to rinse and a clean cloth to dry was the general practice

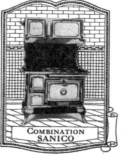

The introduction of porcelain ranges such as this Sanico did away with the need to blacken and polish cast-iron stoves. Manufacturers had found yet another way to bring convenience to the kitchen and eliminate a dreaded job.

for tile and linoleum. Wooden floors were to be swept three times a week and washed, but never soaked, four times a year.

Kitchen walls were to be washed as needed and this would depend a great deal on the type of stove in use. Walls were also to be given a fresh coat of whitewash or enamel paint once a year.

The cookstove or range was to be kept neat and clean by a daily brushing and by blackening and polishing it once a week.

Cooking odors continued to be an ongoing problem and source of irritation for the cook. Washing powder added to boiling water was used to pre-soak pots and pans to eliminate food smells prior to washing. A bottle of soda water poured down the kitchen sink once a week would keep it odor-free.

For kitchens with a broom closet, this space was painted or white-washed and then cleaned with soda water and soap on a weekly basis. A careful scrubbing was done once a month, and burlap squares were ideal for taking up dirt. The closet was allowed to air-dry before restocking the contents.

The china closet received a weekly wiping and twice a year it was emptied so shelf linens could be laundered and shelves wiped with soapy water. The same was done in the pantry, and the icebox and range received weekly attention unless needed more often. Since the hoosier cabinet received daily use as a center of food preparation, it was kept sparkling.

Maintaining cleanliness in the kitchen was of great importance but the other rooms in the house received careful attention as well. In the

WHAT DO YOU DO?

Young Housekeeper— What do you do to keep your sink from stopping up?

Experienced Housekeeper— I frequently pour through mine a boiling hot solution of salsoda or lye.

This small illustration from the March 1914 issue of Woman's World *maga-zine shows the young housekeeper asking advice of a more experienced housekeeper. Keeping the kitchen sink in good order and sweet-smelling was of great importance with the focus on sanitation in the kitchen.*

bedrooms, daily chamber work was just a small portion of the work to be done. Monthly or seasonal cleaning involved emptying closets and dresser drawers so they could be wiped down with an alcohol cloth. Also in the bedrooms, and throughout the rest of the house, draperies were removed and shaken in the fresh air. Mirrors were cleaned and pictures removed from the walls so the glass could be cleaned. Ceilings, moldings, walls, windows, blinds, cornices and exposed pipes were dusted. Rugs were taken outdoors to be "beaten," and if bedrooms, parlors and so on had carpeting laid down, a carpet sweeper was used or dusting was done the old-fashioned way whereby damp sawdust was sprinkled on rugs and then swept with a broom dipped in hot water. This was followed by sweeping with a clean broom, and then a rag soaked in a solution of hot water and ammonia was used to wipe the entire carpet.

After cleaning the rooms of the house, the furniture was closely inspected. Upholstered furnishings were draped with towels and beaten to remove dust, then brushed and wiped with a hot, wet rag and a cloth dipped in alcohol. Walnut, cherry or oak woodwork was washed, dried and polished with a flannel cloth dipped in ker-

Numerous packaged products introduced during the early 1900s were designed to decrease household labor. This Liquid Veneer, a ready-made cleaning and polishing agent allowed the housewife to dust, clean and polish the furniture and woodwork in one easy step.

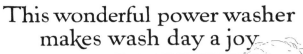

This wonderful power washer
makes wash day a joy

When not washing use the Maytag to operate other household appliances. Has belt power pulley which will operate your churn, cream separator, etc.

For homes without electricity

Here's joy for you women to whom wash day has meant long hours of hard work you women who have given up hope of owning a real power washing machine because your homes are not equipped with electricity.

Here's a wonderful power washing machine —the first and only one of its kind—which is operated by a powerful little gasoline motor *built into the machine!*

This Maytag Multi-Motor Washer brings to you all the advantages of the electric motor —saves all the hard work of wash day.

Set this machine wherever you want to work. Put it in the warm cellar or kitchen in cold weather. Put it on the shady porch or in the cool shade of a tree in summer. Put in the water and soap and the soiled clothes. Give the starting wheel a little flip with your foot and wash day starts. Biggest washes are handled in a few minutes. Heavy pieces or light pieces are spotlessly cleansed, while you do other things.

Then note the swinging, adjustable, reversible power wringer. It wrings from the machine into the rinse tub—from the rinse tub into the blue tub—from the blue tub into the clothes basket—all without moving the machine—all without a bit of work. You merely feed the clothes through this power wringer.

Why make wash day a day of hardship? The Maytag Multi-Motor Washer costs little. It is easy to operate. Comes equipped with a long, flexible metal exhaust tube which carries exhaust outdoors. So you can use it in any room in the house. Gasoline and oil for a big wash cost only a few pennies. And, when the wash is done, you can operate your churn, cream separator, feed grinder, etc., from the pulley wheel on the side of the machine.

Go to your local dealer and see this Maytag Multi-Motor Washer. Have him demonstrate it for you. Any woman can operate it easily. In the meantime, write for a *free* copy of our famous "Household Manual."

THE MAYTAG COMPANY, Dept. 101, NEWTON, IOWA
Branches at: Philadelphia, Pa.; Indianapolis, Ind.; Minneapolis, Minn.; Kansas City, Mo.; Atlanta, Ga.; Portland, Ore.; Winnipeg, Man., Can.
Makers of Maytag Hand Power, Belt Power and Electric Washers

The Maytag Multi-Motor —a wonderful little air-cooled gas engine. Weighs only 35 lbs. Equipped with long flexible metal pipe which carries exhaust out of doors. Engine can be purchased separate for other uses.

Maytag
Multi-Motor Washer
With Built-in Gasoline Engine

Many other appliances can be operated from this power washer. The feed grinder, bone grinder, etc.

Although many households continued doing the laundry the old-fashioned way with boilers, washtubs, scrubboards and wringers, Maytag had introduced a gas motor washer by 1915 that was especially popular in homes without electricity. While Maytag had great success with their early washers, other manufacturers were not so fortunate, as washers were slow to catch on until after 1920.

osene, while mahogany furniture was to be wiped clean and polished with a dry cloth. A rag tied to a stick was ideal for cleaning carvings in the wood.

Wicker furnishings, if natural, were scrubbed with soapy water and placed in the sun to dry. Painted or varnished wicker pieces were dry-wiped with cheesecloth filled with sawdust. Crevices were treated to light cleaning with a rag dipped in linseed oil.

All hardware throughout the house, including knobs, handles and pulls were cleaned as needed, and household repairs made as soon as required. Popular household manuals also recommended the garret (attic) and basement be cleaned twice a year. Floors, walls and shelves were to be scrubbed and everything made neat and orderly. Housekeepers were encouraged to discard useless items and fire hazards such as loose paper, straw and so on. For example, Emily Holt advised that

> Garrets are made for keeping things—but not all things. Old shoes, for example. Bury, burn, give away or sell them. With a single tree at hand it is sinful to keep the shoes out of the ground. Put them at least two feet down—nature and the tree roots will do the rest. A grape-vine will transmute old leather into the fairest fruit and rank green leaves. In the range, under a layer of coal, old shoes make the very hottest ironing-fire. Lastly, the junkman will take them, sometimes for a "thank you," and sometimes for coin enough to buy the young people sweets.[16]

Other cleaning tasks, such as polishing the silver, cleaning the good china, and mending broken household items, were done faithfully but perhaps saved for a rainy day.

The fourth branch of the "science of housewifery," laundry, was a time-consuming, tedious and often cumbersome job that took at least two days a week to complete during the early 1900s. As the new century arrived, the typical kitchen (or laundry room if a separate area adjoining the kitchen was available) included a mind-boggling array of necessary equipment. Whereas a built-in laundry included soapstone or porcelain washtubs, the housewife that had to make do in her kitchen needed several wooden tubs for washing and a sturdy bench to line the tubs up on. Glass washboards (rather than wooden or metal examples, which were considered unsanitary at the turn of the century), and at least two strong wringers in good working order were required. A copper boiler or heavy tin pot was needed to boil the wash and a "boiling bag" of unbleached muslin was recommended for soaking linens or lace. In most

Those households that were unable to take advantage of the new electric irons often found gasoline or alcohol irons more convenient than sadirons, which had to be heated atop the stove. This Imperial Iron was promoted as "Practically indispensable to housewife or servant."

Don't Slave

All Day Ironing

No Stove Required

Get the

Imperial

Self-Heating

Flat Iron

On 10 Days' Free Trial

It Irons in Half the Time

Better, easier, at one-tenth the cost of old style stove heated irons. Saves strength, health and nerves. Heats itself inside with gasoline or de-natured alcohol. No waiting for heat or fussing with half cold irons. No tiresome walking back and forth to ironing board.

Safe Cleanly Odorless

Handier and cheaper than gas or electricity. No wires or tubes. The Imperial is the best self - heating flat iron

Burns 5 Hours for 1 cent

made. We prove it to you by free trial. Steady, easily regulated heat. Handle always cool. Use any-where, indoors or out, home or traveling. Converts into gas stove instantly. Get a quick meal on it. Fully guaranteed. Costs little. Pays for itself in no time. Practically indispensable to housewife or servant.

FREE Illustrated booklet "Ironing Comfort" and 10 Day FREE TRIAL OFFER. Write today sure.

Imperial Brass Manufacturing Co.

Dept. 16, 1200 W. Harrison St., Chicago, Ill.

kitchens the boiler was heated atop the range, but compact gas laundry-stoves were available. Two or three willow baskets and a large number of wooden clothespins were used to cart the clean wash outside and hang the laundry to dry.

Once this day-long chore of washing was completed (either on Monday or Tuesday), a second day was devoted to ironing. The well-equipped housekeeper had several sadirons ("sad" meaning heavy), six or seven pounds each in weight, a polishing iron and a small lightweight iron for delicates, collars and trim. Gas or Kerosene irons were also available and the new electric irons were considered a real step into the "modern" age. Unfortunately few women were able to take advantage of this new appliance since electric power was available only on a limited basis and to a relatively small number of homes during the early 1900s. Trivets on which to set a hot iron, an enameled ware or copper starch kettle and a wooden ironing table, skirt and sleeve boards completed the array of laundry tools.

When wash-day arrived each week, the laundry was sorted in me-thodical fashion, household manuals having recommended washing

A scientific oven heat regulator that places 44 oven temperatures at your command. You set the wheel—the heat never varies, never fails.

The Answer to the Servant Problem

NEVER has the question of domestic help been so serious. Among housewives everywhere it is the chief topic of conversation. It is estimated that but one home in 8 seeking a servant can get one.

Accurately measured heat

Invention has given to housewives the solution for this problem. This wonderful invention is the "LORAIN" Oven Heat Regulator.

With this device on your gas range you can measure your heat as accurately as you do your flour.

As women returned to their kitchens because of a shortage of "domestics," manufacturers routinely advertised new household products as modern-day servants or "The answer to the servant problem" as in this advertisement for Lorain Gas Ranges. With the advent of electric appliances and small, planned kitchens, the middle-class home no longer had a need for domestic servants.

table linens first, followed by bedding, light-color clothing, colored clothes, then stockings and undergarments.

Soiled items benefited from a pre-wash soaking in warm soda water and whiskey, or the housekeeper simply poured boiling water on grass, berry or grease stains to prevent them from setting.

Borax-soaps were added to the copper or tin boiler for washing and a small amount of kerosene could be added to "whiten" linens and so on. Wheat-bran was recomended instead of soaps for washing prints. After boiling for 20 or 30 minutes the laundry was removed to the washtub where it was scrubbed on the glass washboard. After two clean-water rinsings in separate tubs, the wash was put through the wringer. After the wash was completed, everything was hung out to dry and even this required special skill to avoid putting a strain on delicate fabrics and threads or cause folds and wrinkles that would be impossible to remove.

Once dry, shirts were to be starched and if the starch was not properly mixed and cooked before use, it left clothing with a strong odor that was almost impossible to remove. For print fabrics of yellow and/or brown colors, coffee was added to the starch and a special black starch could be purchased for mourning clothes.

Finally, the most tedious of tasks, the ironing was to be done. Ironing cuffs, collars and lacy folds on shirts required enormous patience and manual dexterity. The rest, ironing linens, bedding etc., was simply boring and time-consuming.

Just as improvements were being made in kitchen design and "economy" of time and efforts being realized in regards to cooking (thanks to mass-produced gadgetry and packaged foods), so too did improvements alter the other branches of housework. By 1920 packaged cleaning supplies were on the market, freeing the housekeeper from mixing solutions, disinfectants and polishes. The increased production of electric appliances introduced vacuum cleaners, washing machines and carpet cleaners, and although standardized electric power was not yet available to all homes (especially rural areas), increasing numbers of women were able to employ these new "servants." As new household products were introduced to the public, manufacturers targeted women in their advertisements, fully aware of the housewife's campaign to "get out of the kitchen." She was receptive to any and all labor or time-saving devices that would allow her to spend more time with her children, assist charitable causes and, for many (the suffragette), pursue political action.

During World War I, not only were women encouraged to ration their food staples and cook with the war effort in mind, but their time devoted to household tasks was voluntarily decreased as they joined the ranks of the employed to fill factory jobs left vacant by men called to duty. Many women not employed still allocated time for war-related volunteer programs.

As the year 1920 approached, the combined effects of improved kitchens, mass-produced goods, new appliances and interests outside the home began to alter the "science of housewifery."

The Study of Domestic Science

We cook food to nourish the body, and to make the food more digestible and attractive. But cooking or Domestic Science goes much further than the mere skill to produce palatable and digestible dishes.

Domestic Science
—Ida H. Clark, 1912

By the early 1900s the formal study of domestic science was taking place in public, private and rural schools across the country. Generally incorporated into the curriculum for seventh and eighth graders, with advanced courses offered in high school, the study and practice of basic domestic science was conducted in a laboratory consisting of a kitchen, dining room, laundry area and a dressing room where pupils could put on their aprons and caps.

Laboratory equipment ranged from elaborate to simple and functional, and as Ida Hood Clark advised in her 1912 classroom edition of *Domestic Science,*

> The laboratory should be well-lighted, thoroughly ventilated and comfortably heated. Six separate tables may be made, planned for four girls at each; or one large table may be arranged in a semi-circle around the instructor's table, which should be placed at the point where the half circle ends . . . If gas is used, twelve gas plates are needed, for the work is so arranged that two girls work together at one plate. One extra gas plate is needed for the instructor's use in demonstrating the lesson and in performing experiments before the class. Blue-flame oil stoves may be used.[17]

In addition to tables, gas plates and an icebox, the classroom laboratory was also equipped with gadgets and utensils that were stored neatly in drawers or on shelves. A sampling of the necessary kitchen tools to be shared by two students included the following:

2 common white dinner plates, saucers and cups.
2 tablespoons (nickel plated).
2 teaspoons (nickel plated).
1 large knife, dinner size, wood or bone handle.
1 vegetable knife.
2 forks, wood or bone handle.
2 tin pie-plates (large size).
2 tin pie-plates (small size).
1 potato-masher, wooden or wire.
1 double-boiler (small size).
1 pt. pan (agate ware).
½ pt. pan (agate ware).
1 small saucepan with handle and cover.
1 pt. yellow bowl.
½ pt. yellow bowl.
2 qt. yellow bowl.

1 glass lemon-squeezer.
1 wooden spoon (medium size).
1 bread-knife.
1 dish-drainer.
1 soap-dish.
1 rolling pin.
1 standard measuring-glass (½ pt.).
1 salt-box (tin).
1 pepper-box (tin).
1 match-holder (small).
1 match receiver (small).
1 wire egg beater.
1 Dover egg beater.
1 salt-spoon (ivory or bone).
1 strainer (wire).
1 white pitcher for water (2 qt. size).
1 biscuit-cutter.
1 ginger-snap cutter.[18]

Many early twentieth-century domestic science labs were also equipped with a gas- and/or coal-burning range to teach baking and the operation of stoves.

A large sink was present for preparation and clean-up, and students were instructed in the proper way to wash dishes.

A dressing room off the kitchen or a row of lockers stored the students white caps and large aprons with sleeves. Classes began as soon as everyone was properly dressed.

While the kitchen laboratory was the actual center of operations, an adjoining dining room was equally important in order to teach the class how to set the table and serve a meal. Dining rooms were typically equipped with a table and chairs, a fully- stocked china closet, rug under the table, curtains on the windows and a sideboard filled with clean linens.

During class students took turns observing the preparation of a recipe, doing the actual cooking or acting as "housekeeper" by making sure necessary items were at hand, followed by general clean-up at the end of the period.

During the course of a school year these early domestic science courses focused on cooking, exploring the history of numerous foods and drinks, followed by hands-on preparation. The importance of the

The classroom setting for domestic science courses often included a well-dressed dining room such as this one, the Nathan Falk exhibit in the Idaho State Historical Museum. This circa 1901 room includes ornate oak china cabinet, a built-in sideboard and oak table and chairs. An oriental rug covers the floor and an art glass lamp hangs above the table.

Courtesy of Idaho State Historical Museum.

dining room was discussed and "serving" was routinely practiced. Students were introduced to the practical aspects of furnishing a home, decorating trends and the care of wooden furniture. Clark pointed out that

> . . . times have changed and the most intelligent people of today furnish their dining room very simply and artistically, depending upon perfect cookery, absolute cleanliness and delicate service as an ideal environment in which to entertain their guests . . . The dining room should be well lighted. There should be care to make the table and food pleasing to the eye . . . Ferns or flowers adorn and brighten a table more than anything else that can be used. Such decorations are in place on the humblest as well as the most sumptuous tables. The table linen should be as fine in quality as one's purse can buy.[19]

As the new century progressed, the classroom study of domestic science became more detailed and scientific. By the 1920s, in addition to recipes for breakfast, luncheon and dinner, high school instruction manuals also included lessons on housewifery (kitchen efficiency and charm, budgeting time and money, refrigerators and stoves), health and child care (keeping well, caring for the sick in the home, feeding the baby), food preservation (canned and dried fruits and vegetables), hospitality, food values, tips on selecting kitchen utensils, weights and measures and vitamins.

In *Foods and Homemaking* by Carlotta C. Greer, the author asks students to consider the following questions in regard to kitchen efficiency:

> "How high should a work table be?"
> "What is inlaid linoleum?"
> "How deep should a cupboard shelf be?"
> "If a kitchen has windows facing south, what colors would be suitable for the walls?"
> "Why are present-day kitchens usually smaller than those built years ago?"
> "What is meant by the food preparation center of a kitchen?"
> "Why should a kitchen be an attractive room?"
> "Should all kitchen cupboards have doors?"
> "What is the objection to a wooden tabletop?"
> "What is a good finish for kitchen cupboard shelves?"
> "How many miles of useless walking may be done in the home kitchen?"[20]

Clearly the above were intended to encourage students in planning for kitchen economy. This was not, however, a new concept as Catharine Beecher had explored several of these ideas during the early Victorian period, but in an age when middle-class households were adjusting to modern technology and the down-sized servantless kitchen, convenience was increasingly important.

By 1920 the kitchen was to be planned with two work centers in mind. In preparing food, the icebox, stove, sink and worktable were to be in close proximity to each other to save steps. The dishwashing activity required the sink and storage cupboard be next to each other to promote efficiency. The typical new kitchen was 9x12 feet in size so all furnishings and tools would be close at hand.

Time studies became increasingly popular during the early twentieth century and business-like or industrial methods for maximum productivity were applied to kitchen chores. For example, Greer discussed suggestions for efficiency when she wrote:

> to make the most of one's time, it is necessary to know how to do a piece of work well in the shortest time. After we have efficiently arranged equipment, we need to know how to work efficiently; that is, work with the least waste of energy and time. To do this the following suggestions may help you.
>
> 1. Collect all materials and tools needed for a piece of work . . .
> 2. Use the right tool . . .
> 3. If possible, keep on with one kind of motion before changing to another . . .
> 4. Study the motions made in doing a piece of work.[21]

While the study of domestic science during the early 1900s was concerned primarily with cooking, by the 1920s teachers were instructing both boys and girls regarding other aspects of the home. Decorating the home, etiquette, cleaning and so on were reviewed. Pupils were encouraged to assist their mothers at home so they would receive valuable hands-on experience in housekeeping and cooking. This was considered equally important for boys so they would have a greater appreciation for home life.[22]

The classroom study of domestic science eventually became "home economics." Today middle or high school students receive a brief introduction to homemaking in component courses called "home and careers."

Popular Magazines—
Advice at Hand

I kept house as well as a woman who was also dabbling in business a little could do, and somehow I came to the conclusion that a woman ought to be brave and honest and kind and patient; and I also decided that it takes a little more courage and patience to face the pots and pans than to do any other thing. So I set my kitchen woman up and put her halo on her head as my typification of the ideal. I said that she who actually cooks meals and cleans house and raises children, and still keeps cheerful and intelligent and happy, is the greatest woman in the world. Perhaps my woman deity is obsolete.

> "The Ideas of a Plain Country Woman," Ladies' Home Journal
> —The Country Contributor, June 1912

During the nineteenth century, household advice, protocol and recipes were available through instruction manuals, cookbooks, a small number of magazines and handwritten notes passed from one family member to the next. With the dawn of the twentieth century, changes affecting the average household were taking place at such a fast and furious pace that updated advice and instructions were sought by housekeepers everywhere. Womens' magazines responded, and soon these turn-of-the-century periodicals became as important as their nineteenth-century literary counterparts. In addition to offering household advice and recipes, editorials in womens' magazines debated then-current issues surrounding the role of women both inside and outside the home, child rearing and childhood education and matters of the heart.

There are familiar names in the forefront of magazine history. Louis A. Godey began publication of the most noted women's magazine of the Victorian era, *Godey's Lady's Book,* in 1830. Edited by Sarah J. Hale, *Godey's* dispensed advice on all matters pertaining to the home until publication ceased in 1898.

The Harper brothers established *Harper's New Monthly Magazine* in 1850 and *Harper's Weekly* in 1857. Numerous other publications sprung up during the next twenty years, including an 1879 weekly publication, *The Tribune and Farmer,* which was the brainchild of Cyrus H. K. Curtis. As editor, Curtis allowed his wife Louisa to have full control over the women's section of the small magazine and during the next four years it became so popular that in 1883 Curtis began publication of the *Ladies' Home Journal.*

By the year 1890 widespread effects of the industrial revolution were having a profound impact on the publishing industry. With the multitude of new products, inventions and services available, editors found it a profitable venture to increase advertising in their periodicals. These artistic, creative and soft-sell ads of the late 1800s in no way resembled the outlandish and often ridiculous advertisements found in earlier newspapers, and the public, especially women, were favorably impressed. As a result, circa 1900–1919 magazines included eye-catching ads for such products as Royal Baking Powder, Ivory Soap, Coca-Cola, Cream of Wheat and so on. During this twenty-year period advertising for everything from food products to appliances and household furnishings increased, and reached on an average, over one-half million readers.

Magazines became larger and circulations increased. Thanks to advances in the postal system, monthly publications were going out to homes all across the country. During the early years of the new century there were well over 4,500 periodicals being published in the United States. A sampling of popular women's magazines during this time included *Ladies' Home Journal, The Delineator, Collier's, Cosmopolitan, Good Housekeeping, Homemaker, McCall's, Needlecraft, Red Book, The Farmer's Wife, House and Garden, House Beautiful* and *The Housewife.* While some of these magazines targeted women in rural areas and others concentrated on fashion, current events, needlework or literary content, most were including household advice and recipes by 1900. Many in fact had "household departments" devoted to articles and/or questions and answers on cooking, cleaning, entertaining, household management, raising children etc. Articles were included on healthful menus, new appliances or kitchen gadgetry and instructions for "economy" of use.

Women were also advised on the most efficient way to cope with a "less than perfect" kitchen. For example, the June 1912 issue of *Ladies' Home Journal* included an article, "How We Keep House in Two Rooms: A Practical Plan for a Newly Married Couple," by Barbara Randolph. The author wrote, "With eggs at sixty cents a dozen, butter fifty cents a pound, and rents proportionately high, and with no hope that they will be any lower, is it strange that the young man who earns a moderate salary should look upon establishing a home of his own as a formidable undertaking? . . . I think I have found a solution to this problem, but it applies only to those who care more for one another than they care for unenlightened public opinion." Randolph went on to explain that she and her husband rented a small, two-room apartment in order to save for a house. Of the tiny kitchen/dining area she told readers,

The cover from the March 1914 issue of Woman's World. This was just one of many popular women's magazines published during the early 1900s and like others, this periodical included household advice, recipes, editorials and numerous advertisements that targeted the middle-class housekeeper.

This 1919 advertisement for Swans Down Cake Flour presents an appealing, "soft-sell" approach, which middle-class housekeepers were inclined to respond to. The pages of early nineteenth-century magazines were filled with such ads for food products, appliances, household goods and so on.

Our landlord had a small sink put into one corner, having it built high, at my request, so that I need not stoop over when washing dishes. A few shelves and a two-burner gas stove with an adjustable oven complete our kitchen equipment. A space measuring 30x40 inches is enclosed on one side by a high green cabinet, which acts as a screen between the kitchen and dining area and affords a shelf and space on the kitchen side for hanging the numerous kitchen utensils. The fourth side of the minute kitchen is formed by a chiffonier also painted green. On top of it stand all the plates and bowls I use. The back I have painted white, and on it hang my matchbox, apron, holders, dustpan and brush; under it stands my white enameled bread-box, and the drawers are used for linens, drug supplies, tools, paper, etc. Under the sink a galvanized pail acts as a kitchen waste-basket, except on cleaning days when it does duty as a scrub-bucket . . . Over the sink white canisters contain sugar, flour, coffee, tea and salt. Seasonings stand on a tiny shelf near the stove. Large covered canisters on the shelves under the stove contain cereals . . . It is possible for me to prepare a meal without moving from one spot, and to put it steaming hot on our dining-table less than four feet away . . . The reason this all appeals to me very strongly is because by doing my own cooking, which I love to do, I may have all sorts of attractive cooking utensils.[23]

After describing in detail their newlywed apartment, advising readers on the merits of simplicity in housekeeping and the importance of maintaining a pleasant mood at all times for peaceful harmony, Mrs. Randolph went on to explain her housekeeping routine. She wrote,

Our miniature establishment is easily managed. The good strong woman who does our laundry work comes in two mornings each week, her duties being to keep the floors, windows and bathroom clean. She changes the beds, polishes all of the brass, copper and silver, boils out the garbage-pail and cleans the enameled sink and the zinc under the stove. The kitchen floor is scrubbed twice a week so it is always immaculate. All of this, including the laundry work, is done for a fixed and very reasonable price each week. My own part of the work takes about two hours each day. While we are eating breakfast the beds are airing. After the dishes are washed I make the beds, arrange the room so it becomes a living room once more . . . I then fill the lamp, do the dusting, make out menus for the day, do any ordering that is necessary—and my housework is done, except for the preparations for our two simple meals."

The author went on to tell readers that by living in their small apartment the first few years of married life it helped her prepare for housekeeping on a grander scale. She was of the opinion that all young couples could develop a systemized means of "management" and accurate account keeping by starting out small, and that living within the confines of limited space would teach the "futility of accumulating unnecessary things."[24]

While the Victorian period had officially come to a close by the time this article was written in 1912 (Queen Victoria reigned from 1837–1901), many of the sociological factors associated with this era of excess, rigid custom and material prosperity lingered among the middle and upper classes until the beginning of World War I. However, excerpts from the article above indicate the "modern" age was dawning and simplicity was now viewed favorably, and in fact encouraged in all aspects of house and home. This is clearly indicated in many of the new homes being built during the period 1900–1920. Again, women's magazines were at the forefront in illustrating the popular bungalows and scaled-down homes that opted for plain lines, craftsmanship and careful attention to function (especially in the kitchen) rather than the grand designs and ornamentation found in pre-1900 Victorian dwellings.

During World War I, periodicals played an important role in recruiting women to volunteer for the war effort and as mentioned earlier, encouraged the housewife in wise use of food staples and cooking substitutions to assist the cause. For example, an essay presented in the April 1918 issue of Ladies' Home Journal reminded readers, "The foursquare woman is a volunteer. No able-bodied woman has a right to occupy space in our land who is not doing, or preparing to do, some active service for the right to occupy the space she fills. Are you a foursquare woman? Then register for your place in the ranks of the army at home. There is no lack of opportunity for those with a will to serve, and the foursquare woman will find it."[25]

Women were already getting out of the house. Increasing numbers of women worked in offices, department stores or as professionals (nurses and teachers), and others were out and about campaigning to promote women's right to vote. Volunteer work during the war and additional women entering the work force to fill in for men in action dramatically increased the numbers of women spending time away from home. The woman's world was expanding beyond her kitchen and it wasn't long before home economists suggested she apply the principles of business learned in the outside world to the day-to-day management of her home. Suddenly the "science" that she'd practiced for almost a century was (by the end of the war) a "business." During 1919 and 1920 many magazine articles explored this concept. The May 1919 issue of *Ladies' Home Journal* featured a piece, "Are Business Methods Possible in the Home?" Author C. W. Taber told readers,

> The young wife who steps from a well managed business office into the open door of the new home which her husband has provided for her is more likely to enjoy the management of that home than her sister who has had no contact with the business world. Her keen mind will show her at once how she can apply the same methods to her household that she was expected to follow in her office tasks . . . the average household combines the functions of the factory, the warehouse, the office, and sometimes the farm . . . to think of running such an enterprise as the household without regard to business principles or practices is absurd . . .[26]

The author went on to explain the necessity in realizing the difference between "home," a spiritual atmosphere, and the "household," a physical environment that must be approached with the logic of economics and principles of business. Toward this end, and in regard to the kitchen and housework, women were advised to "employ every machine, device or apparatus that can be applied to the household," and organize the major operations of the home—marketing, laundry, general cleaning, renovating, sewing and cooking—so that these and "all similar processes are carried out in a definite order and routine for the purpose of economy of labor, material and money." Taber then summarized that "Business methods and practices can and must be adapted to every household; and until such becomes the general instead of the exceptional practice, the American household cannot assume or provide the best environment for the expression of that dearest and most sacred of all institutions—the American home."[27]

As increasing numbers of women complained of boredom, the constant drudgery of housework and frustration over their narrowly defined roles in life, popular magazines voiced their concerns and also sought to comfort and reassure them. For example, in an article entitled "Is Housework Pushing Down the Birth Rate?" readers were told:

> recently we have been hearing much about vocational guidance; about the waste involved in our custom of placing round pegs in square holes; about the need to conserve gift and effort as precious assets of the state. This must mean for women as well as for men. Yet on the basis of our present adjustments some mythical voca-

tional guide must have been saying to all women something like this: "You have a gift for designing gowns, drawing, house decoration, accounting, nursing, teaching. These are precious talents . . . These must not be wasted. So now, therefore, proceed to practice these pursuits for one, three, five, seven years after you leave school. *Then* give them all up and turn your attention to 1.) cooking 2.) cleaning 3.) laundry work 4.) chamber work; for it is fitting." But now suppose that the bewildered woman, who is getting in effect this strange brand of vocational guidance replies: "But what of the waste of my aptitude and my training?" The reply will be: "You will be married. And cooking, cleaning, laundry and chamber work belong to marriage." Now suppose the woman ventures once more and says: "But I love the work I can do best, and I don't want to give it up." The old reply has been: "You will forget all this in motherhood." Never until the last few years has the thunder of woman's third question shaken the world: "Why? Why will my time of active motherhood leave me no time for the work I love, but leave me ample time for cooking, cleaning, laundry and chamber work? Why?" Why indeed. Even now the answer is coming in hundreds of thousands of voices.[28]

In contrast, others sought to encourage the housekeeper that her role in the home was paramount. For example, during the early 1900s the *Ladies' Home Journal* featured a regular column, "The Ideas of a Plain Country Woman," by the "Country Contributor." In the March 1918 issue this columnist reminded readers ". . . when we are trying to work by our hands to shelter, to educate, to inspire those who make up our household, we are doing a beautiful service. It is this that glorifys the domestic sense . . . The domestic sense, which I prize so highly, is not a dull contemplation of domestic duties and details. It is a warm sense of appreciation of our home privileges; of warm rooms and good beds and savory meals; of household interests; of good reading and pleasant companionship; of memories and day dreams and friendship and love. It is life in its best and fullest sense, because, of all the many agreeable things of life, the domestic sense remains with us the longest . . ."[29]

As Sheila M. Rothman pointed out in *Woman's Proper Place,* "The Progressive era witnessed the triumph of a new ideal for womanhood . . . Appropriately labeled "educated motherhood" . . . Women had to be trained to the tasks of motherhood. A warm heart was simply not enough . . . In essence, maternal impulses had to give way to maternal insights."[30] We see then that educated motherhood was considered a profession just as the "virtuous woman" acting as keeper of the domestic sphere had been. This new emphasis on children and childhood development prompted the introduction of kindergarten in schools and efforts by "Mother's Clubs" all across the country to educate women to their new tasks.[31] This new focus on how to properly raise children could also be seen in the pages of popular magazines, which included increasing amounts of information on this subject.

Magazines continued to be a vital means of communication with women (and continue to be so today), bringing them the latest advice of home economists, information on new products and services, home design and decoration, child-rearing and so on. For example, when the grocery store as we know it today with carts and cashiers was given a trial run in the southern states prior to 1920, women were advised through periodicals to schedule a "shopping day" each week and plan menus accordingly. The old-fashioned daily meal planning, followed by a call to the grocer for delivery of the required ingredients, was quickly becoming a thing of the past.

Magazines played a significant role in the modernization of the kitchen both in terms of the informative articles published and advice given, and the massive advertising campaigns that sought to put the latest, most modern convenience in each and every home.

Notable Changes: The Hoosier Kitchen Cabinet and the Introduction of Electric Appliances

Feeding and caring for the home has been the woman's job during the long period of the world's pioneering. Considering her lack of training, she has done her work nobly and has brought to it and taken from it spiritual values which are the triumphs often won from hardship. But also, in this pioneering, woman has suffered untold deprivation and waste. And in a civilizing world nobody desires that hardship and waste continue.

"Is Housework Pushing The Birth Rate Down?," *Ladies' Home Journal*
—Zona Gale, May 1919

During the period 1900–1920 both kitchen design and function were advanced considerably as a result of an increase in electric appliances and the widespread popularity of all-purpose, freestanding kitchen cupboards. Massive advertising campaigns promoted these products as "helpmates" and "servants" during a period when employing domestic help was on the decline and, indeed, women were told they'd no longer require help in the kitchen if this room was outfitted with the latest modern furnishings, appliances and tools. In a 1912 article, "The New Home-Making," author Martha B. Bruere proclaimed, "The last year I have kept no maid, having discharged my last one after nearly six years of service, and have enjoyed the year more than the previous one . . . I never hesitate to spend money for any labor-saving device."[32]

Freestanding kitchen cupboards, today generically referred to as "hoosiers" by antiques enthusiasts were modern descendants of the circa 1896–1910 baker's cupboard, constructed of maple or pine. The two-piece baker's cupboard featured pull-out wooden bins beneath the tabletop or wooden work surface (for flour and cornmeal) and utensil drawers. The top portion included small spice drawers and either open shelving or small enclosed cupboards for packaged goods or dishware. These simple, factory-made cupboards underwent a series of changes in design after about 1910, resulting in the rearrangement of bins, additional cupboard space and the introduction of a more sanitary work surface. These hoosier cabinets became quite large, some over six feet tall, thereby providing space for almost every utensil and commodity used in the early 1900 kitchen. Like the baker's cupboard, hoosiers could be purchased through mail-order catalogues or at furniture stores.

Several manufacturers produced these all-purpose cabinets, but it was the Hoosier Manufacturing Company of New Castle, Indiana that was most prolific in both production and advertising. Founded in 1899 by J. S. McQuinn, the Hoosier Mfg. Co. was turning out over 600 cabinets a day in the mid-1920s and its extensive advertising campaign included full-page ads in such national publications as *Ladies' Home Journal, Cosmopolitan* and the *Saturday Evening Post.* "Hoosier" became a household word, and the cabinet, a necessary household item.

Other noted cabinet manufacturers included G.I. Sellers & Sons of Elwood, Indiana; Mutschler Brothers Company of Nappanee, Indiana; The Campbell, Smith, Ritchie Company (Boone Kitchen Cabinets) of Lebanon, Indiana; Showers Brothers Company of Bloomington, Indiana; McDougall Company of Frankfort, Indiana; and Wilson Kitchen Cabinets of Grand Rapids, Michigan.

These efficient, step-saving cabinets were hailed as a revolutionary new concept in modern convenience. Sellers & Sons Company advertised their cabinets as "the best servant in your house," and the Hoosier Manufacturing Company cabinets would "make your dreams

HOOSIER
the Kitchen Cabinet that saves miles of steps

"The Hoosier will help me to stay young"

"RETAIN your youthful energy and girlish appearance," is the wedding-day advice of thousands of mothers. As they look back over the years, they realize that woman's charms soon fade and her health often gives way when drudgery methods rule her days.

But in Hoosier homes, daughters know the miles of needless steps and hours of wasted time that this scientific kitchen helper saves. They honor it for the service it has rendered the "little Mother" who has been able to give more freely of her time to a happy comradeship with her children.

The bride from a Hoosier home will have a Hoosier.

It will be numbered among thoughtful wedding gifts or be first on her list of household needs. Other brides should know what the Hoosier means. And millions of tired Mothers should also learn how the Hoosier reduces kitchen work and frees them from burdensome labor.

The Hoosier merchant is anxious to demonstrate this automatic servant. Will you go and see the many models now? Also send to us for "New Kitchen Short Cuts"—a book every housewife should have.

If you don't know the name of the local Hoosier store, be sure to ask us.

The Hoosier Kitchen Cabinet, promoted in this 1919 advertisement as an "automatic servant," was to be on the wish list of every young bride. These all-purpose cabinets were extensively advertised in leading magazines such as Ladies' Home Journal, Cosmopolitan and others and as a concentrated work center, they brought convenience to the kitchen. The Hoosier Cabinet illustrated here is equipped with a metal flour bin and sifter, sugar bin, circular spice wheel with glass spice jars, a porcelain enamel pull-out work surface, silverware drawer, bread drawer and cupboard space for dishware, pots, pans etc.

National Demonstration Week

SELLERS KITCHEN CABINETS

By Dealers Everywhere May 3 to 10

DURING this one week dealers throughout the entire nation will devote their stores to a great national demonstration of the wonderful Sellers "Mastercraft" Kitchen Cabinet.

This country-wide exhibit to the housewives of America is given by thousands of dealers in recognition of *the cabinet design which offers complete kitchen service.* Every woman, whether she owns a cabinet or not, should plan to visit her local dealer during this period and inspect this masterpiece of kitchen convenience.

"Sellers" has long stood for the most advanced ideas in quality cabinets. Over 30 years of progressive effort are exemplified in this big beautiful model, which women have always wanted.

The Sellers "Mastercraft" offers you 15 long desired features which never before have been combined in any one cabinet.

It is scientifically designed in size and appointments to handle the equipment and supplies of the average family. From 300 to 400 articles are accommodated for greatest convenience.

The Automatic Lowering Flour Bin marks the end of treacherous climbing, of dangerous lifting and straining. This bin comes down level with the work table. You fill it easily. Then it is quickly slipped up into place.

The Automatic Base Shelf Extender is a typical Sellers improvement. When you open the lower cupboard door the pots and pans are automatically brought within reach.

Then there are the clear white Porceliron Work Table, a refinement that all particular housewives demand; the patented Ant-proof Casters, Hand-rubbed Oil Finish and many other long wanted improvements, which cannot be described here.

It is every housewife's duty, to herself and to her family, to own this modern kitchen equipment. It organizes kitchen work. Because of its special features it saves much tiring labor, clips many hours from time in the kitchen and is the means of stopping a costly, though often unknown, waste of food.

Remember, too, that "Sellers," because of honest quality, advanced ideas, and reasonable prices, is today the mark of "dependability" in thousands of homes. While maintaining unusually high standards of quality our prices are always reasonable. Any home can afford a Sellers. No home can afford to be without one. Go see this remarkable cabinet during National Sales Week, at your local dealer's store. He will gladly arrange terms to suit your income.

Famous Recipe Book—FREE

Write at once for a copy of "21 Inexpensive Meals," by Constance E. Miller, A. D. E. This book is now in use in thousands of homes. It gives recipes prepared by a dietetic expert, for a whole week of tasty and economical meals. It also pictures and describes the famous line of Sellers Kitchen Cabinets. There is positively no charge. A postal card will bring you a copy.

G. I. SELLERS & SONS CO.
1501 13th Street   ELWOOD, IND.
F. C. Burroughes Furniture Co., Ltd., Toronto, Canada.
(District Representative)

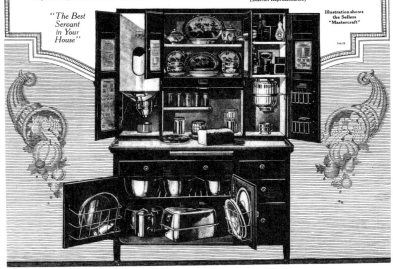

"The Best Servant in Your House"

Illustration shows the Sellers "Mastercraft"

The Sellers Mastercraft Kitchen Cabinet, illustrated in this circa 1919 advertisement and labeled "The Best Servant in Your House," offered a convenient, automatic lowering flour bin. Sellers & Sons Company was second after the Hoosier Manufacturing Company in production and sales. Like other companies, they offered a variety of models in assorted finishes and "terms to suit your income."

come true." The McDougall Company proclaimed their cabinet a "life-long aid to methodical and easy dispatch of kitchen duties."

In general, all these cabinets, regardless of manufacturer, were designed to serve as a helpmate; a multipurpose unit that would ease the housewife's burden in the servantless kitchen. As such they included multiple features standard on all units: metal flour bins with sifters, a metal or glass sugar dispenser, a spice shelf or circular rack, canisters, slide-out cutting board, table of weights and measures, a "want" list for grocery shopping, linen/silverware drawers, storage cupboards, metal bread drawer and aluminum or porcelain-enamel pull-out work surface. Several top-of-the-line cabinets also included clocks, swing-out ironing boards, mirrors and coffee mills. Tambour doors that either rolled down, pulled up or opened side-to-side protected spice jars and bins from dust when the cabinet was not in use.

Early cabinets (1910–1920) were sold with an oak finish or painted white. The more expensive models had decorative frosted, etched or slag glass inserts in top cupboard doors. The standard hoosier cabinet was 40–42 inches wide and 72 inches tall but both larger and smaller models were produced to meet the need of every type of kitchen.

This early, successful attempt at planned organization in the kitchen was designed to save time and strength by eliminating trips back and forth to the pantry; serve as an office for keeping recipes and household accounts in one convenient location; and become the center of kitchen operations where meal preparations could be done without moving from one spot. Even the housewife with the luxury of built-in cupboards in her kitchen was encouraged to invest in a hoosier to avoid scattering her steps.

Whether considered an appliance or a piece of furniture, a hoosier cabinet was indeed an investment for the family of the early 1900s. Prices generally ranged between $20 and $50, a great deal of money at that time. These cabinets, however, were made affordable (thus readily available to a larger number of households) by way of simple payment plans. For example, a circa 1920 advertisement by the Hoosier Manufacturing Company told readers in a national magazine, "The best news of all is the fact that you do not need to go on doing your work in the hard, old-fashioned way while you save up money to buy the Hoosier. Your dealer will put the Hoosier in your home on dignified, easy terms."

By 1920 architects and builders were quick to recognize the proven capabilities of the hoosier cabinet as they incorporated them into new

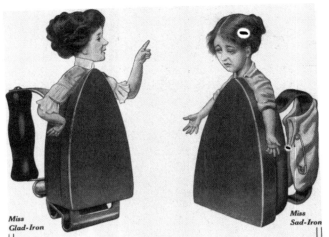

A 1912 advertisement for the Hotpoint electric iron produced by the Pacific Electric Heating Company of Ontario, California. The Hotpoint was early on tested by women who were favorably impressed with the convenience of an electric iron and Hotpoint went on to become a best-seller.

A HOTPOINT BREAKFAST SET

The Beginning of A Perfect Day

As the breakfast goes, so goes the day. And what could be more auspicious than an *electric breakfast* of waffles and coffee, prepared in a jiffy, at the table—with a Hotpoint Breakfast Set!

Like all Hotpoint Servants, Hotpoint Percolators and Waffle Irons are famous for service. Dependability has given them the National preference. Unusual in their refinements and time-saving features.

Many attractive Hotpoint Set *combinations* may be built around this Breakfast Set—including Grill, Table Stove and Toaster, all harmonizing in design and finish.

See this interesting Hotpoint Set—at your dealer's. For dependability, insist always on *Hotpoint.*

Complete Breakfast Sets, as shown above, $49.50 · Waffle Iron, $15.00
Percolator Set, $35.50 · · · Other Percolator Sets up to $65.00

EDISON ELECTRIC APPLIANCE CO., Inc.

Chicago   Boston   New York   Atlanta   Cleveland   St. Louis   Ontario, Cal.   Salt Lake City
Canadian General Electric Company, Ltd. *Head Office:* Toronto

Hotpoint
SERVANTS

WORLD'S LARGEST MANUFACTURER OF HOUSEHOLD ELECTRIC HEATING APPLIANCES

In this 1920 advertisement the Edison Electric Appliance Company refers to all their electric appliances as "Hotpoint Servants." The Breakfast Set was an especially popular "servant," one that the housekeeper could take right to the table to serve her family coffee and waffles.

kitchen designs. At the same time many were eliminating the walk-in pantry, now considered obsolete.

Freestanding hoosier cabinets had additional, far-reaching effects on kitchen design during the 1920s and 1930s, preceeding the "streamlined" kitchen with built-ins and bringing gay or happy colors to the kitchen. (See Chapter Five.)

Electric appliances in the kitchen during the early 1900s was an extraordinarily new concept. While an all-electric kitchen was featured at the 1893 World Columbian Exposition in Chicago, it would be several years before these inventions were perfected and utilized in a limited number of homes.

The more popular electric appliances available between 1900–1920 included irons, toasters, waffle irons, coffee percolators, electric mixers and carpet sweepers. (The electric refrigerator was generally unknown until the GE Monitor-Top made its debut in 1927.)

In 1903 Earl Richardson, plant superintendent for an electric power company in Ontario, California, developed an electric iron with a "hot point." Up until that time electric companies concentrated efforts on supplying power to limited households only during the evening hours for lighting. Two years later Richardson had so perfected his electric iron that the women using it for "testing" were favorably impressed with its operation and convenience. The power companies slowly realized the unlimited opportunities in making power available around the clock and a flood of new electric gadgetry soon followed, originally targeted for businesses—not households. By 1910 electric irons being produced by General Electric and others were advertised in national magazines. The resulting large number of sales prompted electric companies to finally recognize the potential for growth of electric appliances in the household market.

The first electric coffee percolator was introduced in 1908 by Landers, Frary and Clark of New Britain, Connecticut. This "Universal" percolator featured a cold water pump action that would quicken the coffee-making process. The company proved its commitment to excellence in its housewares products by adding a safety plug (which acted as a circuit breaker) to their percolator in 1915.

In 1920 the "Hotpoint Servants" were being nationally advertised by the Edison Electric Appliance Co., Inc. and their "Breakfast Set" was a best-seller. One circa 1920 advertisement proclaimed, "As the breakfast goes, so goes the day. And what could be more auspicious than an *Electric Breakfast* of waffles and coffee, prepared in a jiffy, at the table— with a Hotpoint Breakfast Set! Like all Hotpoint Servants, Hotpoint Percolators and Waffle Irons are famous for service . . . and time-saving

It Now Matters Much

to the housewife just HOW the dirt and dust are removed from her floor coverings

The ELECTRIC SWEEPER-VAC

WITH·MOTOR·DRIVEN·BRUSH

RAPIDLY, THOROUGHLY and SAFELY renovates in ten minutes as many rugs as could be cleaned in three hours by the old-fashioned way.

The correctly speeded MOTOR-DRIVEN BRUSH and the genuinely powerful suction distinguish the ELECTRIC SWEEPER-VAC.

In order to obtain it, insist on the Vacuum Cleaner with THAT LEVER, which places at your instant command in one machine the two accepted types of Vacuum Cleaner now on the market.

Write for the most elaborate book ever written on Vacuum Cleaners. It's free!

PNEUVAC COMPANY

Dept. 6

Worcester .·. Mass.

The electric sweeper was an appliance that caught on right away as women realized the savings in time and manual labor. Rather than sweeping the carpet or removing the rug outdoors and "beating" the dust and dirt out of it, electric sweepers such as this Electric Sweeper-Vac with a motor-driven brush made the job much easier.

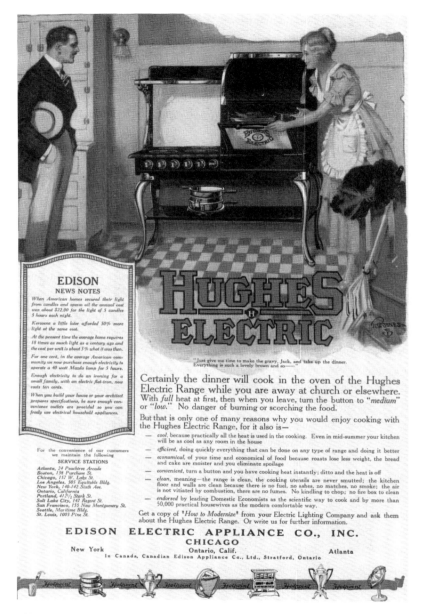

Although electric stoves such as this Hughes Electric model were available by 1920, it was another ten years before they became popular. Women were satisfied with gas stoves and electric power was not yet available to all homes. However, by the 1930s electric stoves saw a marked increase in sales.

features. Complete Breakfast Set (percolator, cream, sugar and waffle iron) $49.50." Although a costly investment, such sets were nevertheless popular in the servantless home.

The pyramid toasters designed to toast bread over the stove burner were slowly replaced by electric models introduced in the early 1900s. Both Westinghouse and General Electric offered these appliances by 1910 and the GE D-12 model was a simple porcelain-based unit with wire framing to hold the bread in place. This porcelain base not only made this toaster attractive but it also served as an insulator. Some of the other electric toasters, such as that produced by Landers, Frary and Clark, had a spring-operated frame to hold the bread in place and, with ornate designs in their metal construction, they were also an attractive addition to the kitchen.

In 1918 Landers, Frary and Clark introduced an electric waffle iron and in 1920, the Armstrong Electric & Manufacturing Company of Huntington, West Virginia brought out an electric waffler with the added feature of a heat indicator to tell the user when the appliance was ready for use.

The Hamilton Beach Manufacturing Company produced a Home motor in 1912 that was intended for use with sewing machines but also included attachments, one of which was a cake batter mixer.

The electric suction sweeper was being produced by the Hoover Company in 1908 and by 1910 Stecher Electric & Machine Company was turning out the Eureka carpet sweeper.

Edison Electric Appliance Company introduced an electric stove prior to 1920, but due to limited access of electric power and the housewife's satisfaction with her gas stove, it would be another ten years before this type of stove gained in popularity.

During this infancy stage of electric household appliances, many housekeepers could only dream of the day they might have one of these modern conveniences. However, those that were able to take advantage of the new gadgetry found themselves released from the old-fashioned, cumbersome ways of performing certain household tasks. Early indicators pointed to strong consumer interest and desire to have electric appliances in the home and the developments through 1920 paved the way for substantial growth in this area during the 1920s, followed by widespread use in most homes by the 1930s.

At the same time the hoosier cabinet was influencing future kitchen design, early electric appliances were setting the pace for domestic economy and laying the groundwork for the evolution of "modern" kitchen development during the 1920s and 1930s.

Post-Victorian Household Hints and Recipes

❧HOUSEHOLD HINTS❧

A coffee mill is a household necessity if one wishes good coffee. Ground coffee quickly looses its strength, and the amount required at any one time should be ground just before using . . . In selecting a coffee mill it is better to take one that stands on a shelf or table than those screwed upon the wall. The former are more apt to be cleaned often, require less time to operate, and save all the coffee and its strength.

The Enterprising Housekeeper
—Helen Johnson, 1906

There may be—in fact, evidence proves that there are—good cooks who seemingly never measure anything, but by "about so much of this," and "a pinch of that," bring about results so delicious that the would-be follower at once determines to throw rules to the winds and try the same way. Good cooks always measure—one by the cup and spoon, because she must; another by the judgment and experience long years of doing the same thing over and over again have given her; and the chances are that, unless you have the rare gift of cooking straight from the gods, you had better cling to the exact measures and weights if you wish the best results every time, instead of once in a while.

The Enterprising Housekeeper
—Helen Johnson, 1906

HOMEMADE RECEIPT BOOK

Have at hand a blank book in which to paste or copy valuable recipes. Cover this with white oilcloth neatly pasted on. Have a special part of this book or a separate book for menus. This will help to solve the problem of what to have for dinner.

Household Discoveries
—Sidney Morse, 1909

TIN CANS

Lard, kerosene, and other oils are sold in various parts of the country in five-gallon cans. These cans can be obtained from the grocer for a small sum and make excellent boilers to wash out small articles too dainty for the regular wash. They can also be used with a small wash-board as tubs. Or they may be used as flour bins, bread or cake boxes, and the like.

Household Discoveries
—Sidney Morse, 1909

CARE OF KITCHEN WARES—ENAMELED WARE

Scraping ruins enameled ware. Utensils of this ware placed directly over the flame of a coal range should be protected by rubbing the bottoms thickly with soap. Any soot which burns on may then be removed by soap and water. If food burns in any enameled ware utensils, put into them a teaspoonful of sal soda or caustic lye to a quart of water and boil for fifteen minutes. This will soften the burned food so that it can be removed without scraping. If not quite clean, scour with find sand soap. For discolored saucepans boil a little chloride of lime in the water. Or boil in them a strong solution of baking soda.

Household Discoveries
—Sidney Morse, 1909

TABLES OF DOMESTIC MEASURE

Domestic Liquid Measure—
10 drops = 1 saltspoon
4 saltspoons = 1 teaspoon
4 tablespoons = 1 basting spoon
2 basting spoons = 1 gill
2 gills = 1 cup
2 cups = 1 pint
2 pints = 1 quart
4 quarts = 1 gallon

Domestic Dry Measure—
4 saltspoons = 1 teaspoon
3 teaspoons = 1 tablespoon
12 tablespoons = 1 cup
8 tablespoons (heaping) = 1 cup

Household Discoveries
—Sidney Morse, 1909

A WORD ABOUT BAKING POWDER

Every housekeeper should understand the nature of Baking Powder . . . Baking Powder is not a food; it is a preparer of food only, and is used only for the leavening gas it produces to make the food light and sweet . . . An example of a perfect powder is the brand called Calumet Baking Powder [William Wright established The Calumet Baking Powder Company in Chicago in 1889]. The makers use the very latest methods and employ competent chemists who analyze all ingredients. The result is a baking powder which gives the maximum of leavening gas and the minimum of residue, and that neutral, left in food . . . A careful study of the various brands of baking powder before the public has led us to believe that the powder which received the "highest award" at the World's Pure Food Exposition at Chicago—Calumet Baking Powder—embodies all the points desired in a perfect baking powder. Greatest leavening power. Moderateness in price. Absolute uniformity. Small amount of harmless residue in food.

Mrs. Curtis's Cook Book
—Isabel Curtis, 1909

The good word for house-cleaning is—make haste slowly. Better one cleaned room a day, and comfort therewith, than an epidemic of brooms, buckets, scrubbing-brushes, and step-ladders, sure to get everybody's temper on edge. Take plenty of time, but never begin before the beginning. Fretting over work to come may hinder, but cannot possibly help.

The Complete Housekeeper
—Emily Holt, 1917

The house-mother who has a laundry apart from her kitchen should rise up and call her home's builder blessed. Still, it is better to do the washing in a big, airy kitchen than to wrestle with it in the basement, ill-lit and poorly ventilated . . . Splashing in a cellar almost invariably means continuing dampness; thus, what is gained in space and kitchen tidiness is very often lost many times over in health and comfort . . . Cellar drying is inadvisable. Daylight, even of the wannest and stormiest, is a wonderful sweetner and disinfectant.

The Complete Housekeeper
—Emily Holt, 1917

HINTS ON MARKETING

First, go to the store yourself; second, select for yourself the article you desire to purchase; third, inquire its price. If quality and price please you, be sure that you get in weight or measure the amount you buy. Watch the scale. Watch the measure . . . Don't buy in small quantities if you can possibly avoid it. Make every effort to get together two or three dollars. This will enable you to buy for cash; buy in larger quantities; buy where you can do the best. In this way you can save two or three dollars in a very short time.

The Complete Housekeeper
—Emily Holt, 1917

❦ R E C I P E S ❦

SAMPLE BREAKFAST MENUS

1.) Fruit, Baked Hash, Corn Bread, Coffee
2.) Quaker Oats, Ham Omelet, Creamed Potatoes, Coffee
3.) Melons, Poached Eggs, Waffles, Coffee

SAMPLE LUNCHEON MENUS

1.) Corn Fritters, Sandwiches, Citron Preserves, Cake
2.) Stuffed Eggs, Cream Sauce, Tomato Salad, Fruit Jelly
3.) Puree of Clams, Ham Toast, Rice Pudding

SAMPLE SUPPER MENUS

1.) Shrimp Salad, Saratoga Potatoes, Brown Bread & Butter Sandwiches, Coffee, Lemon Jelly, Wafers
2.) Lobster Cutlets, Cream Sauce, Potato Puff, Stuffed Olives, Cake, Chocolate
3.) Corn Fritters, Potato Salad, Rolls, Coffee

The Enterprising Housekeeper
—Helen Johnson, 1906

RUSSIAN TEA

4 teaspoonfuls tea, 1 quart boiling water, 1 teaspoonful sugar, ½ slice lemon, 1 Maraschino cherry. Pour the boiling water over the tea, and

allow it to stand for five minutes. Into each cup put the lemon, cherry, and sugar, and pour the tea over them.

Mrs. Curtis's Cook Book
—Isabel Curtis, 1909

BAKING-POWDER BISCUITS

2 cupfuls flour, 2 tablespoonfuls lard, 1 cupful milk, ½ teaspoonful salt, 2 teaspoonfuls Calumet Baking Powder. Sift the salt, baking powder, and flour together, rub in the lard, add the milk, and beat to a soft dough. Turn out on a floured baking board, roll out about an inch thick, and cut into biscuits. Lay in a baking pan, brush the tops with milk, and bake in a quick oven.

Mrs. Curtis's Cook Book
—Isabel Curtis, 1909

BAKED-BEAN SANDWICHES

½ cupful baked beans, 1 tablespoonful horse-radish, 1 teaspoonful celery and parsely minced fine, ½ teaspoonful onion juice, ½ teaspoonful mustard, dash McIlhenny's Tabasco Sauce. Press the beans through a potato ricer, mix with the seasoning, and spread between slices of entire-wheat bread.

Mrs. Curtis's Cook Book
—Isabel Curtis, 1909

MEAT CHARTREUSE IN RICE

2 Cupfuls of Chopped Cooked Meat, 1 Teaspoonful of Salt, ½ Teaspoonful of White Pepper, ½ Tablespoonful of Diced Onion, ¼ Cupful of Breadcrumbs, ¼ Cupful of Melted Butter, Gravy or Stock to Moisten, 1 Beaten Egg, 3 Cupfuls of Cooked Rice, Tomato Sauce. Put the meat into a basin, add the egg well beaten, the salt, pepper, onion, breadcrumbs, and melted butter and enough stock or gravy to moisten. Mix and turn into a mold which has been well buttered and lined with two cupfuls of rice; place the remainder of the rice on the top, cover the mold with buttered paper, and steam steadily for 45 minutes. Turn out on a hot platter and serve at once with hot tomato sauce.

Ladies' Home Journal, June 1912

BROWN BETTY

Place alternate layers of chopped apples and stale bread crumbs in buttered baking-dish, having crumbs on bottom. Add cinnamon and sugar to each layer of apples, using more sugar if apples are sour. The top layer should be buttered bread crumbs. Bake in moderate oven until crumbs are brown.

The Complete Housekeeper
—Emily Holt, 1917

BEEF CROQUETTES

Take cold roast or corned beef. Put it into a wooden bowl and chop it fine. Mix with it about twice the quantity of hot mashed potatoes or boiled rice, well seasoned with butter or drippings and salt. Beat up an egg and work it into the potato or rice and meat, then form the mixture into little cakes the size of fish balls. Flatten them a little; roll in flour or egg and cracker crumbs, fry in hot fat, browning on both sides. Serve piping hot. Almost any cold meat can be used instead of beef.

The Complete Housekeeper
—Emily Holt, 1917

5

The Modern Kitchen 1920–1939

"IT'S ALL IN THE DAY'S WORK"

An early 1930s middle-class kitchen featuring the latest in electric appliances— a GE Monitor-Top Refrigerator and a Hotpoint Electric Stove. Note the kitchen includes the recommended placement of the hoosier cabinet next to the kitchen sink to serve as a "work center" and a porcelain-top table is available for additional work space. The floor is covered with linoleum.

Courtesy GE Appliance Archives.

Engineers, designers and manufacturers have overcome age-old drudgery by making kitchen equipment that is adapted to its purpose. Color and line have also become a part of this once humble room and now it is the most modern room of the house.

"Kitchens of Today," *Needlecraft—The Home Arts Magazine*
—Agnes Heisler Barton, November 1934

*D*uring the 1920s and 1930s the kitchen continued to be strictly an area of food preparation: small in size with all equipment arranged as conveniently as possible. Most urban kitchens designed during this period were square with floor space ranging from 9′ x 10′ in size to 10′ x 12′. A breakfast alcove or "nook" with a table and chairs was often incorporated into a small space adjacent to the kitchen. Porcelain-enamel-top tables were popular at the time and their small size made them the ideal furnishing for the breakfast nook.

The rural or country kitchen was larger to allow additional space for the massive wood/coal burning stove and an area in which to keep a supply of fuel.

Kitchens were still placed at the rear of the house and windows were planned for good ventilation and lighting.

Wall brackets to support gas or electric lighting fixtures were ideally located over the sink, stove and worktable. A single light hung in the center of the room was considered inadequate since it would not properly light "work areas."

While some homes were being constructed without a kitchen pantry, others (especially in rural areas) still included such a space for storage during the 1920s. Only very large homes continued to make use of a butler's pantry.

Kitchen flooring was linoleum tile or hardwood, although wooden floors were used less frequently since they required extra time and effort to keep in good condition.

Linoleum was available in "printed," "inlaid" or "plain" qualities. Printed linoleum referred to flooring in which the pattern or design was only on the surface and could be worn off in time. Inlaid and plain

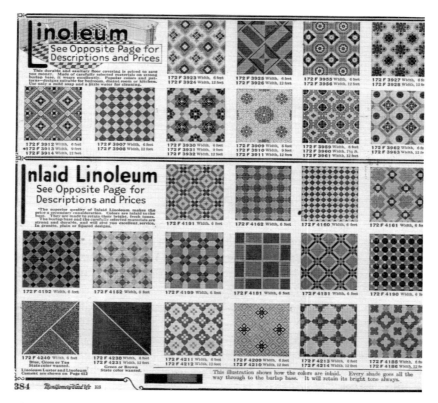

The 1924 Montgomery Ward catalog offered a wide selection of linoleum flooring. Both printed linoleum and inlaid linoleum were available in a variety of colors and patterns but inlaid was noted for being a better quality and longer lasting floor cover.

A bright, cheerful kitchen
—with Valspar-Enamel

"This kitchen I am very proud of," writes Mrs. F. M. Keyser.* "It was finished three years ago, the woodwork in white Valspar-Enamel and the linoleum with clear Valspar Varnish.

"And they've both been put to severe tests. The floor has had boiling water poured on it many times. One evening some vinegar was spilled and forgotten until the next morning. I was very much worried for fear the acid would destroy the color of the linoleum, but the varnish was a perfect protection.

"The woodwork has withstood the smoke and spatters of cooking for three years and still looks as good as new."

You, too, can have a kitchen sparklingly clean and proof against wear. Simply paint your furniture and woodwork with Valspar-Enamel in any color you like. And make your gas range look spick and span with a coat of Valspar Black Enamel.

Anyone can do the work because Valspar-Enamel spreads easily and flows evenly. And besides their cheerful colors, these enamels have a hard, lustrous surface that is easy to clean and absolutely waterproof.

Made in 12 beautiful standard colors: Red—*light and deep*, Blue—*light, medium and deep*, Green—*medium and deep*, Ivory, Vermilion, Bright Yellow, Gray and Brown. Also in Black, White, Gold, Bronze, Aluminum and Flat Black. And by mixing these colors in varying proportions, any desired shade or tint can be obtained.

This 1925 advertisement for enamel paint features a sanitary white kitchen with blue-and-white checkered linoleum flooring. Note the "built-in" sink cupboard and the large hoosier cabinet.

During the 1920s it became common practice to locate the sink underneath a window so the housewife could enjoy a pleasant view as she washed dishes.

linoleum were manufactured with the design or color extending to the back of the flooring. Plain linoleum often featured a solid color such as the then-popular battleship gray. Both inlaid and plain linoleum flooring were recommended since they were of a better quality and longer-lasting.

Tile floors, long thought to be the most sanitary, were also tiring to stand on for any length of time since they had no "cushion" or "give" and soon lost favor among housewives.

During the 1920s lingering concern over sanitation in the kitchen prompted recommendations that walls continue to be painted in light enamel colors such as gray, buff or ivory. Woodwork was also to be given a coat of enamel paint in a light, matching tone. In those middle-class homes where additional money could be spent on the kitchen without concern, tiled walls or a tile wainscoting were still very much in use.

Regarding kitchen equipment, *The House and Its Care* by Mary Lockwood Matthews recommended:

> Every well-planned kitchen should be equipped with cupboards, sink, and work tables or cabinets, preferably built-in, so that there will be no necessity for moving them about to clean underneath or behind them, as must be done with movable cabinets or cupboards . . . The work in the kitchen divides itself into: (1) the center in which the food is prepared, cooked and served, sometimes called the "preparation center," and (2) the center in which dishes are washed and put away, sometimes called the "cleaning-up center." To have a kitchen well arranged, the built-in equipment and small equipment needed in each center must be grouped together. In the preparation center, it is necessary to have the ice-box, the supply cupboard, the work table or cabinet, the stove, and the serving table or tray; in the cleaning-up center, should be found the sink, the drain boards, and the dish cupboards.[1]

While built-in cupboards were recommended and new homes built during the 1920s did include them, they were often quite tall with the top of the cupboard running to the ceiling. Such cupboards were not deep, often a mere 6 or 8 inches—enough to store single items without moving articles from front to back and so forth. Built-in cupboard space was as simple as a single, large cupboard for holding dishware or as elaborate as a wall unit with cupboard space planned around the sink, including drawers for cutlery, utensils, dish-towels etc. Sliding doors on bottom cupboards were suggested for convenience and solid wood doors on top cupboards were favored over glass doors which called for regular cleaning. Built-in kitchen cupboards were often painted the same color as the kitchen walls during the 1920s.

The freestanding hoosier kitchen cabinet grew in popularity as a "work station" during the 1920s, with manufacturers having record sales during this decade. Household manuals recommended the hoosier should be situated near the stove to save steps. Numerous models were turned out, including top-of-the-line cabinets that featured swing-out ironing boards, clocks, mirrors and by the late 1920s, decorative colored finishes. Sanitary enameled work surfaces replaced the zinc or wooden tops found on hoosiers produced during the early 1900s.

Kitchen sinks were porcelain or enameled iron and the practice of constructing sinks on tall legs (leaving the area underneath open for sanitary measures) continued through the 1920s in many homes. An ideal sink had a splash-back and drainboards all cast in one piece with no cracks where dirt could collect.

The icebox was a standard appliance in the majority of middle-class kitchens; however, the introduction of the electric refrigerator in the late 1920s was a significant development that quickly became a "necessity" as more and more homes had access to electric power.

Kitchen stoves in use during the 1920s were fueled by coal/wood, gasoline, kerosene, natural gas or electricity. Natural gas and electric stoves were becoming more popular as gas lines and electric power were made available to an increasing number of homes.

y, 1924

The Ladies HOME JOURNAL

© 1924, The Hoosier Manufacturing Company

YOUR KITCHEN!—FURNISHED AS COMPLETELY AND TASTEFULLY AS ANY OTHER ROOM

—how you can have it so with little trouble and expense

This 1924 advertisement for Hoosier Kitchen Cabinets illustrates their all-purpose "helpmate" as well as a single cabinet unit for brooms and other household supplies. Note the dining nook or alcove with porcelain-top table located just off the kitchen.

THE MODERN KITCHEN 1920–1939 ❦ 229

Fifteen years of development
....but an overnight popularity

WHEREVER you go you hear people praising the General Electric Refrigerator. Almost overnight it has taken a prominent place in the thoughts of homemakers.

One hears of its remarkable simplicity! That it hasn't a single belt, fan or drain-pipe! That it hasn't a bit of machinery under the cabinet—or in the basement! That it never needs oiling. There are many, many comments on the quietness with which it operates. There is enthusiasm expressed for the extreme roominess and the splendid strength of its gleaming cabinets.

Overnight, it seems . . . . but for more than fifteen years the vast laboratories of General Electric have been busy with the development of this truly revolutionary refrigerator. Several thousand refrigerators of nineteen different types, were made, field-tested and improved before this model was finally evolved. It was a long and expensive process—but nowhere in the field of electric refrigeration have engineers and scientists done their work so well.

Write today for booklet E-2 which is completely descriptive.

GENERAL ⚡ ELECTRIC
Refrigerator

ELECTRIC REFRIGERATION DEPARTMENT OF GENERAL ELECTRIC COMPANY · HANNA BUILDING · CLEVELAND, OHIO

When the GE Monitor-Top refrigerator was introduced in 1927 it quickly became a necessity as more and more homes had access to electric power. Housewives no longer had to keep a watchful eye on the drip pan of the old-fashioned icebox and the consistent cool temperature within the refrigerator kept food fresh for longer periods of time.

Kitchen utensils were to be chosen with convenience in mind. If a tool or gadget was well designed, constructed of quality materials, easy to clean, of a handy size and reasonably priced, then it was thought to be a good investment. Generally, kitchen utensils fell into four categories during the 1920s and 1930s. There were gadgets and utensils used in preparing food, cooking or serving food, utensils used in washing the dishes and lastly, miscellaneous tools used in a variety of ways. For example, in preparing meals the houswife might rely on measuring cups, measuring spoons, mixing bowls, a rolling pin, flour sifter, food grinder, chopping bowl, lemon reamer, chopping knife, egg beater, bread mixer, cake mixer, cutters for biscuits, cookies and doughnuts, can opener, graters, spoons, knives, forks etc. In cooking and then serving the meal common tools included the stove, assorted cookware, a tea kettle, frying pans, a griddle, waffle iron, broiler, roaster, soup pot, baking dishes, casserole, cake and bread pans, baking sheets, muffin pans, pie pans, an ice-cream freezer, molds, vegetable press, potato masher, strainers, percolator, teapot and pot holders. For washing the dishes the well-

The 1925 Hoosier Highboy!

the most scientifically designed model and the greatest value ever offered, say domestic science authorities

In an effort to bring additional storage space and "standardization" to the modern kitchen, The Hoosier Mfg. Co. offered cupboards that could be used as an extension of their all-purpose cabinet or separately as needed. Note that this 1925 advertisement features a porcelain sink on sanitary tall legs and a porcelain-top kitchen table.

equipped kitchen had on hand a dishpan, dish drainer, sink strainer, soap dish, soap shaker, dish mop, plate scraper, wire-mesh pot brush, several dish cloths, tea towels, a bottle brush, rack for tea towels, and in some households, a dishwasher (early dishwashers were available that attached to the sink but they were often considered a luxury rather than a necessity). Finally, for miscellaneous kitchen work some women made use of a small cart on wheels to take meals into the dining room, a weighing scale often came in handy, bread and cake boxes stored baked goods, and a clock helped prepare timely meals. The equivalent of today's kitchen junk drawer was a basket or box used to store small items such as paper, string, scissors, household tools, pencils, labels and so on. A serving tray, corkscrew, lidded storage containers (for leftovers) and canister set for coffee, sugar, flour and tea completed the kitchen ensemble.[2]

The majority of kitchenware items were made of the new stainless steel, aluminum, tin, wire, enamel, glass, earthenware (such as yellow ware mixing bowls) or wood.

By the late 1920s changes in kitchen design and furnishings brought the first hint of standardization to kitchen plans and kitchen designs introduced broom closets and utility cupboards made to fit flush against their kitchen cabinets. These narrow cupboards provided additional storage space in the kitchen and were a successful attempt at planned organization.

Coinciding with these early efforts at standardization in the kitchen, color made its debut in furnishings as well as gadgets and utensils. In *Kitchens and Gadgets 1920 to 1950,* author Jane H. Celehar writes that "In the early 1920s, a few housewares manufacturers started to bring color to the kitchen when they put colored wooden handles on kitchen tools. This introduction of color was a revolutionary concept . . . The first colored wooden handles were black, followed by white, and were used prior to and during the 1920s. It wasn't until the late 1920s and 1930s that green became the most popular (or most manufactured . . .) colored handle. Red, blue, and yellow handles were also produced."[3]

It was only a matter of time before color invaded every aspect of the kitchen and, following gadgets and utensils, soon appliances, furnishings, kitchen cupboards and accessories could be bought in many bright and cheerful colors. As early as 1927 major department stores such as Macy's and Abraham & Strauss were promoting a "Color in the Kitchen" campaign that offered an extensive variety of colorful kitchenware items. Given the fact that color in the kitchen was a novelty, manufacturers turned out goods in a variety of "shades," and it wasn't until the 1930s that efforts were under way to develop official standards for color in the kitchen.

Let this radiant sink
gladden every busy hour

A breath of Spring in your kitchen! The invigorating freshness of new things coming to life in a world of sunshine. And beauty, withal! —the sprightly beauty of the rose. What a radiant companion, this sink, in *any* kitchen!

And how sensibly it is proportioned, this "Three 8's" Sink. Its eight-inch back fits snugly under low windows. Warm, soft rays of sunlight come flooding in to speed your work and set your happy thoughts to music. To an eight-inch deep front this sink owes its stately dignity. And you will be delighted to discover that the roomy compartment within is *equally deep* — eight inches. What a comfort to be so well protected from the splash of water in your dish pan.

A vitreous china garbage container, sus-

pended beneath the sink on a folding bracket, contributes to sanitation. Chromard Finish Fittings offer their tarnish-free sheen as a labor-saver. This sink furnishes convenience and efficiency in greater measure.

Rose du Barry is but one of the many soft, rich colors from which you may choose —and white, of course.

Enduringly beautiful, too, these colors. If desired, they are available in Acid-Resisting Enamel which defies fruit acids to spot and stain its hard glass-like surface. The sink portrayed above, and the many other styles of "Standard" sinks, can be leisurely seen at a "Standard" Showroom, where you are always welcome. And a copy of the booklet, in color, "Standard" Plumbing Fixtures for the Home, is yours for the asking.

Standard Sanitary Mfg. Co. PITTSBURGH

The 1920s campaign to introduce color into the kitchen even included the kitchen sink. This 1929 advertisement for Standard Plumbing Fixtures features a "Rose du Barry" or deep pink sink and the ad tells

readers that other colors are also available, including white. The container attached underneath the sink is a "vitreous china garbage container," which contributed to sanitation in the kitchen.

Popular women's magazines played an important role in getting the word on color to housewives all across the country. For example, the November 1930 issue of *Better Homes & Gardens* included a piece, "The Kitchen Has Had Its Face Lifted!" Author Josephine Wylie wrote:

> . . . our ideas about kitchens have changed tremendously in the last decade and more. From a scullery the kitchen has graduated into a new importance and a new beauty. It has had its face lifted, so to speak, its windows made sunnier and more airy, efficient cooking and refrigerating equipment placed in it, cupboards added that are roomy enough to keep each thing in its place; in a word, the kitchen's whole aspect has changed!

The article continued, offering an example of a colorful, modern kitchen built in the new suburban home of a young couple. Wylie wrote:

> The kitchen walls and woodwork are a soft spring-green; its checked-gingham curtains, brilliant yellow. On the floor is linoleum in green and ivory; the sink is in ivory; and the range is yellow and green, one of those new ones made to look like a dresser with a cover that may be let down over the cooking units. The room is just as efficient, just as practical in every way, as if it were void of color and beauty . . . The kitchen is divided into so-called working units . . . There is not a thing about the furnishings of this kitchen that isn't sincere. And it is lovely besides.[4]

In a more detailed look at the use of color in the circa 1930 kitchen, an article entitled "Color Schemes for Your Kitchen" offered several timely suggestions. Author Mabel J. Stegner interviewed Hazel Adler, who was then working with the U.S. Department of Commerce in an effort to standardize color-styling for household equipment. To suggest how women might use color more effectively in their kitchen, Adler told readers that "Quiet colors for backgrounds with a few pieces in high, gay colors to lend interest and accent is my basic principle . . . For the walls, sinks, and cabinets, I should recommend bisque, warm gray, or soft tones of blue or green, known as silver-blue or silver-green . . . So many persons . . . use orange and green; in many cases not because they like the combination for their particular kitchen, nor because it is suited to the individual homemaker, but because they are prone to imitate. There are also other interesting schemes to consider." Adler went on to offer six color schemes for the kitchen, including 1.) Pewter-Gray and Red; 2.) Lavender Accents; 3.) Silver-Green; 4.) Pale Green and Golden

With a black-and-gray printed linoleum
floor, gray walls and bright red and
yellow furnishings and cabinets, this
1926 version was the latest in cheerful
kitchens. According to this Armstrong

Linoleum ad, "gay colors lend wings
to work" and as the workshop of the
home, the kitchen "needs bright
color to gladden the working
hours."

NEW
STYLISH
COLORS
by
SELLERS

Building or Remodeling? Many new homes and up-to-date apartment buildings are being equipped with the new Sellers Sectional Built-in Units. The latest idea. Please write for information.

Who could feel old in so *youthful* a kitchen

SELLERS, they will tell you, has brought style, gaiety, *youth*—into the kitchen of the *modern* home. No longer is this vital room a mere workshop—a place of unescapable duties—with stiff, laboratory-like furnishings.

The modern Sellers *colorful* kitchen is *youthful*—full of sunshine—the cheeriest room in all the house.

Here, with your smartly colored Sellers Kitchenaire to anticipate every need, your heart is light

—your steps are sprightly—your fingers move swiftly—to the rhythm of the gay little song that keeps coming to your lips. Who could feel old in so *youthful* a kitchen?

Try color in *your* kitchen. Plan it around the new, stylish Sellers Kitchenaire. Choose the color you like best. Jade Green! Colonial Ivory! Sellers Grey! Spanish Gold!

Touch up the walls and woodwork. Refinish a chair—clock—waste basket—match holder. Carry color in the curtains. Cover the floor with colorful tile linoleum. See what a marvelous transformation is possible at small expense.

If you are building a new home plan your colorful kitchen around the stunning new Sellers Kitchen Ensemble—the last word in stylish kitchen equipment. Cabinet, utility closets and breakfast set—all finished in the same beautiful colors and design. It is the newest vogue.

You may see these newest kitchen cabinets at a local furniture store. Note the many famous time- and labor-saving features. Because of them millions of homes now use the Sellers. Prices

are very moderate. And most dealers sell on very liberal terms.

Have we your present address?

Your complimentary copy of the new Sellers catalogue is ready. Shows interesting colorful kitchen ideas. Illustrates the stylish Sellers Kitchenaire in actual colors. If we have not your address will you please send it right away? Address Dept. 504.

G. I. SELLERS & SONS CO., *Elwood, Indiana*

SPANISH GOLD

COLONIAL IVORY

SELLERS GREY

SERVER IN JADE GREEN

SELLERS
K I T C H E N A I R E

As color in the kitchen became a popular concept, housewares and furnishings manufacturers began turning out everything from gadgets and utensils to kitchen cabinets in a variety of color choices, with attractive trims and designs. This 1928 advertisement for Sellers Kitchenaire cabinets shows their latest models available in Spanish Gold, Colonial Ivory, Jade Green and Gray.

Yellow; 5.) Dainty Touches of Apricot; and 6.) Bits of Pearl Pink and Blue. Detailed information was offered for each scheme. For example, in decorating the kitchen with "Bits of Pearl Pink and Blue," readers were advised: "Kitchen walls and large pieces of equipment: bisque. Linoleum: blue and bisque squares; curtains: pink and white check gingham. Oilcloth: a soft, luminous pink. Towels: pink and white check or white towels with pink border. Utensils: bisque enamelware with pearl pink trim; a few utensils each of solid color, pink and blue. Accessories: blue kitchen clock, blue-enamel iron skillet, blue earthen coffee pot."[5]

While color in the kitchen was well received by homemakers, an increasing number of housewares manufacturers stepped up efforts to standardize not only colors, but equipment and furnishings used in the kitchen. Applying the principles used in industry remained popular in trying to improve efficiency in the home, and time study results were taken very seriously. Both gas and electric companies joined efforts to make the kitchen as convenient as possible, resulting in the introduction of tabletop ranges that were the same height (36 inches) as other work surfaces (built-in cupboards with a continuous countertop) being introduced into the kitchen. At the same time an increase in the use of electric refrigerators did away with age-old food preservation problems. (See Notable Changes.) Suddenly during the 1930s the kitchen was coming together as a carefully planned, modernized workspace. Celehar writes in *Kitchens and Gadgets 1920 to 1950* that

> The peak period to alleviate household drudgery, when kitchen planning reached a high state of perfection, was during the 1920s and 1930s. By 1935 basic planning principles were well established. These include the concept of work centers, ample storage, work surfaces, and careful placement of equipment to reduce floor space and save steps. Three main centers were now defined [as opposed to two work centers recognized during the 1920s]—storage, involving cupboards and refrigerator; food preparation, dishwashing, and cleaning, centering on the sink; and cooking and serving areas which were centered near the range. The sink was conveniently located between the refrigerator and the range. Around these three centers were grouped cabinets and accessories, appropriate to each, with counters connecting them in a continuous working scheme, thus unifying all appliances with the work process and treating the kitchen as a harmonious whole.[6]

Jane Celehar elaborates in her second book, *Kitchens and Kitchenware,* that "In the mid-1930s, many objects were redesigned as a result of the Depression, mass-production, the need to stimulate sales, and

This young bride is working at a Monel Metal cabinet sink. Just behind her is the newest Magic Chef range, made by the American Stove Co., Cleveland, O. The top is Monel Metal. The Universal Blower Co. of Birmingham, Mich., *makes the Monel Metal range hood, equipped with electric light and exhaust fan. Monel Metal-topped table manufactured by Mutschler Bros. Co., Nappanee, Ind. All cabinets supplied by Whitehead Metal Products Co. of New York, Inc.*

She wouldn't take "No" for an answer...

—and proved that even newly-weds can afford a Monel Metal Kitchen!

MEET Bob and Betty Avery. Yes, you've guessed it—married last June. Bob's salary is not large—yet. So they have to watch their budget when they buy things for their new home.

Said Betty to Bob one day: "Wouldn't it be wonderful if we could have a bright and shining kitchen—with everything *matching* in Monel Metal!"

Said Bob to Betty: "Swell—but those Monel Metal gadgets must cost a fortune."

Betty wouldn't take "No" for an answer. She went to her plumber. And here's what she learned:

— that a silvery Monel Metal sink with a steel base cabinet like the one shown above costs only $104.50.*

—that there is absolutely no increase in price for the Monel Metal top on the new Magic Chef range.

—that the handsome Monel Metal-topped tables and Whitehead steel cabinets cost no more (often cost less) than ordinary, old-fashioned models.

Delightful Discoveries

So Betty has her Monel Metal kitchen. And every day she finds new reasons for patting herself on the back. She's finding that these silvery surfaces have many *sterling* virtues. They're easy to clean, of course. And their resilience subdues the clatter of pots and pans and also helps prevent dish breakage.

Also — she's finding that Monel Metal has more "proofs" than the proverbial pudding! It is rust-proof, proof, crack-proof, accident-proof. It will still have its silvery luster when Betty is a grandmother.

Important: Monel Metal sinks and cabinets to match are now made by the same manufacturer. By buying your sink and all kitchen cabinets from the same maker, you get harmony in every detail... save trouble and expense. For full information write to the manufacturers —Whitehead Metal Products Co. of New York, Inc., 304 Hudson Street, New York, N. Y.

This price applies only to deliveries made east of the Rocky Mountains.

THE INTERNATIONAL NICKEL COMPANY INC. 73 Wall Street New York, N. Y.

| $\frac{2}{3}$ NICKEL | + | $\frac{1}{3}$ COPPER | = | MONEL METAL |

Monel Metal inherits from Nickel its finest qualities—strength, beauty, and ability to withstand rust and corrosion. When you specify metals remember that the addition of Nickel brings toughness, strength, beauty, and extra years of service to steels, irons and non-ferrous alloys.

Monel Metal

EVERY product guaranteed as advertised—see page 6

Monel Metal built-in cabinets and countertops were quite popular during the 1930s and the latest in "modern" kitchen furnishings. This 1936 advertisement features a sink unit, wall-hung cupboards, Monel Metal table and the latest Magic Chef range. Note the addition of a range hood over the stove and the refrigerator styled with rounded corners.

'streamlining.' When units were designed to be integrated around the work centers, the result was the streamlined kitchen. 'Streamlined' originally meant a reduction of wing resistance [in aerodynamics]. Since the mid-1930s, the word has implied a graceful design and has been used interchangeably with the word modern."[7]

Color in the kitchen and the variety of appliances available offered the housewife the opportunity to decorate this room as her heart desired. This 1930 advertisement for Magic Chef Ranges illustrates a modern kitchen remodeled with an "Early American" theme. The stove is finished in marbled black, walls are a pale green with pine wainscoting and a large pine cupboard completes the furnishings.

In creating the modern home, architects were experimenting with floor plans and while the breakfast nook was a popular addition to kitchens built during the 1920s and early 1930s, before 1940 builders were often constructing homes with an "open" floor plan. Generally, this was a design in which the dining room was actually an extension of the living room (creating an L shape). A doorway allowed passage from the dining room into the kitchen where the housewife was still removed from the family as she prepared meals and carried out kitchen chores.

In short, the 1920s were transitional years in regard to kitchen design and decoration. In *The Housewares Story* author Earl Lifshey tells us "A 'new' idea had taken hold. Kitchen design was being revolutionized and the once-wasted wall space was being equipped with built-in kitchen cabinets right at the time the house or apartment was being built . . . The trend toward more up-to-date kitchens got a big boost in 1935 when The National Kitchen Modernization Bureau was established jointly by the Edison Electric Institute . . . and the National Electrical Manufacturers Association to actively promote kitchen modernization throughout the country . . . the new Bureau launched an extensive program that included the creation of model modern kitchen displays; radio programs; distribution of modern electric kitchen plan books . . ."[8]

The ongoing effort to standardize colors used in the kitchen resulted in the formation of the Color Standardization Committee in 1937 (under the U.S. Dept. of Commerce) and Lifshey notes that "Six standard colors were adopted for kitchen accessories: White, Kitchen Green, Ivory, Delphinium Blue, Royal Blue and Red."[9]

The kitchen of the 1930s was the darling of the middle-class home. While it remained essentially a workroom, the kitchen now received as much thought and consideration as any other room in the house. During this period kitchen design and decoration were at the forefront of numerous feature articles in leading magazines. For example, the March 1936 *Home Arts* magazine included a piece, "Color Keeps Your Home Youthful." It told readers " . . . color can also work wonders in the more utilitarian parts of the house, such as the kitchen . . . How does a kitchen appeal to you that has a red painted ceiling to match a cheerful, cherry-red linoleum floor! The walls and the equipment are white, with touches of red in the utensils, and in the interior of the drawers and the cabinets, in the linens, and with red and white plaid gingham curtains."[10]

By 1940, designing modern kitchen work areas in an L or U shape was common. This scheme, combined with standardized built-ins and appliances, has remained the basis for our state-of-the-art kitchens of today.

The Role of the Housewife

It is the personality of the mistress that the home expresses. Men are forever guests in our homes, no matter how much happiness they may find there.

The House in Good Taste
—Elsie De Wolfe, 1920

The term "housewife" began appearing in popular magazines during the 1920s. Rather than referring to women as "housekeepers," the use of the word "housewife" reflected changing attitudes about women's role in the home. New emphasis was being placed on the relationship between husband and wife and more specifically, the wife's role as a "mate." Sheila Rothman writes in *Woman's Proper Place* that "Just as the concept of virtuous womanhood in the post Civil War decades gave way to ideas on educated motherhood in the Progressive era, so in turn did the idea of educated motherhood give way in the 1920s to a view of woman as wife-companion . . . The primary relationship in a woman's life was no longer to be with her children but with her husband; a highly affective and emotive tie between them was now at the core of family life."[11]

During this period advice for women was devoted to keeping romance in the marriage, maintaining youthful beauty and cultivating interests and social contacts that would allow them to entertain their husbands with interesting conversation when they returned home after a hard day at work. This change in how the role of the wife was perceived did not happen overnight but became increasingly important during the late 1920s and on into the 1930s. Magazines reflected this new focus on the "wife" as they printed more and more advertisements for beauty products and devoted space to feature articles about marriage, romantic love, beauty treatments and so on.

While the middle-class housewife was working toward being an acceptable marriage partner, she was also still in charge of the home. Her list of household chores included daily work such as cooking the meals, making the beds, cleaning the bathroom and doing the dishes. She also had weekly tasks to attend to such as the mending, laundry and ironing as well as seasonal or occasional jobs such as heavy cleaning, washing curtains, organizing closets and so on. Women were advised to prepare a schedule or routine that would suit their family and life-style, and whether or not they employed outside help was a factor to be considered. In order to be interesting and entertaining, the housewife was encouraged to have planned activities out in the world such as club membership, church activities, shopping or visiting with friends. It was also wise to plan time during the day to read the newspaper or latest issue of a magazine. In this way she'd be informed and capable of conversing about daily events.[12]

The previous paragraph mentions that the household schedule was influenced by whether or not "household helpers" were employed. During the 1920s and 1930s live-in servants were rarely found in middle-class homes. If there was help at all, it was generally someone hired on a part-time basis to come in certain days of the week for laundry work or heavy cleaning. The modern down-sized kitchen with planned work areas and electric appliances did away with the need for servants.

The "science of housewifery," or the "scientific" methods, applied to cooking and household chores during the early 1900s had given way to more modern business-like methods during the 1920s and 1930s. For

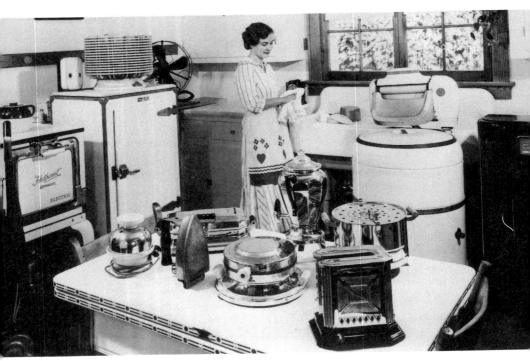

This circa 1920 kitchen displays the wide variety of GE electric appliances available during this period, including stove, refrigerator, washing machine, toaster, waffle iron, coffee pot, sandwich broiler, iron and electric sweeper.

Courtesy GE Appliance Archives.

example, in regard to how housework should be approached, Mary Lockwood Matthews remarked, "It has become an accepted fact to-day that every housekeeper should be as efficient in managing her household as is the man who is managing a big business."[13] In other words, the factory manager would never consider trying to run the business without a planned work schedule. The housewife was to follow this example to achieve success in running her home.

Magazines routinely included articles on the popular business-like methods being put to use in the home. One such piece, entitled "Be a Businesslike Housekeeper," appeared in the May 1925 issue of *The Delineator*. Author Helen Tolman examined the benefits of thorough record keeping in the home and told readers,

> Fortunate is the homemaker who is not satisfied with mere routine, but who is fired with that spark of imagination which gives purpose to her humdrum work and lures her on to delightful experiments in better management . . . records and memos will save you steps as well as worry and will surely improve your system of managing your household. Good records save time and strength and prevent misunderstanding . . . Simple and well-planned records can be divided into three kinds. First, there are memos, or reminders, which will save time . . . and will help produce that orderliness which is not only "the beauty of the house" but balm to the spirit of the dwellers therein. Then there are both temporary and permanent records which serve as guides for the housekeeper who decides to really study the enterprise which she is managing and to play a good and winning game. And lastly there are the records of human interest which form an intimate chronical of family relationships and an interesting story of individual development . . . In home management, as in industry, the manager who is successful both in a business way and in human relationships is generally the one who looks upon her work as a game, and not as a series of unpleasant tasks to be disposed of with the greatest haste possible.[14]

The industrialized household of the modern age, with its compact and colorful kitchen, was host to an increasing number of electric appliances, brandname packaged foods and household products. In order to promote sales, advertisers targeted the middle-class housewife, offered installment plans to make large purchases and sought the endorsement of noted home economists to increase the appeal of their products. The 1920s was a period of active consumerism that ultimately advanced the "de-skilling" of several household tasks or arts such as home canning, cooking from scratch, sewing etc. In her book *Just a*

Housewife, author Glenna Matthews tells us "The 19th century had seen the development of a cultural ideal of 'notable' housewifery whose main properties were skill and frugality. The 1920s version of the good housewife as set forth by the women's magazines had a much more passive quality. Frugality was passé, and skill involved listening to the right experts."[15]

Women did listen to experts during the 1920s and 1930s and were told everything from what products to use to avoid dishpan hands (Ivory Soap) to what breakfast cereal would steady the nerves of a grouchy husband (Postum). Other advertisements told them how to be proud of their laundry (Fels-Naphha Soap), safeguard their husband's health (Post's Bran Flakes), afford a complete house cleaning servant (Hoover vacuum), get rid of gray hair (Mary Goldman's Hair Color Restorer) and how to be a social success (by using Odorono—the underarm toilette). Written in a simple style and language women could relate to, numerous advertisements encouraged women to buy specific personal and household products. More importantly, they encouraged women to become full-fledged consumers. It's therefore not surprising that those years before the Great Depression were an era of massive consumption.

The "drudgery" associated with the circa 1900 kitchen was replaced by "monotony" in the industrialized kitchen of the 1920s and 1930s. While many middle-class women were proud of their modern appliances and colorful workroom, they were still plagued by the boredom that can accompany mindless, repetitive tasks. To deal with this they were advised that scheduling their daily, weekly and occasional chores for peak efficiency would leave more time for enjoyable interests.

Modern bathrooms with indoor plumbing eliminated much of the "chamber work" performed through the early 1900s, but bedrooms still required a daily "airing" and a careful cleaning was done once a week.

In the bathroom a daily ritual of dusting the floor and cleaning the toilet, sink and soap dish was recommended. Weekly washing of bathroom walls was common practice.

In the kitchen, dishes were washed after each meal and the sink rinsed. The worktable was cleaned after each use. If a coal- or wood-burning stove was in the kitchen, ashes had to be removed daily.

Weekly cleaning in the kitchen included washing the floor, windows and curtains, dusting/polishing furniture, cleaning the walls and cupboards.

The other rooms in the house were dusted and vacuumed weekly and the furniture was polished.

The typical middle-class housewife no longer had to keep a stash of homemade cleaning supplies on hand. Everything from disinfectants to soap and furniture polish could be store-bought.

The 1920s and 1930s brought marked change in the way laundry work was done. A laundry room on the first floor, separate from the kitchen was still preferred, or an area of the basement was used to do the wash. Stationary tubs of porcelain, enameled iron or soapstone were found in most houses, doing away with the need for old-fashioned wooden washtubs. Modern washing machines were widely accepted and were powered by electricity, water power or gasoline motors. Different "types" of washers, unfamiliar to us today, were in use in the majority of middle-class homes. Made of either wood or metal, "Dolly" washers had devices with fingers that revolved in the center of the machine, drawing the clothing up through the fingers to remove dirt. Friction washers operated by rubbing clothes between disks or boards. Cylinder washers involved placing the laundry in a small perforated tub that was then placed into a larger cylinder or tub and the two revolved in opposite directions, forcing the water through the laundry. Suction machines included metal cones with levers to press the cones down onto the wash, which then created a suction action. Lastly, oscillating washers rocked from side to side, tossing the wash back and forth to release the dirt. Whatever type of washer a woman chose, the washing machine had

In an ongoing effort to bring convenience to the kitchen as well as the laundry room, Maytag offered a butter churn attachment that could be used with their aluminum gas or electric washing machines that featured a "high center post Gyrator."

Courtesy Maytag Corporation.

achieved status as a household necessity. While women still soaked the laundry (which often meant boiling it) to remove stains, in most cases the washing machine did away with the old-fashioned laboring over a washtub with a tin or glass board for hours on end.

For ironing, sadirons heated atop the stove were considered a bother and most households preferred a new electric or gas iron that didn't require trips back and forth to the kitchen range. The amount of laundry to be ironed, however, had not lessened from earlier years as the use of household linen (especially napkins, tablecloths, doilies) remained in vogue. It took great effort and skill to iron them properly and since most middle-class housewives prized their linen, they often spent hours caring for it.

While some home economists proclaimed that cleaner household appliances combined with careful weekly cleaning eliminated the need for a large, seasonal "spring cleaning" campaign, others advised that seasonal (spring and fall) cleanings were needed to remove all the dirt from the home. For example, in the October 1939 issue of *Woman's Home Companion,* an article entitled "Campaign for a Clean House" offered detailed instructions for seasonal cleaning. Author Lynn-Ray Hunter told readers, "Before the campaign starts I plan the work as nearly as possible according to days—subject of course to interruptions such as bad weather or unexpected company . . . I then make a list of supplies I shall need . . . My cleaning tools are checked over to be sure they are in good order; the vacuum cleaner is cleaned, examined and serviced if necessary . . . In laying out my program I stick to one invaluable rule. Jobs that require the same tools and cleaners are done as far as practicable when the equipment is first taken out; this is the greatest labor-saving I know in house-cleaning."[16] Hunter then went on to offer readers a step-by-step program for cleaning the house top to bottom. She told women to start upstairs, in the bedrooms, where dresser drawers and closets were to be emptied and the contents sorted, walls and woodwork washed, carpets vacuumed, curtains cleaned and hung, furniture polished and so on. A similar cleaning was then done in each room downstairs. In the kitchen the author advised, "Empty cupboards, clean; wash dishes and replace. Wash kitchen walls, woodwork. Clean light fixtures, wash windows. Clean range and refrigerator thoroughly . . . wash kitchen furniture. Wax woodwork. Clean linoleum and apply self-polishing wax. Hang curtains. Clean down the basement stairs. Clean brushes, clothes, sponges; return to proper places. Store all cleaning material."[17]

Being a middle-class housewife during the 1920s and 1930s was considered a profession (according to home economists) and as such a woman was to prepare for this role by obtaining a college education if possible. In this way she'd be better suited to carry out her role as both "housekeeper" (maintaining the house, caring for children, cooking etc.—the physical aspects) and "homemaker" (creating a happy home, raising children, serving as her husband's companion, becoming involved in civic, church and school affairs—the spiritual component). This concept of the middle-class woman as "housewife" would continue on into the next two decades but was briefly interrupted by World War II.

Modern Cooking

To plan a perfect menu requires much more thought today than it did when the ideal company meal was an array of as many and as rich dishes as one could afford. The modern hostess knows that the simplest meal may be a perfect one if it is planned with care and served attractively.

The Boston Cooking-School Cook Book
—Fannie Merritt Farmer, 1933 edition

By the 1920s and especially during the 1930s, the combined efforts of cooking schools, scientists and home economists (not to mention food manufacturers) had elevated cooking to a scientific process. In addition, the introduction of new kitchen equipment and modern appliances changed the way in which cooking was performed. Modern cookery was an area in which the middle-class housewife received a great deal of advice, not only in how to cook but how to use her new kitchen equipment. The Preface to the 1933 edition of The Boston Cooking-School Cook Book told readers, "Of recent years new vegetables, new fruits, and new salad greens have come into use, as well as new ways of preparing the ones formerly known. New equipment, such as mechanical refrigeration, pressure cookers, and the like, have suggested changes in method . . . Although the general character of the work remains the same, a certain amount of rearrangement has been necessary."[18]

The scientific study of food had revealed new information regarding proteins, carbohydrates, vitamins, fats, oils and minerals. Housewives were to have a basic understanding of food composition in order to serve their families meals that would promote good health. As a result, cookbooks published during this period devoted a number of pages to food values. There was also limited information available regarding calories.

In carrying out the actual cooking process women were told successful cooking would be determined by their ability to measure ingredients, properly combine ingredients and then decide upon the appropriate method of cooking. That of course would influence the length of time the food was to bake, broil, boil etc.[19] Gone were the days of trial and error in measuring and mixing, and women no longer had to rely on guesswork to determine the heat of the stove.

To measure ingredients, the measuring cup and a set of measuring spoons had become standard kitchen equipment.

To combine ingredients, women were instructed in the difference between stirring (using a circular motion), beating (repeatedly turning ingredients over and over in the bowl), and cutting and folding (a two-step process used to add one ingredient to another).

Middle-class housewives were familiar with baking, boiling, frying and broiling foods, either through instruction received at home while growing up or from school-based "domestic science" classes. During the 1920s, however, they were also being encouraged to study new cooking methods such as how to fricassee (frying meat to be served with a sauce), sauté (frying with a very small amount of fat), and steam (especially beneficial in preparing vegetables).

Cookbooks and magazines provided a great deal of information on modern cooking but perhaps equally important were the numerous recipe booklets distributed free of charge by many manufacturers. These advertising giveaways instructed housewives on how to operate everthing from mixers and blenders to refrigerators and electric stoves, and gave them a variety of recipes to try as well. For example, *The Silent Hostess Treasure Book*, published by General Electric Company in 1932, offered instructions on the care and use of the new GE refrigerator while at the same time offering recipes and advice on how use of the electric refrigerator could actually be a time-saver in the kitchen. The Foreword told readers, "Not only can it [the GE refrigerator] save the housewife time and energy, but it can actually work for her. With a little planning on her part it can take an active part in the preparation and serving of her meals. This new and latest contribution to efficient homemaking has untold possibilities for the housewife."[20] This GE recipe booklet went on to explain that the refrigerator would safely protect perishables, save trips to the market, allow the housewife to prepare meals in advance, keep leftovers for another meal and help prepare affordable frozen desserts.

Changing life-styles during the 1920s and 1930s influenced what women cooked and continued scientific advances determined the manner in which they cooked it. Armed with the latest advice housewives made every attempt to prepare well-balanced meals and the increased availability of packaged goods added welcome convenience to cooking. Along with canned and boxed goods, the introduction of limited frozen foods added even more variety to meal planning. Thanks to Clarence Birdseye, by the late 1920s a successful method for fast-freezing foods had been developed that would have far-reaching effects on American cookery.

In regard to meal planning, breakfast, luncheon and dinner were the meals of the day, with the exception of Sunday, when "dinner" was served midday, followed by "supper" for the evening meal. Sample menus from *Good Housekeeping's Book of Menus, Recipes, and Household Discoveries* illustrates this. The editors suggested a year-long list of daily menus and for the first Sunday in the month of June they offered the following:

Breakfast— Raspberries, Fish Cakes, Catchup, Corn Bread, Coffee.
Dinner— Jellied Chicken, Baked Potatoes, Buttered Green Peas, Radishes, Olives, Banana Sherbet, Cookies, Coffee.
Supper— Cheese & Pimiento Sandwiches, Sponge Cake with Raspberry Meringue, Iced Chocolate.[21]

For a Monday in June the recommended menu was:

Breakfast— Strawberries, Ready-to-eat Cereal, Cream, Baked Eggs, Bacon Muffins, Coffee.
Luncheon— Grilled Sardines, Asparagus on Toast, Butter Sauce, Sliced Bananas, Cakes, Iced Tea.
Dinner— Baked Ham, Mashed Potatoes, Sauteed Tomatoes, Spinach, Apricot Jelly, Wafers.[22]

Entertaining in the form of the afternoon tea, card party, club or church dinner, luncheon and buffet supper became popular as women were encouraged to become involved in social and community affairs. Preparing hors d'oeuvres as an appetizer for a luncheon or dinner was fashionable and cookbooks published during the 1920s and 1930s often included menus for "French" luncheons and dinners. For example, the revised and updated 1933 edition of *The Boston Cooking-School Cook Book* (the most popular American cookbook during the early twentieth century) offered menus for various social gatherings. For an afternoon tea, "Fannie Farmer's" suggested the hostess might serve "Toasted Mushroom Sandwiches, Chocolate Walnut Wafers and Tea," or perhaps "Watercress Sandwiches, Cherry Tartlets and Tea." Card party refreshments might include "Shrimps a la Newburg, Melba Toast, Sweet Crab Apple Pickle and Coffee," or "Welsh Rarebit, Porcupine Salad and

Coffee." For a club or church dinner women might consider preparing "Scalloped Ham and Eggs, Cabbage and Pineapple Salad, Golden Corn Cake, Chocolate Bread Pudding with Whipped Cream and Coffee," and for a buffet supper, "Molded Salmon with Cucumber Sauce, Chicken à la King, Asparagus en Vinaigrette, Salad Rolls, Olives and Radishes, Coffee, Strawberries and Cream, Chocolate Mint Mold and Cream Sponge Cake." Regarding the buffet, readers were told "Consider color and balance in arranging the table. The guests may serve themselves, or the men may serve the women, or a maid may pass coffee, rolls, and relishes."[23]

While housewives were being instructed in the new "science" of cooking and dabbling in then-popular French cuisine, a new cookbook published during the 1930s was written to show women that creating culinary delights could also be an enjoyable experience. *The Joy of Cooking* remains (after numerous printings and revisions) a popular cookbook today. Author Irma S. Rombauer first wrote this book based on her own accumulation of favorite family recipes. Initially her work was privately printed, but in 1936 the book attracted the interest of a large publisher. Women were encouraged via Rombauer's work to find the "joy" in cooking and this reader-friendly recipe book became a best-seller. The enormous success of *The Joy of Cooking* paved the way for the numerous cookbooks and specialty magazines that would be published in the coming decades. These in turn opened the door to a growing interest in international cooking, vegetarian cooking, gourmet cooking and the low-fat cooking that is in vogue today.

Notable Changes: The Modern Electric Kitchen

> . . . electricity . . . a mystical arena of electron movement that has given to millions relief from performing what once were routine household chores. Those which it hasn't eliminated, it's made easier. It's added to the quality of life, freeing us from daily tasks, increasing our leisure time—for better or worse.
>
> *Electrical Collectibles*
> —Don Fredgant, 1981

While the first two decades of the twentieth century saw the introduction of small electric appliances such as irons, toasters, waffle irons, coffee percolators, mixers and carpet sweepers, the period 1920–1939 brought an increased number of electric appliances to the modern American kitchen.

Problems surrounding standardization of electric power continued and in many rural areas electricity was not yet available; however, the success of, and demand for, early electric appliances (and the convenience associated with having an "electrified" home) encouraged power companies and manufacturers to work towards generation standards.

Electric appliances used in the modern kitchen and laundry were designed for cooking, food preservation and laundry work. The most significant development during the 1920s was the introduction of the electric refrigerator. Early attempts at refrigeration were made between 1916 and 1920, such as the Guardian refrigerator, which was manufactured for a short time in Detroit, but it wasn't until General Motors turned out a steel cabinet Frigidaire in 1926 that refigerators began to attract a great deal of attention.

A circa 1927 advertisement introducing the GE Monitor-Top Refrigerator. This box-like steel cabinet on gracefully curved legs was the first hermetically sealed refrigerator and sales were so impressive that GE claimed a significant share of the domestic market during the first year of production.

Courtesy Friday Historical Business Archives.

Others were also manufacturing electric refrigerators (Philco, Westinghouse and Admiral) and when General Electric debuted its GE Monitor Top model in 1927 it became quite a success. The Monitor Top was the first hermetically sealed refrigerator and consisted of a box-like steel cabinet on tall curved legs with the compressor located on top of the unit. This refrigerator was so popular that GE could claim 7 percent of the domestic refrigerator market during its first year of production.[24]

In their book *A Walk Through the Park* (which explores the history of GE appliances and Appliance Park), authors Franklin Friday and Ronald White, Ph.D., note that "Where none existed ten years earlier, by 1928 there were . . . one-and-a-quarter million refrigerators in the nation's households. The number of electrically wired homes rose in the same decade from seven to 19 million . . ."[25]

By 1929 General Electric was marketing a refrigerator with a freezer space and vegetable compartment and in 1933 adjustable shelving became available. The late 1930s saw the "squared" style give way to

refrigerators with rounded corners, reflecting a more modern design, and other manufacturers followed suit.

A 1936 General Electric advertisement that appeared in several magazines reported "The new General Electric models offer all the latest convenience features: handy temperature, control and defrosting switch, sliding shelves, automatic interior lighting, foot-pedal door opener, quick releasing ice trays, stainless-steel super-freezer, vegetable compartment, and stainless porcelain interiors with rounded corners."

This 1939 General Electric refrigerator sports modern rounded corners. The tall legs found on early models have disappeared and the refrigerator now includes increased storage space.

Courtesy GE Appliance Archives.

Gas cooking ranges dominated the home market during the period 1920–1939 but electric models were growing in popularity. Just as Victorian women had been skeptical of cooking on a gas stove, the modern housewife was concerned about the capabilities of an electric range. Early examples failed to heat as quickly as the gas stove and heating elements had to be replaced quite often since they had a tendency to "burn out."

Electric ranges available during the early 1920s were similar in style to gas models, with tall curved legs and a box-like oven compartment that rose above the range-top burners. This styling gave the appliance a two-tiered look.

Ranges (regardless of whether they were gas or electric) were generally available in black or gray until Hotpoint introduced their white porcelain-enamel range in 1923. This white range was welcome relief from dreary, dark colors and by 1927 when color in the kitchen was becoming very fashionable, Westinghouse and then other manufacturers began offering electric ranges in a variety of colors.

The most noteworthy improvement to the electric range came in the late 1920s when Calrod heating elements were being used by Hotpoint.

This new heating element was a major improvement over the bare wires or wires encased in porcelain brick that had been in use up until that time. Additional improvements in the electric range brought about the style changes to cabinet models in 1934 that were more in keeping with the streamlined kitchen. The tall legs disappeared and the range top was level, designed to fit alongside built-in cupboards with a continuous countertop. This design became the standard in the appliance industry for both gas and electric ranges and even though gas ranges continued to outsell electric models through the 1940s, the gap had narrowed considerably.

Smaller electric kitchen appliances achieved status as necessities in the servantless, modern kitchen. According to Don Fredgant, author of the book *Electrical Collectibles*, "The small kitchen appliance field was America's most active growth industry during 1890–1930. Companies large and small competed for a share of the consumer's dollar, particularly after about 1915."[26]

This early 1930s GE Hotpoint electric stove includes Calrod long-lasting heating elements on the stove top. The oven compartment rises above the stove top in a two-tiered affect and this unit includes an automatic timer, light and range top "set" with clock and salt and pepper shakers.

Courtesy GE Appliance Archives.

Streamling the kitchen and standardizing furnishings and appliances resulted in cabinet model stoves being introduced during the 1930s. This mid-1930s Hotpoint Electric Range featured a level cooktop that was designed to fit flush with built-in cabinets having a continuous countertop.

Courtesy GE Appliance Archives.

AUTOMATIC TOASTERS =

The new 1940
TOASTMASTER
1 slice toaster

= BY TOASTMASTER

NEW beauty for the breakfast table! Two sparkling creations, just released by *Toastmaster*. But— here is beauty that is *more* than chromium-deep! It's *toast-deep.* These automatic pop-up type toasters time the toasting exactly to your taste and pop up the piping-hot slices the instant they're done. No watching, no turning, no burning.

Woman's Home Companion   October 1939

For heavy toast-traffic, choose the two-slice model, $16. For the smaller family, the speedy one-slice is perfect, at $9.95, a new low price. See them both and other *Toastmaster** products ($7.50 to $23.95) wherever fine appliances are sold.

*"TOASTMASTER" is a registered trademark of MCGRAW ELECTRIC COMPANY, Toastmaster Products Division, Elgin, Ill. Copyright 1939, McGraw Electric Co.

Toasters such as this Toastmaster began featuring rounded shapes and chrome-etched designs during the 1930s. Available in one-slice or two-slice models, these latest toasters offered "pop up" convenience, which meant no more "watching, turning or burning."

Toasters underwent continual change and improvement during the 1920s and 1930s and even though the "pincher" type toaster remained popular during the 1920s (bread was held in place by a spring-operated frame), "swing-basket" toasters became available. The "swing-basket" type, first produced by the Manning Bowman Company, had actual bread slots that would swing out to the side and around in order to turn the toast.

An automatic pop-up toaster was developed by the Waters-Genter Company in the early 1920s and after being purchased by the McGraw Electric Company the toaster was marketed under the trade name Toastmaster. A two-slice Toastmaster model was introduced by 1934 and in 1936 the Sunbeam Silent Automatic Toaster, which operated without ticking and had a thermostatic control, could be purchased for $10.95.

While early toasters were almost elegant in design, with subtle decorative touches and soft embellishments such as carved designs, the toasters being manufactured during the 1930s began to reflect the modern age. They sported rounded shapes and their chrome sides were often etched with geometric designs.

The electric coffee percolator remained an important household necessity during the 1920s and 1930s. The practice of selling this small appliance as part of a "breakfast set" (which also included a sugar bowl, creamer and optional waffle iron) continued through the 1920s. In addition, the glass vacuum-drip coffee maker, such as that produced by Silex, proved very successful in the home market throughout the 1930s.

The crude early electric mixers in use during the early 1900s gave way to large, all-purpose mixers in the 1930s. Advertisements encouraged the housewife that this was one appliance she could not do without and when Sunbeam's Mixmaster was introduced in 1930 it was promoted as the appliance of the decade. In *The Housewares Story* author Earl Lifshey tells us "This was a mixer mounted on a heavy cast metal base, equipped with a juicer attachment and two stainless steel mixing bowls for which there was a ball-bearing turntable. While it was not the first mixer with a substantial cast rather than a stamped or wire base, it was the first to be offered under $20.00 . . . The first year, according to Sunbeam, sixty thousand units were sold. By 1936 'Mixmaster' sales reached to more than three hundred thousand units."[27]

The Mixmaster was available with optional attachments, such as a meat grinder, potato peeler and juice extractor. In 1939 a new and improved model with a speed setting was being sold and the line of possible attachments expanded to include a bean slicer, pea sheller, can opener, coffee grinder, drink mixer and knife sharpener.

The darling of the modern kitchen, the Sunbeam Mixmaster was down-sized during the 1930s for convenient handling. By 1939 when this advertisement was published, there were over ten attachments that could be added to the Mixmaster for greater convenience in the kitchen.

This circa 1920s aluminum washer by Maytag featured Gyrafoam action—an agitator that forced water through the clothing rather than pulling clothes through the water. This concept was so gentle on the wash that by the mid-1920s one out five washers in homes across America was a Maytag.

Courtesy Maytag Corporation.

Other small kitchen appliances introduced during this twenty-year period included electric juicers, tabletop broilers, blenders and electric fry pans.

Electric appliances were equally important in household cleaning and laundry work. As increasing numbers of homes had access to electric power, sadirons and irons fueled with gasoline or kerosene were quickly replaced by the electric iron.

Temperature-control irons were being produced by the early 1930s. For example, Proctor Electrical Appliances was selling an Automatic Heat-Adjusting Speed Iron with a dial that offered settings for a variety of fabrics. These irons were still quite heavy and tended to be very large in size. It wasn't until the 1940s that the electric iron was downsized to the trim, sleek design we're familiar with today.

By the early 1920s wooden and wood/steel washing machines were being replaced by all-metal models. Maytag found their aluminum washer to be a huge success and in 1922 the company introduced their Gyrafoam washer, which had an agitator that gently cleaned clothing by forcing water through the clothes instead of pulling the clothing through the water. This feature which eliminated the possibility of damage to clothing, combined with the all-aluminum machine, proved to be so popular that by 1924 one out of five American washers was made by Maytag.[28]

Savvy marketing during the 1920s saw Maytag loaning washers to domestic science departments in those schools across the country that had a student body of at least three hundred pupils. In addition, Maytag produced advertising materials in foreign languages such as French, German and Italian to reach the large immigrant population in the United States.

In 1931 Maytag introduced a washer with a porcelain enamel tub and by 1939 the Master Washer with a larger load capacity was introduced and became available in the white finish that was becoming standard on large appliances.

The 1940s would bring the design change that saw the tub washer on legs shift to the box-like automatic washer we know today.

Electric vacuum cleaners were early on considered a significant improvement in maintaining a sanitary home (far better than "sweeping" or "beating" carpets to remove dirt and dust), and improvements made in the vacuum during the early 1900s brought several models to market during the 1920s and 1930s. Swedish Electrolux vacuums were being produced in the United States by 1924 and several major manu-

Here is high-powered cleaning help FREE

—a Grand Prize Eureka for your use during spring housecleaning

Great Eureka National Educational Offer

Let there be no hesitation or delay in your acceptance of this wonderful special offer of FREE cleaning help.

Old ways of cleaning house were good enough as long as better methods were unknown, but the woman who clings to them today is but dooming herself to cruel and unnecessary hardship.

It is so very easy to obtain the matchless help of the Grand Prize Eureka. Simply telephone the Eureka dealer near you—or, if you do not know his name, sign and mail the coupon below. The Eureka will be delivered to your door and called for after you have finished housecleaning.

This generous offer is made—for a limited time only—as a feature of the great Eureka National Educational Campaign. We want women everywhere to learn what more than a million Eureka users already know—the amazing ease, speed and thoroughness with which the high-powered Eureka performs so vast a variety of cleaning tasks, and the superiority that has made this Grand Prize Cleaner the repeated first choice of world authorities in so many lands.

Should you decide that you want to keep the Eureka, a special low $4.75 down payment and very easy terms are also available for the duration of this offer. But remember that Eureka's housecleaning help is FREE—that you are placed under no obligation in accepting it.

Remember, too, that this great offer holds good for a short time only. Accept it quickly so that you may be sure to have the Eureka when you need it.

$4.75 down

This 1925 advertisement for the Eureka Vacuum Cleaner offered women the opportunity to try the appliance in their home, free of charge, to experience how easy it would make their housecleaning. If satisfied with the results, a $4.75 down payment would allow them to keep the machine and pay the balance on easy terms. This sales approach was most likely successful as the vacuum had achieved status as a necessary household tool.

facturers such as Hotpoint, Regina Corporation, Westinghouse and Sunbeam were turning out home vacuums as well.

An article entitled "Your Household Gods" appeared in the May 1936 issue of *Good Housekeeping* magazine and seemed to explain the importance of the electric vacuum. Author Katharine Fisher noted "Those of us who in earlier years took care of our homes without benefit of carpet sweeper or vacuum cleaner have thankfully emerged from the clouds of dust of the past and made a profound bow to our mechanical maids. No more shaking of small scatter rugs out the window; it's not good for the rugs, and it's bad for passers-by who breath the dust. No more beating of carpets and rugs in the back yard during those long-gone annual upheavals called spring cleaning. Cleaning has become scrubless and dustless and nearly effortless."[29]

Other electric appliances for use in cleaning were introduced, such as the floor polisher and dishwasher, but were slow to catch on since they were considered luxury items at that time rather than necessities or great conveniences.

The modern electrified kitchen that began to emerge in the 1920s was the focus of architects, builders and home economists during the 1930s. Suddenly families were proud of their colorful, conveniently arranged modern kitchens, and the addition of each new electric appliance to the household was a measure of success as well as a status symbol. Just as the Victorians considered their parlor a reflection of their social standing, the modern decades saw the kitchen assume this role. Perhaps Josephine Wylie's 1930 article said it best when she wrote: "One cannot help but think that house-builders of past ages held a particular grudge against the kitchen, because they made it so unlovely. They tacked it to the rear of the house, having it appear just barely to belong, as if it were something for the house to be ashamed of . . . To those who remember the oldtime kitchens more favorably, sentimental recollections add charm—the heavenly smells that came from there on baking days . . . the big room that was spacious enough for everyone without crowding. While we regret the passing of some of these good things we used to enjoy in old kitchens, I suspect that few men and women today would want to trade their colorful kitchens, with handy little breakfast corners and all of the other conveniences, for those places that they remember with such sentimental recollec-tions. And many men these days are as proud of having a tile-surface table and an electric refrigerator as are their wives. We have come a long way in our attitude toward the importance of the furnishings of the kitchen."[30]

Modern Household Hints and Recipes

❦HOUSEHOLD HINTS❦

. . . If you were to ask me how to give a "professional touch" to your every-day desserts, I should tell you not to bother preparing elaborate dishes at all, but to go straight along with your gelatines and tapiocas, fruits, berries, puddings and pastries; looking to your sauces! Chances are, your desserts, excellent in themselves, are eloquently incomplete for want of an appropriate sauce to dress them up!

Hip-O-Lite Professional Recipes, circa 1920s

Beautiful floors are largely a matter of prevention—the great secret is to put them in perfect condition—and keep them that way. Doorways, passages and tracks become worn and unsightly first. You can keep these spots looking well by waxing them frequently—this requires but little time and effort . . . Waxed floors are not only beautiful and satisfactory, but they are economical, for they can be kept in perfect condition at very small expense.

The Proper Treatment for Floors, Woodwork and Furniture
—S.C. Johnson & Son, 1921

Linoleum floors, although most often used in kitchens, are finding their way into other parts of the house. The manufacturers themselves give sound advice about the care of such floor coverings. But this injunction should be in every house-keeper's mental-note book: Do not under any ordinary circumstances scrub linoleums or use strong soap, washing powders or other strong alkalies in cleaning them. Scrubbing and alkalies take the pattern off printed linoleum.

"Care of Floors," *The Delineator*
—Ruth Kellogg, May 1925

CARE IN USING ELECTRICITY

Now that electrical devices of all kinds are so constantly used, many women forget that certain precautions must be taken in their use. Never turn electricity on or off when you are standing on a wet or even damp floor. If you do so, the current is apt to pass through your body. This advice is particularly applicable to the kitchen, bathroom, and laundry where water is most likely to be spilled.

Good Housekeeping's Book of Menus, Recipes and Household Discoveries, 1926

ORDERING ICE BY POUNDS

It is often a great annoyance to the busy housewife to accomplish the necessary household tasks and still keep a watchful eye for the ice man's arrival in order to tell him the amount of ice desired. Eliminate this inconvenience in the following manner: cut out the figures, ten, fifteen, twenty, thirty, etc., from a large-typed calender, and when ice is needed, attach the necessary figure to the ice card with a clip.

Good Housekeeping's Book of Menus, Recipes and Household Discoveries, 1926

A kitchen is a place for the preparation of food; it should not be used as a laundry, a sitting room, or a dining room.

The House and Its Care
—Mary L. Matthews, 1931

At meal time one should be comfortable and happy. A happy state of mind is believed to help digestion. This means the conversation at the table should be pleasant. Such subjects as sickness and operations do not make suitable table talk. Sad or disgusting topics should be avoided. Choose pleasant subjects and wholesome stories that cause amusement and laughter.

Foods and Home Making
—Carlotta C. Greer, 1933

To judge the quality of a can before opening it sometimes is a difficult matter. The label gives you very little help. The brand or the name of the firm distributing the goods may appear on the label . . . certain brands or certain distributing firms are to be relied upon . . .The following terms are used to indicate the quality of canned goods: Extra Fancy—finest quality; Fancy—excellent quality; Choice or extra standard—not quite so good as fancy; Standard—good quality; Second or substandard—inferior to standard.

Foods and Home Making
—Carlotta C. Greer, 1933

TO DETERMINE THE FRESHNESS OF EGGS

Hold in front of candle flame in dark room, and the center should look clear. Place in basin of cold water, and they should sink. Place large end to the cheek, and a warmth should be felt. Rough shell.

The Boston Cooking-School Cook Book
—Fannie Merritt Farmer, 1993

Silver is apt to be marred when it is stored loosely in a drawer; and yet if wrapped in paper or in cloth cases, it is not so easily accessible. One good method is to have a special drawer for silver. Cotton flannel treated to prevent tarnish or dark outing flannel makes a good lining for the drawer and dividers. White or light-colored cloth or tissue paper is not desirable for use with silver because it may have been bleached with sulfur which tarnishes silver.

Kitchen Storage Space
—Clara E. Jonas, 1938

❧RECIPES❧

STEAMED BROWN BREAD

2 cupfuls of graham flour	1 tablespoonful of hot water
½ cupful of rye flour	½ cupful of cornmeal
½ cupful of seeded raisins	½ teaspoonful of salt
2 cupfuls of sweet milk	½ cupful of molasses

1 teaspoonful of soda

Mix together the graham flour, cornmeal, rye flour, salt and raisins. Place the molasses and milk in a separate bowl. Dissolve the soda in 1 tablespoonful of hot water, add to the molasses and milk and stir until the liquids are mixed. Add the flour mixture all at one time and stir until blended and smooth. Pour into 2 greased 1-pound coffee cans. Adjust the lids and steam 3 hours. This may be served hot at once . . . served cold, or rewarmed by steaming again for a few minutes.

Better Homes and Gardens, November 1930

BAKED PEARS

Drain the juice from canned pears, or raw ones pared and cored may be used. Arrange the halves in a baking dish. Sprinkle generously with brown sugar and a bit of cinnamon or nutmeg. Add only enough juice or water to cover the bottom. Bake in a moderate oven (350 degrees) until the water is absorbed, or if raw ones are used bake until they are tender. Chill and serve with thin custard sauce or whipped cream. A macaroon crumbled over each serving adds extra deliciousness.

Better Homes and Gardens, November 1930

CLAM JUICE COCKTAIL

3 cups clam liquor
1 stalk celery
1 teaspoon grated onion

Salt
2 tablespoons catsup
2 or 3 drops Tabasco sauce

Lemon juice

Add celery cut in pieces, onion and catsup to clam juice. Bring slowly to boiling point. Remove from fire and cool. Strain. Add Tabasco and lemon juice, salt and pepper to taste. Chill thoroughly in refrigerator and when ready to serve pour into orange juice glasses.

The Silent Hostess Treasure Book
—General Electric, 1932

STUFFED PEPPERS

6 firm green peppers
2 cups chopped cooked meat (veal, beef, ham, chicken)
½ cup bread crumbs (or leftover cooked rice)

½ cup stock
½ teaspoon salt
1 small onion, chopped
⅛ teaspoon pepper
Buttered bread crumbs

Wash peppers, cut a piece from the stem of each, and remove seeds. Parboil for five minutes. Stuff with a mixture of the meat, bread crumbs or rice, stock, and seasonings, and top with buttered crumbs. Place in baking dish, cover with waxed paper, and keep in refrigerator cabinet until about an hour before meal time. Pour stock or water around them to cover bottom of pan and bake in a moderate over (350° F.) for forty to forty-five minutes. Serve with tomato sauce if desired.

The Silent Hostess Treasure Book
—General Electric, 1932

PINEAPPLE AND CUCUMBER SALAD

2 tablespoons gelatin
1 cup shredded pineapple
¼ cup vinegar
1 cup boiling water
¼ cup cream, whipped
1 cup diced cucumber

½ teaspoon salt
¼ cup cold water
½ cup mayonnaise
Juice of ½ lemon
¼ cup sugar
Paprika

Soak gelatin in cold water five minutes, then dissolve in boiling water. Add sugar, salt, vinegar and lemon juice. Let cool. When mixture begins to thicken stir in cucumber and pineapple and pour into molds. Chill thoroughly. Unmold on lettuce leaves and garnish with mayonnaise to which whipped cream has been added. Sprinkle with paprika.

The Silent Hostess Treasure Book
—General Electric, 1932

PARSLEY OR PERSILLADE POTATOES

1½ pounds of small new potatoes, boiled	Melted Butter
½ cup finely chopped parsley	Juice ½ lemon

Add lemon juice to butter and pour over potatoes. Roll potatoes in parsley.

The Boston Cooking-School Cook Book
—Fannie Merritt Farmer, 1933

MENU FOR A FRENCH LUNCHEON
(serve the Asparagus as a separate course)

Assorted Hors d'Oeuvres	Persillade Potatoes
Fillets of Sole, Marguery	Asparagus, Hollandaise

Crepes Suzette

The Boston Cooking-School Cook Book
—Fannie Merritt Farmer, 1933

STUFFED AVOCADOS

1 c. drained cooked or canned peas	¼ cup mayonnaise dressing
1 c. cooked sliced carrots	3 avocados
½ cup diced celery	Lettuce

French Dressing

Combine the peas, carrots, celery, and mayonnaise. Halve the avocados, remove the stones, and peel the avocados. Arrange the halves, one on each of six individual beds of lettuce. Place about 1 tsp. of French Dressing in each half and then fill each with some of the vegetable mixture. Serves 6. To serve 2 or 3 make half this mixture.

"The Chuckling Cooks Club," *Good Housekeeping*
—Alice Booth, May 1936

LUNCHEON SUGGESTION—WELSH ACCENT

Pour a thin Welsh rarebit—it comes canned to save you trouble—over heated green asparagus to serve with potato chips and cold meat. For a frivolous dessert make meringue cases filled with fresh jam. Tea for grown-ups, milk for children.

Woman's Home Companion, October 1939

6

The Kitchen As We Know It 1940–1990s

"MAN DOES NOT LIVE BY BREAD ALONE,
EVEN PRESLICED BREAD"

During the 1950s color in the kitchen shifted from bold, primary colors to the use of softer shades. This 1955 GE kitchen displays Mix-or-Match appliances, which were available in Petal Pink, Canary Yellow, Cadet Blue, Turquoise Green and Woodtone Brown. GE also offered Textolite countertops, which were compatible with their Mix-or-Match color program. Note this kitchen includes a built-in range top and oven and the whole room has a very "modern" look.

Courtesy GE Appliance Archives.

There is no single, universal kitchen lay-out which is right for everyone . . . The style of your kitchen is something only you can decide . . . The atmosphere . . . will come from the personal details and final touches you give to it . . .

conran's *Creative Home Design*
—Nonie Niesewand and David Stevens, 1986

*W*hile the typical 1940s kitchen may appear at first glance to be very different from the kitchen as we know it today, the concepts of planned space, storage areas, good lighting and work centers have remained constant throughout the second half of the twentieth century. Modern gas or electric appliances, built-in cupboards with a continuous countertop and the work triangle have been the basics of kitchen design for decades.

What has changed, and undoubtedly will continue to change, are the advancements in technology that lead to more efficient appliances and altering styles and trends in home decoration that impact on the kitchen. In addition, the concept of the kitchen as a workroom has been replaced by today's multipurpose kitchen, which is reminiscent of the Colonial-era hall or keeping room. Changing life-styles have brought about this revival in assigning several functions to one large area—as a matter of convenience and as a way for the family to spend time together in today's fast-pace world.

In looking back at the last fifty years, the modernization movement that was transforming the kitchens of the 1930s and early 1940s was temporarily put on hold during World War II as manufacturers turned their attention to the war effort. Production of various appliances and kitchen furnishings were halted but women were assured that refrigerators, stoves, kitchen cabinets (made of metal or wood) etc. would be available again as soon as the war was over. In the meantime, supplies were generally limited to those items turned out during pre-war production.

The typical new kitchen of the 1940s was a square room with a convenient L or U design in placement of the sink, stove and refrigerator. The kitchen sink was commonly placed underneath a window so the housewife would have the pleasure of an enjoyable view as she washed the dishes or prepared meals.

As the "breakfast nook" area began to disappear from many kitchen plans, the room was enlarged somewhat to accommodate a table and chairs in the center of the room or off to the side against a wall. In many homes this was the beginning of the end for the formal dining room. By the 1950s smaller middle-class homes were routinely being built without them.

The popular practice of turning out appliances and sinks in assorted colors during the 1920s and 1930s had given way to the manufacture of standardized appliances in a crisp white enamel finish. Color, however, still dominated in the kitchen and during the 1940s red and black were most stylish, often combined with accents in pink. Tablecloths, napkins and even curtains were made in bright colors (such as red, green, yellow and blue), and a checkerboard design or fruit motifs were in vogue on linens and accessories.

The six "standard colors" that had been adopted for use in the kitchen during the 1930s were forgotten after World War II and leading home magazines such as *House & Garden* began conducting consumer research each year to determine color trends in home furnishing. From this information manufacturers began turning out appliances and housewares in popular new colors.[1]

Linoleum was still the preferred choice for floor covering during the 1940s but modern designs, marbled patterns and solid colors replaced the outdated black-and-white-checkered design. Linoleum was also used as a countertop material.

Throughout the 1940s (but most noticeably after the war had ended), advertisements in national magazines showed families how they could modernize their kitchen a step at a time and as their budget would allow. An old-fashioned sink on legs could first be replaced with a modern built-in sink/cabinet unit and then additional cupboards and a countertop could be installed. The next step was to purchase the wall-hung cabinets followed by upgrading appliances. Those companies that produced kitchen cabinets and sinks (including the mail-order houses) were happy to provide free idea booklets and design service to help the middle-class American family realize the dream of a modern new kitchen. For example, a 1948 advertisement by the Kitchen Maid Corporation told readers, "Your new kitchen need not be cold and institutional. With Kitchen Maid cabinets of wood, it can be efficient, glamorous, yet warm and friendly too . . . Planned especially for you by experienced specialists, with appliances of your own choice. See your dealer or send for our new booklet." For 10¢ a homeowner could receive Kitchen Maid's booklet with ten different plans displayed in color.

During the late 1940s the idea of incorporating a kitchen island or L-shaped counter extension with stools became popular for serving breakfast, lunch and snacks. In addition, many cupboards began to include open corner shelves at the end of the unit that were ideal for displaying and storing small appliances.

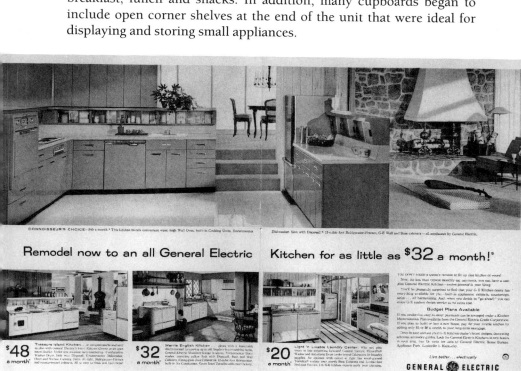

As home remodeling became popular this 1957 GE advertisement showed the public they could create a new kitchen in one of several "styles" with different budget-wise payment plans. Note the open living plan in the "Connoisseur's *Choice" kitchen in the top of the photo. General Electric offered everything needed to remodel the 1950s kitchen, including "Built-in appliances, cabinets, countertops, sinks . . . all harmonizing."*
Courtesy Friday Historical Business Archives.

Kitchen tables, chairs and stools were made of chrome-plated steel, and kitchen tables sported easy-to-clean enamel, linoleum or plastic tops. Companies such as Daystrom Corporation and Chromcraft Dinette Furniture were extremely successful in marketing these modern kitchen furnishings. Red and black were popular colors in the new dinette sets, as well as yellow and gray.

Kitchen appliances still appeared in the "streamlined" designs (with rounded corners) made popular during the 1930s but many were downsized to handle easily and to reduce the weight of the appliance.

New electric appliances appeared during the 1940s, including corn poppers, roasters, a combination clothes washer/dishwasher, garbage disposers (initially called disposers and then later disposals) and freezers for home use.

Electric ranges, offered in numerous models during the 1940s, often included utensil drawers, plate warmers, oven lights, fluorescent range-top lights, an oven timer and extra electrical outlets.

During the 1940s several new electric appliances were introduced, including the home freezer. This late 1940s model by Maytag offered an optional table *attachment that could be special ordered for added convenience in the kitchen.*

Courtesy Maytag Corporation.

The housing boom in the suburbs led to a greater demand for modern new appliances such as this circa 1949 Maytag Washer with the AMP—Automatic

Maytag Pump. Compact and easy to operate, this washing machine proved to be a best-seller.

Courtesy Maytag Corporation.

Refrigerators, a necessity in the middle-class household, began to include larger freezer compartments and some manufacturers offered two-door models with the freezer on top (such as the 1949 Frigidaire).

Small appliances became smaller and easier to handle. For example, the Sunbeam Mixmaster, the darling of the 1930s kitchen, was much smaller and more manageable during the 1940s. Attachments that could be purchased for the all-purpose Mixmaster included (in 1948) a food chopper, drink mixer, slicer/shredder, butter churn, can opener, bean slicer, ice-cream freezer, coffee grinder, knife sharpener, silver polisher, pea sheller and potato peeler.

Changes in cookware and kitchen accessories arrived during the 1940s with the introduction of copper-bottom stainless-steel pots and pans by Revere Ware, and enameled ware, tin and earthenware items (such as canisters) were replaced by plastic.

After World War II there was strong demand for modern kitchen furnishings as suburban developments were being constructed across the country. In their book *A Walk Through the Park,* Franklin Friday and Ronald F. White, Ph.D., note that in 1950 "Company strategists had made optimistic predictions for the . . . appliance industry based on four factors: the increase in population in the United States by two million per year, recent increases in the number of electrically wired homes, increased per-capita earnings and social changes which . . . would elevate the importance of electric appliances in everyday life."[2]

The 1950s were years of rapid development and improvement in housing and kitchen/laundry appliances. Many of the ranch or tract homes being built in suburban areas had reversed floor plans where the eat-in kitchen was located at the front of the house while the living room was in the back, with large picture windows looking out over the yard.

In the 1954 edition of *The Pocket Household Encyclopedia* by N.H. and S.K. Mager, the authors suggested, "Interesting kitchens may be created around a variety of motifs: Mexican, Early American, ranch type, French Provincial, peasant, Pennsylvania Dutch, etc. Color should be used on walls to offset the glare of white equipment. Walls may be covered with a washable covering—paper, fabric, plaster, plastic tile, linoleum, or washable wallpaper . . . Inlaid linoleum floors are generally considered best . . . Drapes or curtains should be bright, conceal or reveal according to the worthiness of the view . . . Modern designers plan kitchen utility rooms in which there is a kitchen and dining area, also a laundry and heater area which may include room for a home freezer . . . Kitchens do a lot of work in a little space."[3]

As new homes were being built in record numbers during the 1950s, the basic U- or L-shaped kitchen plans were most popular but alternate designs included the "Pullman" or "Two Wall" plan and the "Galley" or "One Wall" plan for smaller homes and apartments. Variations of the U and L plans included a "Broken U" and "Broken L" design and the "Individual Center" incorporated an island. The sink, stove area and countertop space comprised the three work centers so crucial to then-modern kitchen design.[4]

The 1950s saw the popularity of bright, primary colors give way to a demand for softer shades of pink, blue, turquoise and yellow. Once again manufacturers began to produce major appliances in an array of colors. At General Electric, not only were kitchen appliances turned out in color, but washers and dryers as well. (Although the electric dryer had been invented years earlier, it was the 1950s before it was successfully manufactured for the home market.)

Maytag Corporation introduced their first electric dryer in 1953 and by 1954 their Supermatics (an automatic electric washer and matching dryer) could be bought in pastel green, yellow or pink.

Continued improvements in laundry appliances saw Maytag introduce washers with a two-speed motor and a delicate cycle, cold water wash/rinse cycles, push-button operation and timed bleach dispensers.

Stoves manufactured during the 1950s included double ovens and high backsplashes with a finger-tip control panel. Old advertisements show that at General Electric the ranges developed during this decade were given appealing names such as "Stewardess" and "Airliner" that reflected America's love affair with airplane travel.

General Electric debuted their Spacemaker refrigerator in the 1950s, a unit with a surprising amount of storage capacity that took up relatively little space. By 1956 GE was selling a refrigerator with easy-open and shut

A modern 1950s GE kitchen with built-in dishwasher, electric range with extra-high backsplash area and a Spacemaker refrigerator. This kitchen *with state of-the-art appliances and built-in cupboards with a continuous countertop was a model of efficiency.* Courtesy GE Appliance Archives.

THE KITCHEN AS WE KNOW IT 1940–1990s   🍂 273

magnetic doors and in 1957 they turned out the first straight-line refrigerator—the rounded corners of the streamlined design were now gone.

Although readily available, dishwashers and garbage disposers had not yet caught on and were found in only a small number of homes.

Regarding smaller appliances, the steam iron was introduced during the 1950s along with the four-slice toaster and the electric can opener.

Plastic tableware, available during the 1950s in attractive colors with decal designs, became quite popular.

"Space-age" or state-of-the-art kitchens with built-in ovens and countertop ranges were being displayed by major appliance manufacturers at building and trade shows before the end of the 1950s.

During the 1960s appliances sported new colors such as copper, avocado and gold. Between 1965 and 1968 Maytag manufactured washers and dryers in these colors (their "California gold" washer and dryer pictured here). This new line of colors was introduced to complement the wood tones now commonly found in kitchen cabinetry.
Courtesy Maytag Corporation.

The 1960s and 1970s found architects designing homes with a variety of open floor plans where the kitchen was no longer isolated or considered a separate room. A harmonious, attractive kitchen became even more important when it could be viewed from other rooms in the house.

Metal, tile or linoleum countertops gave way to new plastic laminates and old linoleum flooring was replaced with new vinyl floor coverings or an all-purpose indoor/outdoor carpeting.

With the United States approaching its two-hundred-year anniversary, decorating the kitchen often focused around a "Colonial" theme or the relatively new "country" decorating theme.

While painted metal kitchen cabinets had been widely used during the 1940s and 1950s, the next two decades saw a shift to wood cabinets in a variety of stains or finishes. To complement the richness of these woodtones, "natural" colors such as sandalwood and avocado became popular on appliances. General Electric introduced their avocado kitchen appliances in 1966 and the following year "harvest gold" appeared.

In 1965 Maytag made washers and dryers available in coppertone, turquoise and sunshine yellow. The company introduced Spanish avocado in 1966 and "California gold" in 1968.

The 1970s brought about yet another change in coloring when major appliances were being manufactured in almond, wheat, onyx and, once again, white. The concept of the kitchen began to change as it was assigned multiple functions and the trend was to make it look more like a room with furnishings and accessories rather than a food preparation center. Now appliances were to blend into the background—not take center stage as the strong avocado and goldtone appliances had done.

Regarding kitchen appliances, the 1960s brought general acceptance of the garbage disposal located underneath the sink (as we're familiar with today) and the portable dishwasher became popular.

The "self-cleaning" oven was introduced during the early 1960s and in 1964 GE introduced its Americana range with a conventional oven as well as an electronic microwave oven.

Side-by-side refrigerator-freezers were being made in the 1960s and washers and dryers with large-load capacities and permanent-press cycles appeared.

The energy crisis of the 1970s brought new importance to the concept of "energy efficiency" and manufacturers focused on this aspect to improve kitchen, household and laundry appliances.

The countertop microwave was being sold during the early 1970s but it wasn't until the 1980s that one could be found in the majority of homes. The microwave is undoubtedly the most significant new development in terms of convenience and time-saving during these past fifty years.

Copper-bottom stainless-steel cookware was still quite popular but the 1960s and 1970s brought Teflon-coated cookware and colorful aluminum cookware with an acrylic coating into the kitchen. The Pyrex glass baking dishes introduced by Corning during the early 1900s expanded into Corning Ware, which could go directly from freezer to oven, by 1958, and in 1970 Corning introduced their Corelle Livingware line of dishware, which was breakage-resistant, affordable and looked like china. Once Corelle was available plastic tableware fell out of favor and was often packed away for the next garage sale.

With an increased use of plastics in making small appliances, they became lightweight (such as irons) and larger items such as stand mixers were replaced by more convenient hand-held models. The blender became popular for use in the kitchen during the 1960s and 1970s both for mixing drinks and cocktails and for preparing health food beverages.

It's interesting to note that several of the smaller gadgets once considered necessities in the old-fashioned kitchen were, by the 1960s and '70s thought to be optional items. With supermarkets full of every conceivable food product, Terence Conran notes in *The House Book* (which was published first in England and then in the U.S. in 1976) that items such as a preserving pan, fish kettle, pressure cooker, meat thermometer, ice-cream maker and oyster opener were now considered "useful luxuries."[5]

During the late 1970s the popularity of "Colonial" or "Early American" decorating evolved into "Country" style. Due in part to a renewed awareness of our American heritage (inspired by the 1976 bicentennial celebrations), a growing interest in folk art and crafts and alternate life-styles, "Country" proved to be an ideal style for the relaxed, all-purpose kitchens that were coming into vogue.

By the 1980s, lavish attention was being showered on many middle-class homes and especially the kitchen. Books, magazines and specialty publications devoted to kitchen design and decoration proved quite successful and "how to" books for home remodeling and decorating showed homeowners everything from how to stencil kitchen walls to distressing a new wood floor to give it an aged look.

Just as the circa 1920–1930 kitchen was updated during the 1940s and '50s, the 1980s saw many families remodel kitchens in homes built during the 1960s and '70s. Different life-styles as well as updated appliances, new color schemes and trends in kitchen cabinetry were largely responsible for the rush to kitchen showrooms and home building centers. Others sought professional advice from architects, interior designers and custom cabinetry outfitters.

In determining their needs for the kitchen of the 1980s, middle-class families were encouraged to examine their life-style. For example, working couples often required enough space and work area for two cooks. Those who entertained at home often requested a large open area so guests could join them in the kitchen. Perhaps children found the kitchen an ideal spot to do homework or work on the computer. Moving the laundry area back into the kitchen was often convenient and space-saving, an office area proved ideal for keeping things organized and adding a small greenhouse area off the kitchen or inserting a greenhouse window was especially popular.

The latest in modern appliances, this 1978 GE kitchen included a refrigerator/freezer with automatic ice and ice-water maker, a Potscrubber dishwasher, trash compactor and stove with self-cleaning oven. Note the microwave is built into the wall next to the stove and the room as a whole is large, including table and chairs and access to a patio. A tongue-and-groove wooden ceiling and walls add warmth and a personal touch to this kitchen.

Courtesy GE Appliance Archives.

Families became more affluent.

The pantry reappeared in many new homes or remodeled kitchens during the 1980s. While a small, separate room or area was incorporated into many kitchens for additional storage space and as a "cold spot" for wines, staples and so on, the concept was also updated to include various built-in pantry cupboards or cabinets with pull-out or swing-out drawers and shelves.

Energy efficiency continued to be very important and consumers found major appliances labeled with government-mandated "Energy Guide" stickers that offered information on the appliance's energy consumption. This helped consumers comparison shop for the most cost-effective appliances.

The country decorating style that was coming into its own during the late 1970s was in full-swing by the early 1980s and expanded beyond the scope of a "style" to become a way of life for many middle-class Americans. The essence of "country" was a return to basics, enjoying simple pleasures and having a comfortable home. As such (both a style and a way of life), country-inspired kitchens were dressed in colors evoking charm and warmth and accessorized with vintage antiques and collectibles recalling earlier kitchens, hearths and pantries.

Although "country" received notable attention, other decorating schemes were at home in the kitchen. For example, Better Homes and Gardens 1983 book *Your Kitchen* includes suggestions for the "city slick" style (also known as high- tech), which " . . . is as close to the modernist credo of 'form follows function' as kitchens have ever come." Regarding contemporary styling the editors suggest " . . . the true beauty of contemporary design is that it's timeless. This enduring style goes from decade to decade without dating itself, as less classic looks might." Other decorating styles were mentioned as well, including Traditional and Eclectic which "gives you a chance to do what you like, do as little or much as you like, and live with all the things that are closest to your heart."[6]

In addition to the above, by the late 1980s a Victorian revival in decorating was under way and the Victorian-inspired kitchen became the object of many a remodeling project.

Industrial kitchens, taking their cue from the hard-working kitchens found in restaurants, incorporated sleek design with optimum efficiency. In his 1989 book, *Kitchens and Dining Rooms*, Terence Conran tells us "An industrial-looking kitchen tends to have a formal, high-tech atmosphere . . . The two qualities valued most by professional chefs are durability and ease of cleaning. It is not easy to turn the industrial kitchen into a part of the living room nor to make it cozy. This is a style for a separate kitchen . . ."[7]

bring back in style, almost to re-create what was lost with two working adults.

Depending upon the decorating style, kitchen walls during the last decade were either painted with an easy-to-clean high-gloss or semi-gloss paint, covered with scrubbable, paper-backed vinyl wallcovering, outfitted with ceramic or mosaic tiles—or some combination of the above.

Popular floor treatments included a return to wood floors, vinyl flooring or tiles and ceramic or quarry tiles.

Countertops came a long way during the 1970s and 1980s. Materials were vastly improved to withstand heat, stains and moisture. Plastics in the form of laminate (Formica) and vinyl were widely available in assorted colors and patterns. "Butcher block" wooden counters, reminiscent of the nineteenth-century chopping table were in vogue, and tile, granite and synthetic marble, while a bit more costly, were quite durable.

In remodeling during the 1980s replacement of kitchen cupboard doors became a less expensive alternative to installing all new cabinetry.

working families meant more money to be spent.

This 1990s Maytag kitchen includes a full array of Deco White Maytag appliances and combines function and convenience with beauty and style. Kitchens of today are planned with "work triangles" and are designed to *meet individual homeowner's needs, often serving as a family center combined with a dining area and family room or living area extension.*

Courtesy Maytag Corporation.

There was such a wide variety of kitchen furnishings, appliances and accessories available during the 1980s that simply choosing a faucet could be a complicated affair. Consumers routinely comparison-shopped to determine the best value for their hard-earned money.

Today, the kitchen of the 1990s incorporates the best in planning and design while maintaining a personal character and charm that continues to make it the center of the home.

As high-tech industries and manufacturers continue to bring us the latest for the kitchen, vinyl flooring has been renamed "resilient" flooring and durability has been improved.

Non-porous, solid surface materials for countertops, such as Corian and Fountainhead, are even more durable than laminates, and if cut or stained, an abrasive cleaner will restore them to new.

The focus on the environment finds us recycling glass, plastic and paper goods in our kitchen and "environmentally-friendly" appliances such as Whirlpool's 22 cubic-foot refrigerator that is chlorofluorocarbon-free are being introduced.

Just as the housekeeper of the nineteenth century could never have imagined the state-of-the-art convenience and multiple functions associated with today's kitchen, it will be interesting to see what the new century has to offer as the history of the American kitchen moves forward.

From "Housewife" to "Individual"

It was a strange stirring, a sense of dissatisfaction, a yearning that women suffered in the middle of the twentieth century . . . Each suburban wife struggled with it all alone. As she made the beds, shopped for groceries . . . chauffeured Cub Scouts and Brownies, lay beside her husband at night, she was afraid to ask . . . the silent question, "Is this all?"

> The Feminine Mystique
> —Betty Friedan, 1963

The concept of the middle-class housewife, so clearly defined in the 1930s, was subject to upheaval during the 1940s as a result of World War II. Husbands and sons were called to duty in large numbers, leaving wives and mothers to fill the void in factories across America and run their households alone.

While concerns over being a model wife were temporarily set aside to contribute to the war effort, as soon as the war came to a close women returned home to pick up where they'd left off. Between 1945 and 1960 the typical middle-class housewife was to focus her energy on her husband and being a good marriage partner, overseeing the children and taking care of the home.[8]

As in the previous decade, magazines during the 1940s (with the exception of the war years) included more advertisements for beauty products than kitchen products and more articles about fashions, beauty and romance than food and homemaking. Women still looked to the experts for advice. For example, an article in the June 1942 *Ladies' Home Journal* told wives how to make their marriage a partnership. Author Paul Popenoe suggested " . . . in marriage, if each has a different goal, they will always be in trouble. The best goal is the success of the marriage ~togethers~ itself; and if each refers everything to the test of whether it will promote success of their marriage, there will be little occasion for squabbling."[9]

In addition to magazines, television commercials targeted women in advertising for beauty products, and programing during the 1950s and 1960s stereotyped the middle-class housewife. (Remember "Leave It to Beaver," "Ozzie and Harriet," "Father Knows Best"?)

The economic boom during the 1950s saw a record number of homes being built in the newly developed suburbs. Roles were clearly defined for the husband who went off to work during the week and spent weekends tinkering at this workbench or tending the yard, and the wife who stayed at home caring for the house, preparing the meals, raising the children and joining the PTA.

Just as the early years of the Victorian period saw the home considered a "safe haven" from rapid industrialism and problems in the city, during the 1950s the suburban American family looked to their home as an escape from fears associated with the Cold War. For the housewife, however, despite the fact that the suburbs held the promise of a new home with a modern kitchen, a backyard for the children to play in and, ultimately, fulfillment of the American dream, as the novelty wore off many women found themselves bored and lonely.

Bridge parties and afternoon teas gave way to the morning coffee klatch, and cocktail parties became popular for at-home entertaining during the 1950s and 1960s. Except for such get togethers the housewife spent a great deal of her day alone in the suburbs.

Taking care of the house still included daily, weekly and occasional chores that had to be done. In a housedress and apron, the suburban middle-class wife and mother fixed breakfast for her family, packed their lunches and saw them off to school and work. After doing the morning dishes, beds were made and the bathroom cleaned. Dusting was done and rugs were vacuumed. The dinner menu was planned and the evening meal prepared.

Many housewives did their laundry on Tuesday so they could spend Monday catching up with chores after the weekend, but the practice of assigning different days of the week to various household activities had virtually disappeared during the modern age.

Weekly chores included grocery shopping, although staples such as milk, bread and butter were delivered to many homes once or twice a week by the milkman.

A thorough cleaning throughout the house was also done weekly, including dusting pictures, lamps, blinds or shades and baseboards, moving furniture to vacuum underneath, washing the kitchen floor, turning mattresses and changing the bedding.

Occasional tasks such as washing curtains, cleaning and organizing closets and dresser drawers, polishing or waxing the furniture and so on were recommended every few months.

With automatic washers and dryers, efficient gas or electric stoves and the variety of other large and small appliances at her disposal, the time spent doing certain chores was reduced from previous decades, but new tasks, such as chauffeuring children, quickly filled in the gap. Despite the fact that the middle-class housewife could find herself busy with the demands of small children, caring for her home and running countless errands, she nevertheless experienced overwhelming feelings of isolation.

In short, her physical surroundings had vastly improved; manual labor within the home had lessened; and cooking had become a matter of opening a series of boxes and cans and then turning knobs on the stove. There was little work the housewife could perform that actually involved great skill—this in turn resulted in few opportunities for feelings of self-satisfaction.

Through the late 1950s and early 1960s women grew increasingly discouraged with the narrow confines of their role and their identity as a "housewife." Their self-worth was in jeopardy at the same time that *The Feminine Mystique* by Betty Friedan was published in 1963. Friedan's book explored the plight of the housewife and her encouragement that women seek fulfillment via creative work or a career helped establish a movement that would eventually recognize women as individuals in their own right, rather than as servants within their own home.[10]

Without delving too deeply into the feminist movement, we tend to think of it as a twentieth-century phenomenon when in fact a feminist movement (as it relates to the housewife) had been under way since the nineteenth century. When Charlotte Perkins Gilman wrote her book,

Women and Economics, in 1898, she encouraged women to work towards economic equality with men. She saw the woman's role in the home as an economic asset to men, allowing them to amass more wealth than would otherwise be possible. In short, women were simply considered economic factors. (Gilman noted in her book that horses were too.) She staunchly believed that the home and all manner of housework was archaic and should be dealt with via large laundries and kitchens outside the home that the general public could utilize to obtain meals etc.

The battle over opposing views was quietly waged into the new century. In August 1950 an article by Agnes E. Meyer entitled "Women Aren't Men" appeared in *The Atlantic Monthly*. Meyer wrote in support of the role of the housewife, telling readers

> . . . For woman is the cement of society. Since time immemorial it has been woman who has held the family, society, and life itself together . . . Instead of apologizing for being a mere "housewife," as so many do, women should make society realize that upon the housewife now fall the combined tasks of economist, nutrition expert, sociologist, psychiatrist, and educator. Then society would confer upon the status of housewife the honor, recognition, and acclaim it deserves. Today, however, the duties of the homemaker have become so depreciated that many women feel impelled to work outside the home in order to retain the respect of the community.[11]

In contrast, a 1949 article, "Women Are Household Slaves," by Edith M. Stern told readers:

> . . . When a man marries and has children, it is assumed that he will do the best work along lines in which he has been trained or is at least interested. When a woman marries and has children, it is assumed that she will take to housewifery. But whether she takes to it or not, she does it. Such regimentation, for professional or potentially professional women, is costly both for the individual and society. For the individual, it brings about conflicts and frustrations . . . The educated individual should have a community, a national, a world viewpoint; but that is pretty difficult to get and hold when you are continually involved with cleaning toilets, ironing shirts, peeling potatoes, darning socks and minding children.[12]

It was not, however, until Friedan's work in 1963 that women united in unprecedented numbers for the common cause of the feminist movement. The timing was right; many a suburban housewife saw herself very clearly in *The Feminine Mystique* and a younger generation of women had actively been supporting the Civil Rights movement.

The National Organization for Women (NOW) was established in 1966 and by the early 1970s the "women's liberation" movement was well under way. Whereas only 25 percent of American women held a job away from their home in 1940, by 1974 statistics indicated that almost half of the married women with children were employed either full time or part time.[13]

During the late 1970s and the 1980s, as increasing numbers of women went to work, use of the word "housewife" virtually disappeared from our vocabulary. To be politically correct, those who remain at home without outside employment are now referred to as "homemakers."

During the late 1970s economic factors such as the cost of living, housing and so on impacted on the number of women entering the work force. The two-income family became a necessity for many middle-class couples to maintain their standard of living. As women went to work a great deal of attention was focused on child care and the division of labor within the home. Husbands were expected to share household chores and while this was wonderful in theory, it was far from the norm. Many women realized they had not one job but two—the cooking, cleaning and laundry work was being done by them during the evenings and on weekends. Judith K. Sprankle explored this problem in her 1986 book, *Working It Out: The Domestic Double Standard*. She wrote, "The fact is that equal employment, without appropriate adjustments for the performance of essential, previously unpaid work done by women in the home, has resulted in each women's assumption of dual and even triple full-time roles, and juggling them to her own and society's satisfaction is still viewed as her problem alone . . . Our liberated society has . . . created a widely imbalanced new system of labor that penalizes women at home for every gain we have made at work."[14]

In Betty Friedan's second book, *The Second Stage* (published in 1981), the author addressed such conflicts, encouraging women that the feminist movement did indeed make great changes but the time has come for men and women to work together for the good of the family and the future.

As women achieved status as individuals, the idea of marriage as a "partnership" has taken on a whole new meaning. During the 1980s and on into the 1990s this "partnership" has focused not only on the good of the marriage but also on the survival and good of the home and family unit. The role of the husband, once the "breadwinner," continues to evolve into a position of shared-responsibility in terms of household chores, child rearing, cooking, laundry work and so on.

With the increase in the number of working couples, those middle-class families that can afford to often have a part-time cleaning woman come into the home or hire a cleaning service to do periodic, thorough cleanings. Other services have sprung up in response to growing needs, such as day care centers, which provide child care during business hours. In other areas, lawn services can be hired to provide weekly maintenance of the yard, catering has proved popular and time-saving for entertaining at home and gourmet deli shops mean dinner can be picked up on the way home from work. While the milkman no longer brings staples to the house (except in smaller communities where a local dairy may still provide such services), corner grocery stores have been replaced by huge "supermarkets" for one-stop shopping and "mini-marts" are on almost every street corner for a quick stop to buy necessities during the week.

From housewife to individual or working woman, the journey thus far has not been an easy one. What began as a civil rights movement grew to encompass a battle of the sexes. In addition, a backlash during the 1980s found full-time homemakers speaking up in support and defense of their role in opposition to ardent feminists. Many "super women," finding the balancing act between home and career too demanding and stressful, sought creative alternatives such as flex-time and shared jobs at work or home-based businesses.

While the kitchen is still considered predominantly a woman's domain, the concept of "family" has changed these past few decades to include working couples, house-husbands, single-parent households and multi-generational families living together under one roof. As a result, in today's home we are apt to find any family member doing the laundry, grocery shopping or preparing the meals. Children at a young age are as adept at working the microwave as they are the VCR. Judith K. Sprankle notes in *Working It Out: The Domestic Double Standard* that "As soon as the kids are old enough to understand the concept of sharing, they're ready to get in on the act [housework]; and if women ever hope to banish the domestic double standard, we must orchestrate the performance, not continue to play all instruments. It doesn't really matter . . . who does what. What does matter is that everyone shares the total load—sequentially or concurrently, but so far as possible, equally."[15]

During the 1980s and 1990s information on homemaking has come to us in various forms. Numerous television shows on network and cable channels are geared to the home, offering advice on decorating, cleaning, gardening and cooking. Magazines and special-interest publications are available for virtually every aspect of homeownership, homemaking and so on. Popular women's magazines such as *Better Homes and Gardens*,

Woman's Day and *Family Circle* devote a large portion of their editorial content to child rearing, cooking, cleaning tips, decorating, remodeling, organizing one's time etc. Other periodicals such as *House Beautiful, Country Living* and *Metropolitan Home* focus more closely on decorating, life-styles, cooking and gardening. Books too are published on the various aspects of homemaking. The 1989 publication of Better Homes and Gardens' *Household Hints and Tips* (a modern-day counterpart of the nineteenth-century all-purpose home manual) offers a reflection of our times and tells readers that "Keeping a home running smoothly can be hard work. Making sure everything is in working condition, preparing healthy, varied meals, maintaining appliances and other items, and coping with illness, children and pets are major responsibilities . . ."[16] Toward this end, efficient home management today focuses on adequate storage areas for belongings, making lists to stay organized, planning meals in advance as a time-saver and "picking up" as we go along to help keep the house neat and clean.[17]

From mistress of the house and then housekeeper during the 1800s to housewife during the twentieth century, women have found their way from the home and a stereotyped role into a world of achievement, self-esteem and possibilities. With each step forward there have been personal rewards and conflicts. As the journey continues it will be interesting to see where the new century takes us. One thing is for certain, if middle-class women return to their kitchens it will be because they want to—not because the precepts of womanhood deem that they have to.

As Rosalind Miles so eloquently writes in her 1989 book, *The Women's History of the World*, "This story has no ending, as the history of women, so long in the making, is in one sense only just begun . . . The new spirit of women's self-discovery and self-reliance has permeated every aspect of contemporary life."[18]

Trends in American Cooking

. . . American food truly reflects American history, and vice versa. Each is the story of a coming together of diverse cultures and peoples to form a vital unity of spirit and taste. Ours is such a young history that we can still see the process, and taste it.

"Digesting History," *Bon Appetit*
—William J. Garry, Editor in Chief, November 1993

America's culinary history since 1940 has brought us numerous changes in what we eat as well as how we cook it. Today, visit any bookstore or your local library and you're liable to be overwhelmed by the vast number and variety of cookbooks available. Cooking has become, in many instances, an art form. Americans enjoy cooking more than any previous generation and feel free to experiment, create and dabble in the unknown.

During the 1940s there were food shortages just as there had been during the first World War and housewives had to make do with substitutions and try alternate meal plans. They were of course taking full advantage of the canned, boxed and frozen foods filling the shelves and freezer cases at the grocery store, and popular magazines gave them recipes and tips on how to take advantage of time-savers (a whole dinner could be planned around canned Spam) rather than cook from scratch.

Cookbooks popular during the 1940s and 1950s, such as *The Betty Crocker Cookbook, Better Homes and Gardens New Cook Book* (many a bride-to-be received one of these kitchen bibles as a shower gift), revised editions of the *Boston Cooking-School Cook Book* and the popular *Joy of Cooking* offered a broad range of recipes. The relatively small number of books available did not yet target specific types of cooking or cuisine. Instead, comfort foods such as meat and potatoes were the basic standard around which the family meal was planned.

During the 1950s, advertising on television and in magazines brought the housewife news of the latest in modern-day cooking. While packaged Jello and other instant desserts were all the rage during the 1920s and '30s, packaged cake mixes and frozen TV dinners were now staples in middle-class kitchen cupboards and refrigerators all across America. As Evan Jones points out in his book *American Food* ". . . national advertising created national rather than regional appetites and tastes."[19] *killing the palate*

Even as the nation was paying homage to convenience foods and frozen entrees, there was a small but growing movement under way to inspire the American public that good living was, in essence, good food. For example, *Gourmet* magazine, which premiered in 1941, was quite popular by the 1950s when Americans became infatuated with travel, international cuisine and fine wine.

In 1940 James Beard, considered by many to be the father of American food, published his first book, *Hors d'Oeuvres and Canapes*. As a newspaper columnist, free-lance writer, teacher and author, Beard brought well-loved recipes and much deserved recognition to creative American cooking throughout the 1950s and '60s. His 1959 book, *The James Beard Cookbook,* was especially popular and was updated in 1970. With a lifetime devoted to American cuisine and inspiring others to pursue excellence in cookery, in 1981, at the age of eighty-two, Beard wrote his nineteenth book, *The New James Beard*. In the introduction he told readers, "The culinary world was never livelier than now, restaurants were never more experimental, and great cooks were never more appreciated. Taste responds to feedback—well named, because it does nourish the imagination. The razzle-dazzle is a great stimulant. But what truly stimulates, sustains, and rewards good cooking is honor at home. It gives me joy to see so many couples cooking together these days, and to watch their children growing up where they belong, right in the kitchen, as I did long ago."[20]

During the flight to the suburbs in the 1950s a new twist on cooking became popular thanks to the outdoor grill. All across America families were barbecuing and recipe books began including instructions for cooking over hot charcoal fires. For example, the 1953 edition of *Better Homes and Gardens New Cook Book* devoted a new section to "Outdoor Cooking." Information was presented on the type of equipment to use, building a fire, selecting meats to barbecue, barbecue sauces and meal planning.[21] Cooks were told that "To round out the grill-cooked meat, good choices for kitchen-cooked main dishes include creamed potatoes; scalloped potatoes; spoonbread; green beans with cream of mushroom soup; and vegetables scalloped in cheese sauce."[22]

In contrast, today's picnic-style barbecue with hamburgers, hotdogs, steaks etc. might include lighter fare such as fresh vegetables, a tossed salad and condiments. For a dinner, main dishes such as potatoes might be baked or dressed with a low-fat sauce.

While there are those that would never foresake a charcoal fire and would swear by the excellent results in flavor, the gas grill was introduced during the late 1950s and many found it time-saving, more convenient and more reliable than the old grills. The gas grill has become a necessity in the middle-class backyard or on the patio, and barbecuing is as popular today as it was over thirty years ago.

Just as James Beard reawakened an interest in American cooking during the 1950s and '60s, Julia Child made Americans fall in love with French cooking. First a student, and then an instructor of French cuisine while living in Paris during the 1950s, Child went on to co-author *Mastering the Art of French Cooking* with Louisette Bertholle and Simone Beck in 1961. In a ten-year period their book went through twenty printings. In the foreword, the authors told readers, "This is a book for the servantless American cook who can be unconcerned on occasion with budgets, waistlines, time schedules, children's meals, the parent-chaffeur-den-mother syndrome, or anything else which might interfere with the enjoyment of producing something wonderful to eat . . . Cooking is not a particularly difficult art . . . The most important ingredient you can bring to it is love of cooking for its own sake."[23]

The American public enthusiastically embraced Child's book and then the woman herself when her public television show, "The French Chef" premiered during the 1960s. Here was a cook the homemaker could relate to. Child would dive into her recipe with great gusto and little concern if a mess should happen to be made. She showed housewives that cooking could indeed be enjoyable.

Child's second book, *The French Chef Cookbook,* was published in 1968 and a second volume of *Mastering the Art of French Cooking,* which she wrote with Simone Beck, appeared in 1970. She has since published additional cookbooks and appeared in other cooking shows such as "Julia Child & Company." Child taught America the fine art of French cooking—and made it fun every step of the way.

The initial success of Child's first book indicated there was a market for specialty cookbooks during the 1960s and 1970s. Evan Jones noted this trend when he wrote, "In the 1960s the character of the best American cookbooks changed from catch-all collections of recipes to skillfully written books that had themes, vibrancy and eclecticism . . . American publishers had issued 49 cookbooks in 1960, and a dozen years later, the annual total, according to *Publishers Weekly* had jumped to 385 new titles (not to mention paperbacks and reprints)."[24]

While a great many middle-class Americans turned their kitchens into learning labs and taught themselves new culinary skills, others were reveling in the convenience of "fast food." What began with a single hamburger stand in California during the 1950s was parlayed into an American institution known as McDonald's. Others soon followed, including Burger King, Wendy's, Kentucky Fried Chicken, Taco Bell and so on. From the 1960s through the present day, fast-food restaurants, many now with convenient "drive-thru" windows, have provided the answer to a need in our hurry-up, have-to-have-it-now, no-time-to-cook world.

Fast food and all, Americans were doing a great deal of cooking during the 1970s and much of it was experimental. Middle-class couples found entertaining at home (with guests gathered in the kitchen to socialize while the meal was being prepared) a relaxing and casual way to spend the evening with friends. In addition, college students and other young adults who'd risen to the cause of the civil rights movement and the feminist movement, and protested the Vietnam War, were looking to alternative life-styles. Communes sprang up across the country where groups of people strove to live together in harmony and provide for their own needs by living off the earth. They farmed the land and prepared simple, wholesome dishes without food additives, relying on natural grains, beans, legumes, fruits and vegetables as staples.

The concept of communal living didn't last but the diets and eating habits of this younger generation during the 1970s resulted in a growing awareness of the health benefits associated with a vegetarian diet. Consequently, health food stores and specialty shops became commonplace as Americans tried to improve their eating habits.

During the 1980s there was a move away from red meat or limiting consumption of red meat, and poultry (with the skin removed, of course) became a popular alternative. Pork was advertised as the new "white meat"; we took the salt shaker off the kitchen table; and with new information on the negative effects of high cholesterol, low-fat cooking was recommended. Suddenly the supermarkets were full of low-fat, low-cholesterol and high-fiber products, and oat bran became the darling of the 1980s. In *The Oat Bran Cookbook* by Kitty and Lucian Maynard (published 1989), the authors wrote in the preface that "now more than ever, Americans are becoming aware of their health needs and the various diets and foods available for good eating. More people are walking, jogging, and running today . . . Since this is a trend—and not a fad—it signifies America's movement toward becoming a healthier society."[25]

Inspired then by cooking shows, cooking classes, a vast selection of cookbooks and magazines such as *Gourmet, Bon Appetit, Food and Wine, Cooking Light, Vegetarian Times* and others, middle-class America got out their state-of-the-art food processors and bread machines and began to create an assortment of healthful, tasty dishes. Fresh fruits and vegetables became vital for a healthy life-style, especially those noted to include cancer-fighting agents such as the beta carotene found in carrots, sweet potatoes, spinach, broccoli, apricots, cantaloupes and peaches. New recipes were tried and new (healthier) ways of preparing and cooking old-time comfort foods such as meatloaf and mashed potatoes were practiced.

As this trend continues on into the 1990s, the U.S. Department of Agriculture has given us a new Food Guide Pyramid on which to base our daily diet. This replaces the "Basic Four" food groups (milk, meat, bread/cereal, vegetables/fruit) that children have long been taught in elementary school. The new pyramid illustrates the recommended increase in daily servings of bread, cereal, rice or pasta; fruits; and vegetables; and limited servings from the milk and cheese group; the group including meat, poultry, fish, dry beans, eggs and nuts; and lastly, very small amounts of fats, oils and sweets.

Since the 1940s, scientific advances and discoveries, state-of-the-art medical tests, alternate life-styles, pioneering modern-day cooks such as James Beard and Julia Child and improved quality/variety at the supermarket have brought marked change to American cuisine. An article entitled "Great American Dinners," by Kristine Kidd and Karen Kaplan appeared in the September 1992 issue of *Bon Appetit* and this timely piece sums it all up by telling us: "Much has changed over the years . . . Our dining options, once prescribed, are now limitless—we can bring the world to our own tables . . . The basic American Dinner may not seem so basic or so American anymore."[26]

American food means different things to different people. Some might think of a Thanksgiving dinner, apple pie, a steak on the grill, a fast-food hamburger and French fries or a huge tossed salad with bean sprouts and fresh vegetables. This versatility of modern-day foods is what makes it all so interesting.

Notable Changes: The Kitchen Has Come Full Circle

From families with young children to empty nesters, everyone wants to be in the kitchen.

Country Kitchen Ideas
—A Better Homes and Gardens Special Interest Publication, Spring 1993

All of the changes affecting the kitchen during the second half of the twentieth century are notable. Kitchen design planned around work triangles in a basic U, L or galley floor plan have brought convenience to today's kitchen. Modern, energy-saving appliances are more efficient than ever and innovative improvements continue to be made. Long-wearing, durable and low-maintenance flooring and countertop materials are cost-efficient and easy to clean. Gloss and semi-gloss paints along with washable wallpapers allow for numerous decorating possibilities. The microwave brought us speed cooking and the variety of fresh and packaged foods in the supermarket allow us to cook and serve anything imaginable.

In closing, perhaps the most significant development in regard to the kitchen during this time period has been a change in concept—what a kitchen is, what a kitchen does and who works there. Simply put, the kitchen has become the focus—the heart—of the home. In this way, the kitchen has come full circle.

In the early Colonial kitchen or hall, with its massive cooking hearth, the family gathered together for meals, conversation and home-related activities. Today's all-purpose kitchen is not so very different.

Several factors (looked at individually throughout this chapter) combined over the past thirty years to lead the kitchen away from its status as a utility room. For example, as the feminist movement opened the doors to women in the work force, they found their homes, especially the kitchens, no longer suited their life-style. Returning home from a hard day at work, middle-class women during the 1960s and '70s had to prepare dinner, perhaps do a load of wash, tend to young children or catch up with their school-age children and husband. A kitchen isolated from the rest of the house by walls and doors wasn't conducive to family togetherness and the kitchen itself was usually too small to accommodate children at play without them being underfoot.

For avid cooks and those who enjoyed home entertaining during the 1970s, the kitchen became like the stage in a theater. Family and friends would gather in the kitchen to socialize and watch the cook prepare the evening meal. A too small kitchen was a problem to be reckoned with.

Storage space often proved inadequate with the selection of canned and packaged goods available. Homeowners began looking for innovative ways to increase space. A shortage of kitchen cupboards often meant a surplus of kitchen goods had to be stored in the basement or some other inconvenient spot.

While architects and builders responded to these needs by building homes with open floor plans during the late 1960s and the 1970s, the kitchen in many cases was still closed off from the living room by a long wall separating the two areas. Middle-class families called for something more and by the 1980s many people were building houses with large kitchen-dining-family room areas that became the center of the home. Those remodeling older homes were knocking out walls to enlarge their kitchen space and incorporate a family room, office area or computer center.

As the kitchen broke free from its stereotyped role (as simply a workroom), people began to pay close attention to architectural details such as cabinetry and windows. Decorating takes into account the entire "living" area.

As today's family plans their kitchen according to what works best for them, we draw from the rich history of the past to bring warmth, charm and comfort to this multi-functional room. As we move toward the new century the kitchen's place of honor in the home is firmly established.

Contemporary Household Hints and Recipes

❦HOUSEHOLD HINTS❦

Do you have trouble separating ground beef when you're browning it for spaghetti or chili? To do it fast, get out your potato masher, and tromp, tromp, tromp—the job is done.

Better Homes and Gardens New Cook Book, 1953

HOW TO SET THE TABLE

Set each place 24 inches from the next one—that's a minimum distance for comfort. Line silverware up evenly 1 inch from the edge of the table, in the order it will be used. Knives and spoons go on the right of the plate, forks on the left. Always place the pieces you're going to use first on the outside.

Better Homes and Gardens New Cook Book, 1953

If the dining area is connected with the living room, the decor should be carried over or blended . . . If the dining-living room are one, the table may be a drop-leaf against the wall.

The Pocket Household Encyclopedia
—N. H. & S. K. Mager, 1954

SERVING WINE

Aperitifs (Vermouth, Dubonnet, Sherry) or cocktails (Martini, Manhattan) may be served before the meal. White wines (Sauterne, Rhine) are served with fish or shellfish or poultry. Meat . . . cheese and nuts bring out the qualities of a red wine. Avoid salads dressed with vinegar, sweet vegetables, and any other sweet dish. Sweet wines (Port, Madeira) or cordials are served with desserts or after the meal.

The Pocket Household Encyclopedia
—N. H. & S. K. Mager, 1954

Pots, pans and casseroles should be heavy-bottomed so they will not tip over, and good heat conductors so that foods will not stick and scorch. With the exception of heavy copper, the best all-purpose material, in our opinion, is heavy, enameled cast iron.

Mastering the Art of French Cooking
—Julia Child, Louisette Bertholle and Simone Beck, 1961

To ripen fruit, place in well-ventilated area at room temperature; avoid direct sunlight. Tomatoes, peaches, bananas, avocados, pears, and plums can be ripened. Refrigerate ripened fruit, except bananas, till ready to use.

Better Homes and Gardens New Cook Book, 1972

To serve ice cream that won't spoon out because it is too hard, peel off the carton and slice neatly with a cake breaker.

Better Homes and Gardens New Cook Book, 1972

HOW TO THOROUGHLY CLEAN A ROOM

1.) Open all of the windows to air out the room. 2.) Remove scraps of paper, newspaper, and dead leaves of plants or old flowers; empty . . . wastepaper baskets; put away any out-of-place items like papers or books. 3.) Pick up any rugs. If cleaning a living room or bedroom, move all the small pieces of furniture out of the room . . . 4.) Remove cobwebs and brush out closets. 5.) Dust everywhere, including bric-a-brac . . . clean all windows. 6.) Vacuum the drapes and upholstery. 7.) Mop and polish the floor, or vacuum. 8.) Shake rugs outside . . . 9.) Replace all furniture, accessories, and ornaments, and polish them if necessary.

Better Homes and Gardens Household Hints and Tips, 1989

Don't be a pack rat—Throw out what you don't need. A house full of old belongings means a house difficult to clean, and things going unused because you can't find them.

Better Homes and Garden Household Hints and Tips, 1989

❦RECIPES❦

MACARONI 'N' CHEESE

1 6-ounce package 7-minute macaroni	1 teaspoon grated onion
1 10½- or 11-ounce can condensed mushroom soup	½ teaspoon salt
½ cup of milk	Dash pepper
	½ pound American cheese, cubed

Cook macaroni in boiling, salted water; drain and rinse. Combine the mushroom soup, milk, onion, and seasonings. Alternate layers of macaroni, soup, and cheese in greased 1½-quart baking dish. Bake in moderate oven (350) about 45 minutes. Makes 6 servings.

Better Homes and Gardens New Cook Book, 1953

SPINACH SALAD (Makes 4 Servings)

1 pound leaf spinach

1 sweet onion

Soy Dressing:

6 tablespoons olive oil
1 tablespoon soy sauce
2 teaspoons Dijon mustard

1 1/2 tablespoons lemon juice
Salt and freshly ground
black pepper to taste

Wash the spinach well, removing the heavy stems, and dry thoroughly. Put in a salad bowl with the sliced onion. Combine the dressing ingredients, blending them well, and pour over the salad just before serving. Toss thoroughly.

The New James Beard
—James Beard, 1981

BRAISED RUMP ROAST

3 1/2 to 4 lb. boneless beef rump roast
1/4 cup dry red wine or water
1 large onion, sliced

2 teaspoons instant beef bouillon
1 teaspoon salt
1/8 teaspoon pepper

Place roast fat side down, in water-soaked clay pot. Add wine and sprinke on remaining ingredients; cover with water-soaked lid. Microwave for 15 minutes on HIGH. Turn roast over; recover. Microwave for 55 to 65 miutes on MEDIUM (Simmer), or until meat is fork tender. Let stand, covered, 10 minutes before serving. 9–12 Servings.

Microwave Cooking from Litton, 1981

PECAN PIE

3 tablespoons butter or
    margarine
3 eggs, slightly beaten
1 cup dark corn syrup
1/4 cup packed brown sugar

1 1/2 teaspoons all-purpose flour
1 teaspoon vanilla
1 1/2 cups pecan halves
1 (9 inch) Baked Pastry Shell
    in glass pie plate

Place butter in medium glass mixing bowl. Microwave for about 1 minute on MED. HIGH (Roast), or until melted. Stir in remaining ingredients, except pastry shell; mix well; pour filling into shell. Microwave for 20–25 minutes on MEDIUM (Simmer), or until almost set in the center. Let cool and set before serving.

Microwave Cooking from Litton, 1981

SALSA (Makes 1 Serving)

1 teaspoon vegetable oil
2 tablespoons each diced onion
    and green bell pepper
1/2 cup canned crushed tomatoes

1/8 teaspoon garlic powder
Dash salt
1 to 2 drops hot sauce
1/2 teaspoon chopped canned
    chili peppers

In small saucepan heat oil over medium heat; add onion and bell pepper and saute until onion is translucent. Reduce heat, add remaining ingredients, and let simmer until sauce thickens slightly, 5 to 6 minutes. Use immediately or let cool, transfer to container, cover, and refrigerate until ready to use.

Weight Watchers Fast & Fabulous Cookbook, 1983

SUNNY BRAN MUFFINS

1 cup 3-minute Quick Oats
1 teaspoon baking powder
1 teaspoon cinnamon
1 1/2 cups orange juice
2/3 cup vegetable oil
1 1/2 cups whole wheat flour

1/2 teaspoon baking soda
3/4 cup oat bran
4 egg whites
1 tablespoon grated orange peel
1/2 cup orange marmalade
    (with no sugar added)

Stir together the dry ingredients in a large mixing bowl. Set aside. Combine the orange juice, egg whites, vegetable oil, and orange peel, and mix until well-blended. Add the liquid mixture to the dry ingredients all at once, stirring just until moistened. Gently fold in the orange marmalade, blending well. Fill greased muffin tins 2/3 full. Bake at 375 for 20 minutes or until done. Makes 12 muffins.

The Oat Bran Cookbook
—Kitty & Lucian Maynard, 1989

ITALIAN BREAD PIZZA

4 thick slices Italian bread, cut from a
    large loaf
2 garlic cloves, halved
4 teaspoons sun-dried tomato paste
8 small plum tomatoes, thinly sliced
12 to 16 basil leaves, shredded

5 ounces mozzarella cheese,
    thinly sliced
1 tablespoon capers in brine,
    drained
12 pitted green olives, halved
Olive oil

Preheat oven to 475°F (240°C). Cut each bread slice in half crosswise. Under a hot broiler, toast bread lightly on both sides. Rub with garlic. Spread one side of each piece with tomato paste. Arrange tomatoes over tomato paste; spinkle with basil leaves. Top with cheese, capers and olives. Drizzle with a little oil. Bake 8–10 minutes or until cheese melts. Serve hot. Makes 4 servings.

The Book of Vegetarian Cooking
—Louise Pickford, 1993

APPENDIX

Authentic or Recreated Kitchens on Display

Across the country historical societies, patrons and volunteers have been working to preserve and restore bits and pieces of America's history. Since the 1970s there has been heightened interest in saving old buildings and historically significant properties from the wrecking ball, especially fine examples of Victorian architecture. As a result, there are numerous nineteenth-century house museums that can be visited for a glimpse of the past and while many of them do not include kitchens on display, others do.

Living-history museums allow visitors to stroll among historic buildings in an open-air setting and often participate in hands-on activities. The majority of these museums hark back to the Colonial era but there are others that span the decades.

Museums frequently include historic room settings or special exhibits that draw our attention to women's history (especially as it pertains to the home and the kitchen), as in the 1993 exhibition Mechanical Brides: Women and Machines from Home to Office at the Smithsonian Institution's Cooper-Hewitt National Museum of Design in New York City.

Another noteworthy exhibition, True Love and a Happy Home: Cultural Expectations and Feminine Experiences in Victorian America was featured at the DAR Museum in Washington, D.C. The focus of this exhibit was more than one hundred images capturing nineteenth-century women in their various roles as wife, mother, housekeeper, cook and so forth.

To truly appreciate the history of the American kitchen and the women who labored there before modern-day conveniences, visiting authentic or recreated kitchens of the past can be an enriching experience.

The following is a selected listing (alphabetical by state) of historic house museums, living-history museums and museum exhibits where Colonial and Victorian kitchens (authentic or recreated) can be viewed. It is wise to write or call ahead if a phone number is included to verify hours of operation as they can be subject to change. In addition, by contacting your state or local historical societies you may learn of other kitchen exibits or displays.

COLONIAL KITCHENS ON DISPLAY

Constitution Hall Village, 404 Madison Street, Huntsville, Alabama 35801, phone # (800) 678-1819.

The location of the 1819 drafting of the state constitution, Alabama's Constitution Hall Village is a living-history museum with early nineteenth-century buildings, many of which include recreated kitchens with cooking hearths.

AGRIRAMA, P.O. Box Q, I-75, Exit 20, Tifton, Georgia 31793, phone # (912) 386-3344.

A living-history museum that spans the decades and includes early nineteenth-century buildings, a rural farm community of the 1870s, a progressive farmstead circa 1890 and a rural town that includes the Victorian home of the town founder. Several kitchens can be toured and special events are conducted all year long.

Conner Prairie, 13400 Allisonville Road, Noblesville, Indiana 46060, phone # (317) 776-6000.

A living-history museum including the 1836 village of Prairietown, the Pioneer Adventure Area where visitors can try hands-on activities and the Conner Prairie Museum. Prairietown consists of approximately 30 historical buildings, several with recreated kitchens. The museum's centerpiece, the 1823 Federal-style William Conner home, includes a fully functional kitchen with cooking hearth where demonstrations are done. An herb garden is located outside the kitchen and a spring house is close by.

Living History Farms, 2600 N.W. 111th Street, Urbandale, Iowa 50322, phone # (515) 278-5286.

A 600-acre, open-air museum depicting life of the midwestern agricultural community. Spanning the decades from the early nineteenth century through 1900, the site includes a circa 1900 farmhouse with a restored kitchen that serves suppers to the public between November and April. This unique dining experience offers hearth foods, a horse-drawn wagon ride to the farmhouse, parlor games and pump organ music. Special programs are conducted all year long.

Norlands Living History Center, Washburn Norlands Foundation, RFD 2, Box 3395, Livermore Falls, Maine 04254, phone # (207) 897-2236.

Norlands not only includes a Colonial-era house with a circa 1790 kitchen (complete with cooking hearth and brick bake oven), but a Farmer's Cottage kitchen, circa 1870, where cooking is done on a cast-iron wood-burning stove. The 1870 Victorian home of the Washburn family includes a large and cheery kitchen with stove, and special programs often include Saturday night kitchen dances where ice cream is made or corn is popped the old-fashioned way. This living-history center is unique in that live-in programs are available for adults and children to experience life during another time in truly authentic fashion.

Old Sturbridge Village, 1 Old Sturbridge Village Road, Sturbridge, Massachusetts 01566, phone # (508) 347-3362.

An outdoor living-history museum of early New England life circa 1790 to 1840, this site contains forty historic buildings, many with kitchens centered around the cooking hearth.

Storrowton Village Museum, Eastern States Exposition, 1305 Memorial Avenue, West Springfield, Massachusetts 01089, phone # (413) 787-0136.

An authentic, recreated village with nine eighteenth- and nineteenth-century buildings on the site of the Eastern States Exposition. The circa 1776 Potter Mansion contains a recreated kitchen, as does the 1794 Gilbert Farmstead, with cooking hearth, worktable, step-back cupboard and period gadgets and utensils.

The Village of Waterloo, 525 Village of Waterloo, Stanhope, New Jersey, 07874, phone # (201) 347-0900.

The Village of Waterloo includes a recreated colonial village and several of the homes feature old-time kitchens with cooking hearths. This living-history museum also has on display antiques, furnishings and craftwork objects that span both the Colonial and Victorian eras as well as an exhibit displaying artifacts of Native American culture.

The Millard Fillmore House Museum, 24 Shearer Avenue, East Aurora, New York 14052, phone # (716) 652-3280.

The early home of Millard and Abigail Fillmore before the former's presidency, this small Federal-style home reflects the late 1820s through the early 1830s period. The kitchen has been recreated, including a cooking hearth with bake oven. Wide pine boards used as wainscoting are original and have been painted mustard—a color uncovered during restoration work. A kitchen door leads to Abigail's herb garden.

Museum Village in Orange County, Museum Village Road, Monroe, New York 10950, phone # (914) 782-8247.

As a nonprofit educational institution, Museum Village includes over twenty-five different exhibition buildings. Two kitchens can be seen in the village, one in the log cabin and another in the Visitor's Center.

The Hermitage, 4580 Rachel's Lane, Hermitage, Tennessee 37076, phone # (615) 889-2941.

President Andrew Jackson's home, this brick Federal-style building was originally built between 1819 and 1821, enlarged in 1831 and then rebuilt during 1835 after a fire had destroyed a portion of the house. It was during this reconstruction that a freestanding kitchen was built at the rear of the house and connected to the main building by a covered passageway. The kitchen includes a massive cooking hearth, worktable, pie safe, a beaten-biscuit table (small dough table) and assorted nineteenth-century accoutrements.

Colonial Williamsburg, P.O. Box 1776, Williamsburg, Virginia 23187-1776, phone # 1-800-HISTORY.

Set in the 1770s, Colonial Williamsburg includes eighty-eight original eighteenth- or nineteenth-century homes and buildings, many of which include Colonial kitchens. Especially noteworthy is the kitchen in the Governor's Palace, complete with massive cooking hearth, an array of copper pots and kettles, pottery, iron hearth utensils and so on.

VICTORIAN KITCHENS ON DISPLAY

John Muir National Historic Site, 4202 Alhambra Avenue, Martinez, California 94553, phone # (415) 228-8860.

A three-story, 17-room Victorian Italianate-style home built in 1882 by John Muir, a man whose life was devoted to writing articles and books that championed the wilderness, conservation and land preservation. The Muir family had a Chinese chef who was in total command of the large kitchen. This room features a coal range with water heater, wooden icebox, storage pantry etc.

The General Phineas Banning Residence Museum, P.O. Box 397, 401 East M Street, Wilmington, California 90748, phone # (310) 548-7777.

A 23-room Greek Revival house built in 1864, the Banning Residence has been restored down to the last Victorian detail. Eighteen rooms are open to the public, including the kitchen, which recently underwent restoration to reflect the late 1880s–1890s period. Museum programs include tours, kitchen demonstrations, lectures and theme programs such as a Summer Social and a Victorian Christmas.

The Molly Brown House Museum, 1340 Pennsylvania Street, Denver, Colorado 80203, phone # (303) 832-4092.

This Victorian Queen Anne–style home was built in 1889 of Castle Rock lava stone and sports wood trim. The kitchen has been reconstructed to reflect the late Victorian period, complete with Majestic stove, an oak table and chairs and worktable.

The Harriet Beecher Stowe House, 77 Forest Street, Hartford, Connecticut 06105, phone # (203) 522-9258.

This cottage-style house was built in 1871 and the kitchen reflects many of the recommendations included in *The American Woman's Home,* which was written by Catharine Beecher and her sister, Harriet Beecher Stowe.

Westville, P.O. Box 1850, Lumpkin, Georgia 31815, phone # (912) 838-6310.

A living-history museum with relocated and authentically restored original circa 1850 buildings that reflect early Victorian preindustrial life. Several homes include kitchens with cooking hearths or cast-iron stoves where cooking demonstrations are conducted.

Idaho State Historical Museum, 610 N. Julia Davis Drive, Boise, Idaho 83702, phone # (208) 334-2120.

This museum includes detailed interiors and exhibits that explore Idaho's ethnic groups, technology and industry. On display are an Idaho kitchen, circa 1905, complete with cast-iron stove, worktable, hoosier cabinet, porcelain sink, wooden flooring, and wainscoting on the walls. The Nathan Falk Dining Room is another noteworthy exhibit, which features a circa 1901 golden oak interior commonly found in the middle-class home at the turn of the century.

The Glessner House, Chicago Architecture Foundation, 1800 S. Prairie Avenue, Chicago, Illinois 60616, phone # (312) 922-3432 or for recorded tour information, (312) 782-1776.

This 1887 Victorian home with granite exterior was designed by noted architect Henry Hobson Richardson. The kitchen features sanitary walls of white glazed brick and includes a butler's pantry with a copper and oak sink. The kitchen has an iron cookstove with a copper range hood (replicas of the original), a soapstone sink on brass legs and the flooring features Minton Encaustic ceramic tiles in a checkered design. There is a food pantry with oak cupboards and shelves and a servants call system can be seen on the kitchen wall. Mrs. Glessner's collection of over fifty cookbooks are in the house library.

Old Cowtown Museum, 1871 Sim Park Drive, Wichita, Kansas 67203, phone # (316) 264-0671.

An open-air history museum that recreates the Victorian West from 1865 to 1880. The museum includes six historic homes, five of which have furnished kitchens such as the 1869 log Munger House and the 1874 Victorian Murdock House. Along with tours, special events are held throughout the year.

Baltimore City Life Museums, 800 East Lombard Street, Baltimore, Maryland 21202, Phone # (410) 396-3523 or (410) 396-4545 on weekends.

The Baltimore City Life Museums includes *1840 House,* a reconstructed nineteenth-century row house depicting life in 1840 Baltimore. The kitchen includes a cooking hearth and the museum offers a variety of programs that include hands-on participation.

Orchard House, 399 Lexington Road, Concord, Massachusetts 01742, phone # (508) 369-4118.

The home of author Louisa May Alcott, Orchard House was the setting of her well-loved work, *Little Women.* A Colonial structure dating from the early 1700s, Louisa's father, Bronson Alcott, added porches and a gable to the house, which gave it a distinctly Victorian appearance. The kitchen is interpreted as it may have been between 1858–1877 while the family was in residence there and contains many of their kitchenware items. Among the kitchen furnishings are a cast-iron stove, a drying rack, a soapstone sink Louisa May Alcott purchased for her mother with earnings from her books and a hutch table. The kitchen is painted a yellow or "straw" color popular during the period.

The Ella Sharp Museum, 3225 Fourth Street, Jackson, Michigan 49203, phone # (517) 787-2320.

A Greek Revival farmhouse built in 1857, the restored kitchen features a cast-iron stove, early washing machine, bead-board cupboards and assorted kitchen items.

The Glenn House, 325 South Spanish Street, Cape Girardeau, Missouri 63701.

Built in 1883, this Victorian Eastlake-style home originally housed the kitchen in a separate building but at the turn of the century an addition made a passageway between the dining room and kitchen. The kitchen, typical of the kitchens that servants worked in includes a cast-iron stove, icebox, pie safe, servants call box and wooden wainscoting on the walls.

The Martin Franklin Hanley House, 10 North Bemiston Avenue, Clayton, Missouri 63105.

A Greek Revival farmhouse built in 1855 that interprets the 1855–1894 period. The restored outdoor kitchen building includes a bucket bench, dough table, homespun curtains, butter churn, cast-iron stove, an 1875 pine kitchen cabinet and brick flooring.

Wornall House Museum, 146 West 61st Terrace, Kansas City, Missouri 64113, phone # (816) 444-1858.

A restored antebellum Greek Revival farmhouse built in 1858, the Wornall House living kitchen includes cooking hearth, dry sink, wood box, cast-iron stove and worktable. Special programs interpret daily life in the pre–Civil War years in a farming community and open hearth cooking demonstrations are held to bake cookies, vegetable stew, tomato herb soup, biscuits or apple pie.

Old Merchant's House, 29 East Fourth Street, New York, New York 10003, phone # (212) 777-1089.

An 1832 row house with late Federal exterior and Greek Revival interior, this home reflects upper middle-class nineteenth-century Victorian life. The kitchen retains the original fireplace with beehive oven. An Abendroth York cast-iron stove and a sink with pump are among the kitchen furnishings.

The Rich-Twinn Octagon House, 157 Main Street, Akron, New York 14001.

Built in 1849, this octagonal house includes an English-style basement kitchen, pantry, scullery, maid's room, family dining area and sitting area. The kitchen includes a brick cooking hearth, furnishings and the dumbwaiter used to send meals to the formal dining room on the first floor.

Strong Museum, One Manhattan Square, Rochester, New York 14607, phone # (716) 263-2700.

This museum displays and interprets the Margaret Woodbury Strong collection of cultural objects circa 1820–1940 from the northeastern United States. More than 20,000 artifacts housed in glass storage cases are displayed and preserved, including numerous and diverse household items such as kitchen tools, dishware, laundry items etc. In the exhibition area a hands-on learning center for children ages 3–7 (accompanied by an adult) includes a recreated turn-of-the-century kitchen. Other exhibits featured include Changing Patterns: Household Furnishings 1820–1839 and Neither Rich nor Poor: Searching for the American Middle Class.

Sunnyside, Historic Hudson Valley, 150 White Plains Road, Tarrytown, New York 10591, phone # (914) 631-8200.

Washington Irving purchased this farmer's cottage in 1835. Regarding the kitchen with cooking hearth, Irving bought a cast-iron range during the late 1840s or early 1850s and also installed an iron sink with a gravity-fed running water system. The kitchen includes pantries, a laundry room, servant's room a kitchen yard with a root cellar, wood shed and ice house.

Biltmore Estate, One North Pack Square, Asheville, North Carolina 28801, phone # 1-800-543-2961.

George Vanderbilt had this house, modeled after a French château, built during the 1890s. Biltmore once completed, was the largest private home in the United States. The kitchen, located on the basement level, includes a main kitchen, a rotisserie room, pantries and a mechanical refrigeration system that used ammonia and salt water brine solution as cooling agents.

President Warren G. Harding Home, The Ohio Historical Society, 380 Mount Vernon Avenue, Marion, Ohio 43302. Phone 1-800-BUCKEYE for information on hours of operation and special events.

This Victorian home was built in 1891 when Warren Harding was a U.S. senator. He and Mrs. Harding lived here until they left for Washington, D.C. in 1921. The kitchen is typical of the late Victorian period and features a large gas stove and water heater, oak table and chairs, icebox, linoleum flooring, and wooden wainscoting on the walls.

The Calvin Coolidge Homestead, Plymouth Notch, Vermont. For information, write to the Agency of Development and Community Affairs, Vermont Division for Historic Preservation, Pavilion Building, Montpelier, Vermont 05602.

The home of President Calvin Coolidge, the kitchen remains as it was in 1923, at which time it was a typical early Victorian kitchen since it had never been modernized. The kitchen includes an iron sink, cast-iron stove, woodbox and drying rack.

Glossary

of Old Kitchen Terms

American isinglass	Gelatin. Often called for in recipes to make desserts and jellies.
Arrowroot	A powder obtained from tuberous plants found in the West Indies. Frequently used as a thickening agent in puddings during the nineteenth century.
Beetle	A wooden masher. As a verb it means to beat. These were crafted in a variety of sizes to mash everything from herbs to vegetables.
Blancmange	A molded dessert popular during the Victorian era. Means "white food" or jelly and was often made with cornstarch, tapioca or arrowroot.
Butter Spad	A small wooden paddle used to work butter after it was churned in order to remove excess liquid.
Cabbage cutter	A large, oblong wooden utensil with metal blades used to chop cabbage.
Caster	A small container or vessel for the table that held vinegar, mustard or other condiments. Usually made of glass and often adorned with a silver or silver-plate trim.
Caudle	To add wine or ale to rice gruel. This mixture was then lightly seasoned with sugar and nutmeg and served to the sick.
Coffee biggin	A French coffee pot with a removable mid-section designed to filter water through the coffee. This eliminated the need to strain the coffee once brewed.
Confection	Used in nineteenth-century cookbooks, the term refers to a concoction of fruit and sugar or a sweet-meat. Today confection is often considered to mean candy.

Confectionery	The ornamental branch of cooking that includes the manufacture of cakes, pies, candies and other dessert dishes. Today confectionery often means candy store.
Crumpets	Small batter cakes baked in muffin tins.
do.	Means "ditto" in many eighteenth- and early nineteenth-century recipes.
Dredging-box	A wooden box with small holes used to sift flour on meat while it is roasting.
Egg separator	A small tin or aluminum utensil used to separate the yolk from the egg white. Used during the late nineteenth century.
Emptins	A semiliquid prepared yeast used in baking bread. Called for in Colonial recipes.
Fair water	Clean water. Referred to in Colonial recipe books.
Flummery	A confection or dessert in which thin slices of sponge cake are moistened with white wine and covered with a custard and meringue.
Gill	A measurement used in cooking during the eighteenth and nineteenth centuries, equivalent to eight tablespoons.
Greens	Found in various recipes, it refers to a mixture of boiled spinach, dandelions, beet tops, turnip tops etc.
Griddle spad	A spatula.
Gruel	A thin porridge often made by cooking rice or oatmeal in a boiling mixture of water and milk. A dish served frequently to the sick.
Herb spirit	Used in recipes in place of dry herbs. Created by adding sifted herbs such as thyme, basil etc. to brandy and allowing it to steep for two weeks.
Hog-scraper	A tin candlestick with a push-up mechanism so none of the candle would be wasted.
Match-safe	A tin box used to store matches. Usually hung by the stove.
Mush-stick	A large stick used to stir mush (cornmeal boiled in water).
Pearlash	A salt obtained from the ashes of plants and used as a leavening agent in early baking.
Pippin	A type of apple often called for in Colonial recipes.

q.s.	A term often encountered in old recipes to indicate "as much as needed." Actually an abbreviation for *quantum sufficit*.
Quick oven	A hot oven.
Receipt book	A housekeeper's handwritten collection of culinary and medicinal recipes. During the early Victorian period the mistress of the house would copy a recipe from her book and give the "receipt" to the cook.
Roasting kitchen	Also called a tin roaster. A tin vessel in which meat could be placed and then set before the hearth to cook. The open side faced the fire and a small door facing the room would allow the housekeeper to baste her meat and check its progress.
Salamander	A round, long-handled iron plate, which, once heated, was passed over foods to brown the tops.
Saleratus	Baking soda.
Scum	To skim.
Shaddock	A citrus fruit quite similar to a grapefruit mentioned in nineteenth-century recipes.
Slack heat	Refers to a moderate oven in old recipes.
Slapjack	Refers to a cake cooked on a griddle. Today called a pancake, flapjack or griddle cake.
Sugar nippers	Shears used to cut a large cone of sugar into smaller pieces.
Sweet milk	Pure, alkaline cow's milk diluted with one-fourth water and sweetened with a dash of white sugar. This was often given to infants when mother's milk was not available.
Syllabub	A frothy drink popular during the eighteenth and early nineteenth centuries created by mixing milk or cream with wine or cider.
Tea ball	A small, round wireware container with a hinge used to hold tea leaves when brewing tea. Widely used before tea bags were introduced.
Unbolted	Unsifted.
Viand	A choice dish of food. This word is frequently encountered in Colonial recipe books.
Whortleberry	Often called for in old recipes, this refers to a variety of American edible berries (such as the huckleberry) that are considered to be in the same family as the blueberry.

NOTES

CHAPTER ONE

1. Carl Holliday, *Woman's Life in Colonial Days*. New York, Frederick Ungar Publishing Company, 1960, p. 95.
2. Mary Caroline Crawford, *Social Life in Old New England*. New York, Grosset & Dunalp, 1914, p. 236.
3. *Ibid.*, p. 236.
4. Carl Holliday, *Woman's Life in Colonial Days*. New York, Frederick Ungar Publishing Company, 1960, p. 107.
5. Douglass L. Brownstone, *A Field Guide to America's History*. New York, Facts On File, Inc., 1984, p. 261.
6. Edwin C. Whittemore, "Baking in a Brick Oven," in *The Spinning Wheel's Complete Book of Antiques*. New York, Grosset & Dunlap, 1977, p. 446.
7. Alice Morse Earle, *Home Life in Colonial Days*. New York, The Macmillian Company, 1923, pp. 100–101.
8. Carl Holliday, *Woman's Life in Colonial Days*. New York, Frederick Ungar Publishing Company, 1960, p. 105.
9. C. Kurt Dewhurst, Betty MacDowell and Marsha MacDowell, *Artists in Aprons: Folk Art by American Women*. New York, E.P. Dutton in association with the Museum of American Folk Art, 1979, pp. 8–9.
10. Carl Holliday, *Woman's Life in Colonial Days*. New York, Frederick Ungar Publishing Company, 1960, p. 105.
11. *Ibid.*, p. 105
12. Mary Tolford Wilson, "The First American Cookbook," Introduction to Amelia Simmons, *American Cookery*. New York, Oxford University Press, facsimile edition, 1958, p. 10.
13. *Ibid.*, p. 11.
14. *Ibid.*, p. 20.
15. Barbara L. Feret, *Gastronomical and Culinary Literature: A Survey and Analysis of Historically-oriented Collections in the U.S.A.* Metuchen, N.J., The Scarecrow Press, Inc., 1979, p. 45.
16. Mary Beth Norton, *Liberty's Daughters: The Revolutionary Experience of American Women, 1750–1800*. Boston, Little, Brown, 1980, p. 38.
17. Carl Holliday, *Woman's Life in Colonial Days*. New York, Frederick Ungar Publishing Company, 1960, p. 113.
18. Mary Caroline Crawford, *Social Life in Old New England*. New York, Grosset & Dunlap, 1914, pp. 251–253.
19. Carl Holliday, *Woman's Life in Colonial Days*. New York, Frederick Ungar Publishing Company, 1960, p. 111.
20. Mary Caroline Crawford, *Social Life in Old New England*. New York, Grosset & Dunlap, 1914, pp. 253–254.
21. Julianne Belote, *The Complete American Housewife 1776*. Concord, Ca., Nitty Gritty Productions, 1974, p. 7.
22. C. Kurt Dewhurst, Betty MacDowell and Marsha MacDowell, *Artists in Aprons*. New York, E.P. Dutton in association with the Museum of American Folk Art, 1979, p. 26.

23. Faye Dudden, *Serving Women: Household Service in Nineteenth-Century America.* Hanover, N.H., University Press of New England, 1983, p. 44.
24. Catharine E. Beecher & Harriet Beecher Stowe, *The American Woman's Home or, Principles of Domestic Science; Being a Guide to the Formation and Maintenance of Economical, Healthful, Beautiful and Christian Homes.* Hartford, Conn., The Stowe-Day Foundation, 1987 reprint of the original 1869 edition, pp. 307–334.
25. Mrs. L. H. Sigourney, *Letters to Young Ladies.* New York, Harper & Brothers, Publishers, 1854, pp. 69–72.
26. *Ibid.,* p. 77.

CHAPTER TWO

1. Lewis F. Allen, *Rural Architecture.* New York, 1852, pp. 84–94.
2. *Ibid.,* pp. 84–94.
3. Catharine E. Beecher, *Miss Beecher's Domestic Receipt-Book.* New York, Harper & Brothers, Publishers, 1860 (3rd edition), p. 218.
4. Joseph B. & Laura E. Lyman, *The Philosophy of Housekeeping: A Scientific and Practical Manual for Ascertaining the Analysis and Comparative Value of All Kinds of Food, Its Preparation for the Table, the Best Mode of Preserving Articles of Diet, The Proper Care of Health, Remedies in Sickness, and the Intelligent and Skillful Performance of Every Household Office With an Appendix of Recipes.* Hartford, Conn., S.M. Betts & Company, 1869, p. 192.
5. Catharine E. Beecher, *Miss Beecher's Domestic Receipt-Book.* New York, Harper & Brothers, Publishers, 1860 (3rd edition), pp. 253–254.
6. Catharine E. Beecher & Harriet Beecher Stowe, *The American Woman's Home . . .* Hartford, Conn., The Stowe-Day Foundation, 1987 facsimile of 1869 edition, p. 75.
7. Catharine E. Beecher, *Miss Beecher's Domestic Receipt-Book.* New York, Harper & Brothers, Publishers, 1860 (3rd edition), pp. 254–258.
8. *Ibid.,* pp. 258–259.
9. Catharine E. Beecher & Harriet Beecher Stowe, *The American Woman's Home . . .* Hartford, Conn., The Stowe-Day Foundation, 1987 facsimile edition of 1869 publication, p. 24.
10. *Ibid.,* pp. 32–36.
11. *Ibid.,* pp. 371.
12. Joseph B. and Laura E. Lyman, *The Philosophy of Housekeeping . . .* Hartford, Conn., S.M. Betts & Company, 1869, pp. 389–393.
13. *Ibid.,* p. 402.
14. *Ibid.,* pp. 393–398.
15. *Ibid.,* pp. 402–403.
16. *Ibid.,* p. 409.
17. Catharine E. Beecher, *Miss Beecher's Domestic Receipt-Book.* New York, Harper & Brothers, Publishers, 1860 (3rd edition), Preface, pp. III–IV.
18. *Ibid.,* pp. 183–184.
19. *Ibid.,* p. 276.
20. Catherine E. Beecher & Harriet Beecher Stowe, *The American Woman's Home . . .* Hartford, Conn., The Stowe-Day Foundation, 1987 facsimile of 1869 publication, p. 22.
21. *Ibid.,* pp. 463–470.
22. Anna Fergurson, *The Young Lady's Guide to Knowledge and Virtue.* New York, G.W. Cottrell & Company, 1848, p. 20.

23. Glenna Matthews, *"Just a Housewife."* New York, Oxford University Press, 1987, pp. 31–32.
24. Catharine E. Beecher, *Miss Beecher's Domestic Receipt-Book.* New York, Harper & Brothers, Publishers, 1860 (3rd edition), p. 270.
25. *Ibid.,* pp. 247–248.
26. *Ibid.,* pp. 227–233.
27. *Ibid.,* pp. 236–237.
28. Faye E. Dudden, *Serving Women: Household Service in Nineteenth-Century America.* Middletown, Conn., Wesleyan University Press, 1983, pp. 51–52.
29. Joseph B. & Laura E. Lyman, *The Philosophy of Housekeeping* . . . Hartford, Conn., S.M. Betts & Company, 1869, p. 304.
30. Linda Campbell Franklin, "Victorian Factory-Made Antiques," in Ronald S. Barlow's *Victorian Houseware, Hardware and Kitchenware.* El Cajon, Ca., Windmill Publishing Company, 1992, p. 20.
31. Florence Thompson Howe, "Collecting Cast-Iron Comfort," in *The Spinning Wheel's Complete Book of Antiques.* New York, Grosset & Dunlap, 1977, p. 491.
32. Catharine E. Beecher, *Miss Beecher's Domestic Receipt-Book.* New York, Harper & Brothers, Publishers, 1860 (3rd edition), p. 43.
33. Linda Campbell Franklin, *300 Years of Kitchen Collectibles.* Florence, Alabama, Books Americana, 1991, p. 469.
34. Faye E. Dudden, *Serving Women: Household Service in Nineteenth-Century America.* Middletown, Conn., Wesleyan University Press, 1983, p. 136.
35. Mary Virginia Terhune, *Common Sense in the Household: A Manual of Practical Housewifery.* New York, Charles Scribner's, 1882 (revised edition), p. 9.
36. Linda Campbell Franklin, *300 Years of Kitchen Collectibles.* Florence, Alabama, Books Americana, 1991, pp. 176–177.
37. *Ibid.,* p. 22.

CHAPTER THREE

1. Palliser, Palliser & Co., *American Victorian Cottage Homes.* New York, Dover Publications, Inc., 1990, (unabridged replication of original 1878 *Palliser's American Cottage Homes*), Preface.
2. Walter F. Keith, "A Model $2000. House," *Ladies' Home Journal,* March 1897, p. 19.
3. Sarah Tyson Rorer, "Markets and the Household," *Ladies' Home Journal,* March 1897, p. 25.
4. Sarah J. Cutter, *Palatable Dishes: A Practical Guide to Good Living.* Buffalo, New York, Peter Paul Book Co., 1891, p. 820.
5. Catharine E. Beecher, *The New Housekeeper's Manual: Embracing a New Revised Edition of the American Woman's Home or, Principles of Domestic Science.* New York, J.B. Ford & Company, 1873, p. 371.
6. *Ibid.,* p. 371.
7. Alexander V. Hamilton, *The Household Cyclopaedia of Practical Receipts and Daily Wants.* Springfield, Mass., W.J. Holland & Co., 1873, p. 17.
8. Charles L. Eastlake, *Hints on Household Taste.* New York, Dover Publications, Inc., 1969, (unabridged replication of 1878 fourth, revised edition), p. 287.
9. Richard A. Wells, A.M., *Manners, Culture and Dress of the Best American Society.* Springfield, Mass., King, Richardson & Co., 1890, p. 473.
10. The Editors, *Smiley's Cook Book and New and Complete Guide for Housekeepers.* Chicago, Smiley Publishing Co., 1889, pp. 671–675.

11. Mrs. F. L. Gillette & Hugo Ziemann, *The White House Cook Book*. Akron, Ohio, Saalfield Publishing Company, 1915 (revised edition), pp. 589–590.
12. *Montgomery Ward & Co. 1895 Spring & Summer Catalogue*. New York, Dover Publications, Inc., 1969, (unabridged replication), pp. 431–432.
13. Sarah Tyson Rorer, "Small Leakages of a Household," *Ladies' Home Journal*, September 1897, p. 24.
14. Marion Harland, *Breakfast, Luncheon and Tea*. New York, Charles Scribner's Sons, 1875, pp. 196–202.
15. Mrs. John A. Logan, *The Home Manual*. Philadelphia, The Royal Publishing House, 1889, p. 321.
16. *Ibid.*, pp. 321–325.
17. D. Sturgis, "The Planning and Furnishing of the Kitchen in the Modern Residence," *Architectural Record*, 16, 1904, p. 391.
18. Richard A. Wells, A.M., *Manners, Culture and Dress* . . . Springfield, Mass., King, Richardson & Co., 1890, p. 396.
19. The Editors, "Domestic Service," *Harper's Bazar*, May 2, 1874, p. 284.
20. Faye E. Dudden, *Serving Women: Household Service in Nineteenth-Century America*. Middletown, Conn., Wesleyan University Press, 1983, p. 145.
21. Harvey Green, *The Light of the Home*. New York, Pantheon Books, 1983, p. 59.
22. Mrs. John A. Logan, *The Home Manual*. Philadelphia, The Royal Publishing House, 1889, pp. 282–283.
23. Helen Campbell, *The Easiest Way in Housekeeping and Cooking*. New York, Fords, Howard & Hulbert, 1881, pp. 46–47.
24. Elizabeth Nicholson, *The Home Manual, or the Economical Cook and House Book: Hints on the Daily Duties of a Housekeeper*. Philadelphia, Duffield Ashmead, 1889, p. 106.
25. The Editors, *Smiley's Cook Book and New and Complete Guide for Housekeepers*. Chicago, Smiley Publishing Company, 1898, pp. 653–654.
26. Sarah Tyson Rorer, "Markets and the Household," *Ladies' Home Journal*, March 1897, p. 25.
27. Glenna Matthews, *"Just a Housewife."* New York, Oxford University Press, 1987, p. 64.
28. Editorial, *Ladies' Home Journal*, January 1899, p. 14.
29. Glenna Matthews, *"Just A Housewife."* New York, Oxford University Press, 1987, p. 65.
30. *Ibid.*, p. 117.
31. *Ibid.*, pp. 114–115.
32. Sheila M. Rothman, *Woman's Proper Place*. New York, Basic Books, Inc., 1978, p. 84.
33. Emily S. Bouton, *Life's Gateways or How to Win Real Success*. Toledo, Ohio. Published by the Author (Blade Printing & Paper Co.), 1897, pp. 53–59.
34. Alexander V. Hamilton, *The Household Cyclopaedia of Practical Receipts and Daily Wants*. Springfield, Mass., W.J. Holland & Co., 1873, p. 22.
35. *Ibid.*, p. 107.
36. Marion Harland, *Breakfast, Luncheon and Tea*. New York, Charles Scribner's Sons, 1875, pp. 5–15.
37. Miss E. Neil, *The Everyday Cookbook and Family Compendium*. Chicago, M.A. Donohue & Co., Circa 1880s, p. 284.
38. *Ibid.*, p. 312.
39. Helen Campbell, *The Easiest Way in Housekeeping and Cooking*. New York, Fords, Howard, & Hulbert, 1881, pp. 5–9.
40. Mrs. John A. Logan, *The Home Manual*. Philadelphia, The Royal Publishing Company, 1889, p. 1.
41. The Editors, *Smiley's Cook Book and New and Complete Guide for Housekeepers*. Chicago, Smiley Publishing Company, 1898, pp. 670–671.
42. *Montgomery Ward & Co. 1895 Spring & Summer Catalogue*. New York, Dover Publications, Inc., 1969 (unabridged replication).
43. *Ibid.*, pp. 418–424.

CHAPTER FOUR

1. Sidney Morse, *Household Discoveries: An Encyclopaedia of Practical Recipes and Processes.* Toledo, Ohio, The Success Company, 1909, p. 74.
2. *Ibid.,* p. 74.
3. Emily Holt, *The Complete Housekeeper.* New York, Doubleday, Page & Company, 1917, pp. 14–15.
4. *Ibid.,* p. 17.
5. *Ibid.,* pp. 61–62.
6. Gustav Stickley, *More Craftsman Homes.* New York: Dover Publications, Inc. (unabridged republication of 1912 publication), 1982, p. 5.
7. Sheila M. Rothman, *Woman's Proper Place.* New York, Basic Books, Inc., 1978, p. 14.
8. *Ibid.,* p. 5.
9. Glenna Matthews, *"Just a Housewife."* New York, Oxford University Press, 1987, p. 166.
10. Dr. Frank Crane, "Wise Counsel on the Need of Clean and Beautiful Thoughts," *Woman's World,* March 1914, p. 14.
11. Barbara Randolph, "How We Keep House in Two Rooms," *Ladies' Home Journal,* June 1912, p. 74.
12. Dr. Herrick's Family Medicines, *Herrick's Almanac for the Year of Our Lord 1906,* p. 27.
13. Dr. Anna Howard Shaw, "Chairman of the Woman's Committee, Council of National Defense," *Ladies' Home Journal,* April 1918, p. 43.
14. Advertisement for Libby's Canned Meats, *Ladies' Home Journal,* July 1920, p. 57.
15. Sidney Morse, *Household Discoveries* . . . Toledo, Ohio, The Success Company, 1909, pp. 146–147.
16. Emily Holt, *The Complete Housekeeper.* New York, Doubleday, Page & Company, 1917, p. 78.
17. Ida Hood Clark, *Domestic Science.* Boston, Little, Brown and Company, 1912, p. 2.
18. *Ibid.,* pp. 3–4.
19. *Ibid.,* pp. 161–163.
20. Carlotta C. Greer, *Foods and Home Making.* Boston, Allyn & Bacon, 1928, p. 141.
21. *Ibid.,* pp. 192–193.
22. *Ibid.,* Introduction, pp. III–V.
23. Barbara Randolph, "How We Keep House in Two Rooms," *Ladies' Home Journal,* June 1912, p. 74.
24. *Ibid.,* p. 74.
25. Dr. Anna Howard Shaw, "Chairman of The Woman's Committee, Council of National Defense," *Ladies' Home Journal,* April 1918, p. 43.
26. C. W. Taber, "Are Business Methods Possible in the Home?" *Ladies' Home Journal,* May 1919, p. 75.
27. *Ibid.,* p. 75.
28. Zona Gale, "Is Housework Pushing Down the Birth Rate?" *Ladies' Home Journal,* May 1919, p. 41.
29. The Country Contributor, "The Ideas of a Plain Country Woman," *Ladies' Home Journal,* March 1918, p. 63.
30. Sheila M. Rothman, *Woman's Proper Place.* New York, Basic Books, Inc., 1978, p. 97.
31. *Ibid.,* p. 103.
32. Martha B. Bruere, "The New Home-Making," *Outlook,* March 16, 1912, p. 592.

CHAPTER FIVE

1. Mary Lockwood Matthews, *The House and Its Care*. Boston, Little, Brown and Company, 1931, pp. 75–77.
2. *Ibid.,* pp. 87–88.
3. Jane H. Celehar, *Kitchens and Gadgets 1920 to 1950*. Radnor, Pa., Wallace-Homestead Book Company, 1982, p. 58.
4. Josephine Wylie, "The Kitchen Has Had Its Face Lifted," *Better Homes and Gardens,* November 1930, pp. 13–14 & p. 55.
5. Mabel J. Stegner, "Color Schemes for Your Kitchen," *Better Homes and Gardens,* November 1930, p. 26.
6. Jane H. Celehar, *Kitchens and Gadgets 1920 to 1950*. Radnor, Pa., Wallace-Homestead Book Company, 1982, p. 12.
7. Jane H. Celehar, *Kitchens and Kitchenware*. Radnor, Pa., Wallace-Homestead Book Company, 1985, p. 64.
8. Earl Lifshey, *The Housewares Story*. Chicago: National Housewares Manufacturers Association, 1973, pp. 132–133.
9. *Ibid.,* p. 144.
10. Agnes Heisler Barton, "Color Keeps Your Home Youthful," *Home Arts Magazine,* March 1936, p. 22.
11. Sheila M. Rothman, *Woman's Proper Place*. New York, Basic Books, Inc., 1978, p. 77.
12. Mary Lockwood Matthews, *The House and Its Care*. Boston, Little, Brown, and Company, 1931, pp. 134–136.
13. *Ibid.,* p. 138.
14. Helen Tolman, "Be a Businesslike Housekeeper," *The Delineator,* May 1925, p. 48.
15. Glenna Matthews, *"Just a Housewife."* New York, Oxford University Press, 1987, p. 190.
16. Lynn-Ray Hunter, "Campaign for a Clean House," *Woman's Home Companion,* October 1939, pp. 44–45.
17. *Ibid.,* pp. 44–45.
18. Fannie Merritt Farmer, *The Boston Cooking-School Cook Book*. Boston, Little, Brown, and Company, 1933, Preface.
19. *Ibid.,* p. 11.
20. General Electric Company, *The Silent Hostess Treasure Book*. Cleveland, Ohio, GE Corporation, 1932, p. 3.
21. Good Housekeeping Institute, *Good Housekeeping's Book of Menus, Recipes, and Household Discoveries*. New York, Good Housekeeping, 1926, p. 28.
22. *Ibid.,* pp. 28–29.
23. Fannie Merritt Farmer, *The Boston Cooking-School Cook Book*. Boston, Little, Brown, and Company, 1933, Foreword.
24. Franklin Friday & Ronald F. White, Ph.D., *A Walk Through the Park*. Louisville, Ky., Elfun Historical Society, 1987, p. 16.
25. *Ibid.,* p. 10.
26. Don Fredgant, *Electrical Collectibles*. San Luis Obispo, Ca., Padre Productions, 1981, p. 58.
27. Earl Lifshey, *The Housewares Story*. Chicago, National Housewares Manufacturers Association, 1973, p. 267.
28. *The Spirit of Maytag,* Maytag Corporation, 1993, p. 11.
29. Katharine Fisher, "Your Household Gods," *Good Housekeeping,* May 1936, pp. 88–89.
30. Josephine Wylie, "The Kitchen Has Had Its Face Lifted," *Better Homes and Gardens,* November 1930, pp. 13–14, 55.

CHAPTER SIX

1. Earl Lifshey, *The Housewares Story*. Chicago, National Housewares Manufacturers Association, 1973, pp. 144–146.
2. Franklin Friday and Ronald F. White, Ph.D., *A Walk Through the Park*. Louisville, Ky., Elfun Historical Society, 1987, p. 30.
3. N. H. and S. K. Mager, *The Pocket Household Encyclopedia*. New York, Pocket Books, Inc., 1954, pp. 135–136.
4. *Ibid.*, p. 136.
5. Terence Conran, *The House Book*. New York, Crown Publisher Inc., 1976, p. 251.
6. Gerald M. Knox, ed., *Better Homes and Gardens: Your Kitchen*. Des Moines, Iowa, Meredith Corporation, 1983, pp. 24–43.
7. Terence Conran, *Original Designs for Kitchens and Dining Rooms*. New York, Simon & Schuster Inc., 1989, p. 10.
8. Rosalind Miles, *The Women's History of the World*. Topsfield, Mass., Salem House Publishers, 1989, pp. 225–246.
9. Paul Popenoe, "Make Your Marriage a Partnership," *Ladies' Home Journal*, June 1942, pp. 31, 64.
10. Sheila M. Rothman, *Woman's Proper Place*. New York, Basic Books, Inc., 1978, p. 226.
11. Andrea Hinding, *Feminism: Opposing Viewpoints*. St. Paul, Minn., Greenhaven Press, 1986, pp. 78–85.
12. *Ibid.*, pp. 86–92.
13. Sheila M. Rothman, *Woman's Proper Place*. New York, Basic Books, Inc., 1978, p. 229.
14. Judith K. Sprankle, *Working It Out: The Domestic Double Standard*. New York, Walker and Company, 1986, p. 23.
15. *Ibid.*, p. 69.
16. Gerald M. Knox, ed., *Better Homes and Gardens Household Hints and Tips*. Des Moines, Iowa, Meredith Corporation, 1989, p. 8.
17. *Ibid.*, pp. 12–55.
18. Rosalind Miles, *The Women's History of the World*. Topsfield, Mass., Salem House Publishers, 1989, pp. 245–246.
19. Evan Jones, *American Food: The Gastronomic Story*. Woodstock, N.Y., The Overlook Press, 1990, p. 171.
20. James Beard, *The New James Beard*. New York, Alfred A. Knopf, 1981, Introduction, p. XI.
21. *Better Homes and Gardens New Cook Book*. Des Moines, Iowa, Meredith Publishing Company, 1953, pp. 290–300.
22. *Ibid.*, p. 292.
23. Julia Child, Louisette Bertholle and Simone Beck, *Mastering the Art of French Cooking*. New York, Alfred A. Knopf, 1971, Foreword pp. VII-VIII.
24. Evan Jones, *American Food: The Gastronomic Story*. Woodstock, N.Y., The Overlook Press, 1990, p. 179.
25. Kitty and Lucian Maynard, *The Oat Bran Cookbook*. Nashville, Tenn., Rutledge Hill Press, 1989, p. 7.
26. Kristine Kidd & Karen Kaplan, "Great American Dinners," *Bon Appetit,* September 1992, p. 49.

BIBLIOGRAPHY

American Heritage. *The American Heritage Cookbook and Illustrated History of American Eating and Drinking.* New York: American Heritage Publishing Company, Inc., 1964. A two-volume set exploring American gastronomy from the Colonial era through the first half of the twentieth century. Recipes included.

Aresty, Esther. *The Delectable Past.* New York: Simon & Schuster, 1964. Explores the history of food and cooking.

Bank, Mirra. *Anonymous Was a Woman.* New York: St. Martin's Press, 1979. Explores via words and images the variety of hand-crafted objects (quilts, samplers etc.) anonymous women produced during the nineteenth century.

Barlow, Ronald S. *Victorian Houseware, Hardware and Kitchenware.* El Cajon, Ca.: Windmill Publishing Company, 1992. A pictorial guide full of vintage advertisements depicting assorted houseware/kitchenware of the nineteenth century.

Beard, James. *The New James Beard.* New York: Alfred A. Knopf, 1981. A popular, very successful cookbook in the 1980s.

Beecher, Catharine E. *Miss Beecher's Domestic Receipt-Book.* New York: Harper & Brothers, Publishers, 1860. Published as a supplement to Beecher's *Treatise on Domestic Economy,* this work is primarily a recipe book with limited information on housekeeping.

———. *The New Housekeeper's Manual.* New York: J.B. Ford & Company, 1873. Actually an expanded edition of *The American Woman's Home,* which was published in 1869.

Beecher, Catharine E. and Harriet Beecher Stowe. *The American Woman's Home or, Principles of Domestic Science; Being a Guide to the Formation and Maintenance of Economical, Healthful, Beautiful and Christian Homes.* New York: J.B. Ford & Company, 1869. The most noted of all nineteenth-century household manuals, with information pertaining to every aspect of housekeeping.

Better Homes and Gardens. *Better Homes and Gardens Household Hints and Tips.* Des Moines, Iowa: Meredith Corporation, 1989. A modern-day version of the old-fashioned household manual that is full of ideas for time-saving and labor-saving methods throughout the home.

———. *Better Homes and Gardens: Your Kitchen.* Des Moines, Iowa: Meredith Corporation, 1983. Includes kitchen plans and advice for creating a convenient kitchen.

Bouton, Emily S. *Life's Gateways or How to Win Real Success.* Toledo, Ohio: Blade Printing & Paper Company, 1897. Essays expressing the author's viewpoints on various facets of life.

Bridgeman, Harriet and Elizabeth Drury. *The Encyclopedia of Victoriana*. New York: Macmillian Publishing Company, 1975. Text exploring Victorian culture, artifacts and furnishings.

Brownstone, Douglass L. *A Field Guide to America's History*. New York: Facts On File, Inc., 1984. Explores early American industrial structures, methods of transportation, architecture and artifacts and shows the reader how to recognize the landmarks indicating their long-ago existence.

Buehr, Walter. *Home Sweet Home in the 19th Century*. New York: Thomas Y. Crowell Company, 1965. Subject matter is the cultural aspects of home and the everyday tools of housekeeping.

Campbell, Helen. *The Easiest Way in Housekeeping and Cooking*. New York: Fords, Howard and Hulbert, 1881. A small volume devoted to household hints and recipes.

Celehar, Jane H. *Kitchens and Gadgets 1920–1950*. Radnor, Pa.: Wallace-Homestead Book Company, 1982. A historical look at the popular kitchen tools and furnishings in use between 1920 and 1950 that have achieved "collectible" status today.

———. *Kitchens and Kitchenware*. Radnor, Pa.: Wallace-Homestead Book Company, 1985. Explores the changes in the kitchen during the late nineteenth century on through the 1950s with a focus on kitchenware items of interest to collectors today.

Child, Julia, Louisette Bertholle and Simone Beck. *Mastering the Art of French Cooking*. New York: Alfred A. Knopf, 1971. The celebrated cookbook that showed women that French cooking could be enjoyable. Full of easy to follow recipes and helpful advice.

Clark, Ida Hood. *Domestic Science*. Boston: Little, Brown and Company, 1912. Instructional domestic science manual used in the classroom.

Conran, Terence. *The House Book*. New York: Crown Publishers Inc., 1976. A large volume that explores the house room by room, with decorating tips, advice on colors, furnishings etc.

———. *Original Designs for Kitchens and Dining Rooms*. New York: Simon & Schuster Inc., 1989. A planning guide as well as a decorating "how to" book.

Crawford, Mary Caroline. *Social Life in Old New England*. New York: Grosset & Dunlap, 1914. A cultural view of home, home life, religion etc. in Colonial New England.

Curtis, Isabel Gordon. *Mrs. Curtis's Cook Book*. Toledo: Ohio: The Success Company, 1909. A large cookbook typical of such works during the early twentieth century.

Cutter, Sarah J. *Palatable Dishes: A Practical Guide to Good Living*. Buffalo, N.Y.: Peter, Paul & Bros., 1891. A large, hardcover cookbook published as an advertising premium.

Dewhurst, Kurt C., Betty MacDowell and Marsha MacDowell. *Artists in Aprons*. New York: E.P. Dutton, 1979. Explores the artwork and hand-crafted items created by women during the nineteenth century that are now considered folk art.

Duffey, E. B. *The Ladies and Gentlemen's Etiquette: A Complete Manual of the Manners and Dress of American Society*. Philadelphia: Henry T. Coates and Company, 1877. A deportment manual addressing the proper way of conducting one's self in social situations, business matters, letter writing, table etiquette and so on.

Earle, Alice Morse. *Home Life in Colonial Days*. New York: The Macmillian Company, 1923. Explores the cultural aspects of the home during the colonial period.

Eastlake, Charles L. *Hints on Household Taste*. New York: Dover Publications, Inc., 1979 (replication of 1878 edition). The noted household guide that influenced furniture design, home decoration and household accessories during the late Victorian era. This work helped establish the Arts & Crafts movement in both England and the United States.

Farmer, Fannie Merritt. *The Boston Cooking-School Cook Book*. Boston: Little, Brown and Company, 1933. The famed cookbook that influenced American cooking with recipes calling for careful and exact measurement of ingredients.

Feret, Barbara L. *Gastronomical and Culinary Literature: A Survey and Analysis of Historically-Oriented Collections in the U.S.A.* Metuchen, N.J.: The Scarecrow Press, Inc., 1979. A study conducted to identify U.S. collections of printed materials on cooking and gastronomy.

Franklin, Linda Campbell. *300 Years of Housekeeping Collectibles*. Florence, Ala.: Books Americana, 1992. Explores all manner of housekeeping items from the eighteenth, nineteenth and twentieth centuries with numerous vintage advertisements. Of special interest to the historian, the Victoriana enthusiast and the collector.

————. *300 Years of Kitchen Collectibles*. Florence, Ala.: Books Americana, 1991. A large volume devoted to kitchenware items of the eighteenth, nineteenth and twentieth centuries. A complete price guide for modern-day collectors included.

Fredgant, Don. *Electrical Collectibles*. San Luis Obispo, Ca.: Padre Productions, 1981. Text with photos exploring the history and development of electric household appliances.

Friday, Franklin and Ronald F. White, Ph.D. *A Walk Through the Park*. Louisville, Ky.: Elfun Historical Society, 1987. Explores the history of General Electric and Appliance Park.

Good Housekeeping. *Good Housekeeping's Book of Menus, Recipes and Household Discoveries*. New York: Good Housekeeping Magazine, 1926. A selection of recipes and household hints from the early twentieth century.

Greer, Charlotta C. *Foods and Home Making*. Boston: Allyn and Bacon, 1928. A domestic science guide intended for classroom use.

Grow, Lawrence. *The Old House Book of Kitchens and Dining Rooms*. New York: The Main Street Press, 1981. A historical look at the development of kitchens and dining rooms.

Guild, Robin. *The Victorian House Book*. New York: Rizzoli International Publications, Inc., 1989. A room-by-room guide through the various aspects of Victorian architecture, style and decoration.

Hamilton, Alexander V. *The Household Cyclopaedia of Practical Receipts and Daily Wants*. Springfield, Mass.: W.J. Holland & Company, 1873. An all-purpose household manual complete with recipes and advice on a number of topics especially geared to rural living.

Harland, Marion. *Breakfast, Luncheon and Tea*. New York: Charles Scribner's Sons, 1875. A recipe book with commentary on various household topics and concerns of the day by the author.

Harrison, Molly. *The Kitchen in History*. New York: Charles Scribner's Sons, 1972. A historical look at kitchen development and the culinary arts.

Green, Harvey. *The Light of the Home*. New York: Pantheon Books, 1983. A social history of Victorian women, their homes and home life.

Hawke, David Freeman. *Everyday Life in America*. New York: Harper & Row, Publishers, 1988. Explores the cultural history of America in days gone by.

Hinding, Andrea. *Feminism: Opposing Viewpoints*. St. Paul, Minn.: Greenhaven Press, 1986. Excerpts and essays that explore both sides of feminist issues.

Holliday, Carl. *Woman's Life in Colonial Days*. New York: Frederick Ungar Publishing Company, 1960 reprint of 1922 first edition. Writings from the Colonial period portray the everyday lives of Colonial women.

Holt, Emily. *The Complete Housekeeper*. New York: Doubleday, Page & Company, 1917. A household manual complete with recipes and detailed advice on house cleaning, home furnishings etc.

Jones, Evan. *American Food: The Gastronomic Story*. New York: E.P. Dutton & Company, 1975. Explores the history of American cookery and includes over 500 regional, traditional and contemporary recipes.

Leopold, Allison Kyle. *Victorian Splendor*. New York: Stewart, Tabori & Chang, 1986. The history of Victorian style and decorating complete with stunning color photos of Victorian Revival interiors.

Lifshey, Earl. *The Housewares Story*. Chicago: National Housewares Manufacturers Association, 1973. Chronicals the history of the National Housewares Association and explores the development of numerous household and kitchenware items.

Logan, Mrs. John A. *The Home Manual*. Philadelphia: The Royal Publishing House, 1890. The complete homemaker's guide, with information on etiquette, hygiene, dress, decorating the home, recipes, household cleaning, raising children and so on.

Lyman, Joseph B. and Laura E. *The Philosophy of Housekeeping*. Hartford, Conn.: S.M. Betts & Company, 1869. A household manual including recipes, kitchen floor plans, advice on cleaning, caring for animals, children, the sick etc.

Mager, N. H. and S. K. *The Pocket Household Encyclopedia*. New York: Pocket Books, Inc., 1954. A paperback version of earlier household manuals including advice on home repair, decoration, furniture, cooking, shopping and how to use electric household appliances.

Matthews, Glenna. *"Just A Housewife."* New York: Oxford University Press, 1987. A cultural look at the history of women in the role of "housewife" during the nineteenth and early twentieth centuries.

Matthews, Mary Lockwood. *The House and Its Care*. Boston: Little, Brown And Company, 1931. A text devoted to decoration, furnishing the home, cleaning and home maintenance.

Miles, Rosalind. *The Women's History of the World*. Topsfield, Mass.: Salem House Publishers, 1989. Examines the lives of notable women and the contributions they made in all aspects of history.

Morse, Sidney. *Household Discoveries*. Toledo, Ohio: The Success Company, 1909. A large volume of recipes, household advice and hints on entertaining.

Neil, Miss E. *The Every-Day Cook-Book & Family Compendium*. Chicago: M.A. Donohue & Company, circa 1880s. A small book full of recipes and select advice for the city dweller.

Nicholson, Elizabeth. *The Home Manual, or the Economical Cook and House-Book*. Philadelphia: Duffield Ashmead, circa 1880s. A small manual including recipes and household advice on cleaning, decoration and so on.

Niesewand, Nonie and David Stevens. *conran's Creative Home Design*. Boston: Little, Brown and Company, 1986. A sourcebook of ideas for room plans, furnishings and decoration.

Palliser, Palliser & Company. *American Victorian Cottage Homes*. New York: Dover Publications Inc., 1990 unabridged replication of 1878 catalog. An architectural plan book of Victorian cottages, homes and townhouses.

Partnow, Elaine. *The New Quotable Woman*. New York: Facts On File, Inc., 1992. Notable quotes by women through the centuries.

Plante, Ellen M. *Kitchen Collectibles: An Illustrated Price Guide*. Radnor, Pa.: Wallace-Homestead Book Company, 1991. Explores kitchenware from the early 1800s through 1940 with modern day values for same. A sourcebook for collectors of vintage kitchenware items.

Simmons, Amelia. *American Cookery*. New York: Oxford University Press, 1958 facsimile of the 1796 first edition. Considered the first American cookbook complete with recipes and cooking advice.

Smiley Publishing Company. *Smiley's Cook Book and New and Complete Guide for Housekeepers*. Chicago: Smiley Publishing Company, 1898. A large volume including recipes and detailed advice on housekeeping, cleaning etc.

Sprankle, Judith K. *Working It Out: The Domestic Double Standard*. New York: Walker and Company, 1986. A contemporary look at the issues of shared housework, raising children etc. in the day and age of the two-income family.

Thompson, Frances. *Antiques from the Country Kitchen*. Lombard, Ill.: Wallace-Homestead Book Company, 1985. Explores Colonial- and Victorian-era kitchen tools and equipment with values for the antiques enthusiast.

Tunis, Edwin. *Colonial Living*. Cleveland, Ohio: The World Publishing Company, 1957. A historical view of life during the Colonial period.

Wells, Richard A. *Manners, Culture and Dress of the Best American Society*. Springfield, Mass.: King, Richardson & Company, 1891. A deportment manual with information on everything from letter writing to entertaining, raising children and proper dress.

Wissinger, Joanna. *Victorian Details*. New York: E.P. Dutton, 1990. Explores Victorian architecture, home decoration, styles and so on. Full color photos.

Young, John H. *Our Deportment or the Manners, Conduct and Dress of the Most Refined Society*. St. Louis, Mo.: F.B. Dickerson & Company, 1882. An etiquette manual with information on decorating the home, how to behave in public, everyday good manners etc.

Ziemann, Hugo and Mrs. F. L. Gilette. *The White House Cook Book*. Akron, Ohio: Saalfield Publishing Company, 1909. A large recipe book with information on furnishing the kitchen, household hints etc.

PERIODICALS

The American Home Magazine, 1930s and 1940s issues.
The Delineator, 1920s issues.
Godey's Lady's Book, 1850s and 1860s issues.
Good Housekeeping, 1930s, 1940s and 1950s issues.
The Housewife, 1890s issues.
Ladies' Home Jounal, 1896, 1912, 1919, 1920 and 1942 issues.

GENERAL INDEX

Entries are filed letter-by-letter. *Italic* locators indicate illustrations and captions. Locators followed by "g" indicate glossary; locators followed by "r" indicate recipe.

A

Abendroth York (manufacturer) *36*
Abraham & Strauss (department store) 232
Acorn Soap *141*
Adler, Hazel 234
Admiral refrigerator 251
advertising 144, 244, 248, 287 *see also Ladies Home Journal;* trade cards
Agate Ware (cookware) 103, *105*
agitator (washing machine feature) 258
Agriculture, U.S. Department of 290
AGRIRAMA (Tifton, Georgia) 298
Airliner range 273
Alaska icebox *145*
alcoholic beverages
 beer 18
 cherry bounce 35*r*
 wine 158*r*
Alcott, Bronson 301
Alcott, Louisa May 301, 302
Allen, Lewis F. 39
almanacs 181
almond (color) 275
Aluminum Cooking Utensil Company (New Kensington, Pennsylvania) 178
aluminum cookware 178, 276
aluminum washers 258
America Eats: Forms of Edible Folk Art (William Ways Weaver) 26
American Agriculturist (publication) 69, *84*
American Citron 21*r*

American Cookery (Amelia Simmons) 21, 22, 23, 28, 32, 34, 35
American Food (Evan Jones) 287
American Frugal Housewife, The (Lydia Marie Child) 25, 26, 33
American Home Economics Association 173
American isinglass 304g
American Linoleum Manufacturing Company (New York City) 93
American Revolution (1776–83) 28
American Stopper Company (Brooklyn, New York) 144
American Woman's Home, The (Catharine E. Beecher and Harriet Beecher Stowe) 55, *56, 57*
 on early colonial women 30
 on family happiness 52
 on flooring 93
 on floor plans *45, 45–47, 46*
 on household management 78–79
 on stoves 41, *42*
 on utensils 66
Amish (Pennsylvania Dutch) 25
ammonia 121, 132, *184*
andirons (firedogs) 12
antiseptics 122
apple butter 25
apple cheesecake 82*r*
apple cider 18
Appledore Cook Book (Maria Parloa) 135
apple jam 80*r*
apple parers 70–71, *101*
apple pie 81*r*

D

Farmer, Fannie Merritt   127, 135, 247   *see also* Boston Cooking-School Cook Book
farmer's markets   40
Farmer's Wife (magazine)   200
fast foods   289
Father Knows Best (TV show)   281
Fels-Naphha Soap   244
Feminine Mystique, The (Betty Friedan)   280, 282, 284
feminist movement   282–284
Feret, Barbara L.   25
Ferguson, Anna   58
Field Guide to America's History, A (Douglass L. Brownstone)   9
Filley foundry, M.L. (Troy, New York)   69
Fillmore, Millard and Abigail   299
firedogs (andirons)   12
fireplaces   *see* hearths
fish   33–34r
Fisher, Katharine   260
flax   19
flooring
    colonial (1700–1839)   7
    early Victorian (1840–69)   41
    late Victorian (1870–99)   93–94
    post-Victorian (1900–19)   162, *164,* 165, 185, 187
    modern (1920–39)   226, 261
    contemporary (1940–present)   268, 275, 279
floor plans
    early Victorian (1840–69)   *38, 45, 45–51, 46, 49*
    late Victorian (1870–99)   *86, 87, 88, 89*
    modern (1920–39)   240
    contemporary (1940–present)   272, 275, 292
Florence Cook Stoves   *163*
Florence Kerosene Stoves   *140*
flour   *174, 202*
    receptacles   *107*
    sifters   72
flummery   305g
fluting irons   75
fly traps   78

Food and Wine (magazine)   290
food choppers   72
food grinders   *107*
Food Guide Pyramid (U.S. Department of Agriculture)   290–291
Foods and Home Making (Carlotta C. Greer)   197, 262
Formica   279
Fountainhead (countertop material)   280
Frankfurth Hardware Company, Wm. (Milwaukee, Wisconsin)   *101, 102, 103*
Franklin, Benjamin   67
Fredgant, Don   253
freezers, electric   270, 271
French Chef, The (TV show)   289
French Chef Cookbook, The (Julia Child)   289
French cooking   250, 265, 288, 289
fresh-air closets   165
fricassee (cooking method)   248
Friday (day of week)   16, 18, 60, 78, 119
Friday, Franklin   251, 272
Friedan, Betty   280, 282, 284
Frigidaire (refrigerator)   251, 271
fritters   156r
frozen foods   249
Frugal Housewife, The (Susannah Carter)   21
fruit   9, 70   *see also specific fruits* (e.g., apples)
frying pans   99
furniture polish   150

G

gadgetry   *see* utensils
Gale, Zona   205, 207
"Galley" (floor plan)   272
garbage disposals   275
garrets (attics)   190
Garry, William J.   286
gateleg tables   10
General Electric Company (GE)   *see also* Monitor Top
    appliance colors   *266, 273,* 275
    electric irons   214

scrapple 25, 82r
"scullery" 40
scum 306g
seafood
    baked oysters 155r
    chowder 25
    lobster sandwiches 158r
Second Stage, The (Betty Friedan) 284
Sellers & Sons Company (Elwood, Indiana) 208, *210, 236*
Serving Women: Household Service in Nineteenth-Century America (Faye E. Dudden) 29, 70, 114
Seventy-Five Receipts for Pastry, Cakes, and Sweetmeats (Eliza Leslie) 25, 35
sewing 79
shaddock 306g
Shake Hands? (Lilly Martin Spencer painting) 65
shoofly pie 25
Showers Brothers Company (Bloomington, Indiana) 208
Shredded Wheat 145
Sigourney, Mrs. L. H. 31
Silent Hostess Treasure Book, The (General Electric Company) 248, 264, 265
Silex percolator 255
silver polishing cloths *184*
silverware 263
Simmons, Amelia *see American Cookery*
Simmons Hardware Company *145*
sinks
    early Victorian (1840–69) 43
    late Victorian (1870–99) *92,* 92–93
    post-Victorian (1900–19) 165, *187*
    modern (1920–39) 229, *233,* 237
slack heat 306g
slapjack 306g
slaves 20, 25
"Small Leakages of a Household" (Sarah Tyson Rorer article) 153, 154
smallpox 122

Smiley's Cook Book and New and Complete Guide for Housekeepers (Smiley Publishing Co.) 97–98, 123, *124,* 137, 139, 154, 158–159
Smith, Eliza 21, 34
Smith-Lever Act of 1914 173
smokehouses 9
soap 16, 18, *121,* 152, 193
soups *143,* 155r
South (region) 9, 15, 20, 25, 37
"space-age" kitchens 274
Spacemaker (refrigerator) 273, *273*
Sparrow Kneader & Mixer Company (Boston, Massachusetts) 72
Spencer, Lilly Martin *65*
spice mills 72
spinach salad 295r
spinners 19
spinning bees 27
Sprankle, Judith K. 284, 285
spring cleaning 120, 246
springhouses 9
spring soup 155r
spruce beer 34r
squash pudding 34–35r
Standard Sanitary Mfg. Company (Pittsburgh, Pennsylvania) *233*
starch 18, 193
steaming (cooking method) 248
Stecher Electric & Machine Company 217
Steero Bouillon Cubes 182
Stegner, Mabel J. 234
Stern, Edith M. 283
Stevens, David 267
Stewardess range 273
stew pie 34r
Stickley, Gustav 172
stoneware 13
Storrowton Village Museum (West Springfield, Massachusetts) *5, 6,* 299
stove polish *108,* 150
stoves *see* ranges and stoves
Stowe, Harriet Beecher 55, 300 *see also American Woman's Home, The*
strainers 99
streamlined design 239, 270

T

U

V

vacuum cleaners, electric *215, 258, 259,* 260
Van Camp (food company) 144
Van Camp's Pork and Beans *144,* 182
Vanderbilt, George 303
vegetables 9, 12
vegetarian diet 290
Vegetarian Times (magazine) 290
veneer *188*
viand 306g
Victoria, Queen (Great Britain) 204
Victorian period
> early (1840–1869) 36–83
> late (1870–1899) 84–159
vinyl 275, 279
Virginia Housewife, Or Methodical Book of 1824, The (Mary Randolph) 25, 33
"virtuous woman" 30, 125
vitriol 122
Vollrath Manufacturing Company, Jacob J. (Sheboygan, Wisconsin) 103
Vollrath Ware (enameled kitchenware) 103
volunteer work 204
Vose & Company (Albany, New York) 69

W

waffle irons, electric 217
waffles 25
Wagner Manufacturing Company (Sidney, Ohio) 178
wainscoting 94, 162, 228
waiter's pantry 87
Walk Through the Park, A (Franklin Friday and Ronald F. White) 251, 272
wall finishings 94, 162, 187, 228, 279
walnut (wood) 188
Walton, Federick 93
washboards 75, 109
"wash day" 16
washing *see* laundry
washing machines
> electric 245–246, *257,* 258, *271*

gasoline *189,* 245–246
manual *74, 75,* 110
washrooms 40
Waterloo Village (Stanhope, New Jersey) 299
Waterman, Nathaniel 73
watermelon 21r
Waters-Genter Company 255
Wear-Ever aluminum cookware 178
Weaver, William Ways 26
Wednesday (day of week) 16, 18, 60, 78, 117, 119
weights and measures 77, 151, 219, 248
Weight Watchers Fast & Fabulous Cookbook 296
Weir Stove Company (Taunton, Massachusetts) *167*
Welch's Grape Juice 182
Wells, Richard A. 97, 113
Welsh accent 265r
Wendy's (fast food restaurant chain) 289
Wesson Oil 182
Westinghouse (manufacturer) 217, 251, 260
Westville (Lumpkin, Georgia) 300–301
wheat (color) 275
Whirlpool (manufacturer) 280
white (color) 51, 171, 232, *233,* 240, 252, 268, 275
White, Ronald F. 251, 272
White Enamel Refrigerator Company (St. Paul, Minnesota) 146
White House Cook Book, The (Mrs. F. L. Gillette and Hugo Ziemann) 100–101, 132
whitewash 79
whortleberry 306g
wicker furniture 190
"wife-companion" 241
Willcox, Philip 67
Williamsburg, Virginia *see* Colonial Williamsburg
Wilson, Mary Tolford 22, 23
Wilson Kitchen Cabinets (Grand Rapids, Michigan) 208

windmill power   43

Windsor stove   148

wine   158r, 293

Woman in America (Mrs. A. J. Graves)   76

Woman's Committee of the Council of National Defense   181

Woman's Day (magazine)   286

Woman's Home Companion (magazine)   246, 265

Woman's Life in Colonial Days (Carl Holliday)   16, 27

Woman's Proper Place (Sheila M. Rothman)   127, 173, 206, 241

Woman's World (magazine)   175, *187, 201*

Women and Economics (Charlotte Perkins Gilman)   283

"Women Are Household Slaves" (Edith M. Stern article)   283

"Women Aren't Men" (Agnes E. Meyer article)   283

Women's History of the World, The (Rosalind Miles)   286

women's liberation movement   284

wooden floors   165

woodenware   13, 52

wool   19–20

Working It Out: The Domestic Double Standard (Judith K. Sprankle)   284, 285

worktables   10, 43, 44

"work triangles"   267, *279,* 291

World Columbian Exposition (Chicago, 1893)   214

World War I (1914–18)   181, 193–194, 204

World War II (1939–45)   267–268, 280

Wornall House Museum (Kansas City, Missouri)   302

Wright, William   220

Wylie, Josephine   234, 260

Y

yellow (color)   232, 237, 268, 270, 272, 273, 275

Young, John H.   85

Young Housekeeper's Friend, or, A Guide to Domestic Economy and Comfort, The (Mrs. Mary Hooker Cornelius)   76, 80

Young Lady's Guide to Knowledge and Virtue, The (Anna Fergurson)   58–59

"Your Household Gods" (Katharine Fisher article)   260

Your Kitchen (Better Homes and Gardens)   278

Z

Ziemann, Hugo   100, 132

zinc, chloride of   122

zinc work-tops   90

Recipe index